HABITAT Meerkats live in the desert areas of the southern part of Africa.

YOUNG Meerkats are adults when they are about one year old.

HABITAT Each meerkat has a job to do in its community.

SENSES Meerkats rely on their sense of smell to identify one another and to find food.

Science

Meerkat

Harcourt
SCHOOL PUBLISHERS

Orlando   Austin   New York   San Diego   Toronto   London

Visit *The Learning Site!*
www.harcourtschool.com

ISBN 0-15-340061-7

3 4 5 6 7 8 9 10 048 13 12 11 10 09 08 07 06

Meerkat

Consulting Authors

Michael J. Bell
Assistant Professor of Early Childhood Education
College of Education
West Chester University of Pennsylvania

Michael A. DiSpezio
Curriculum Architect
JASON Academy
Cape Cod, Massachusetts

Marjorie Frank
Former Adjunct, Science Education
Hunter College
New York, New York

Gerald H. Krockover
Professor of Earth and Atmospheric Science Education
Purdue University
West Lafayette, Indiana

Joyce C. McLeod
Adjunct Professor
Rollins College
Winter Park, Florida

Barbara ten Brink
Science Specialist
Austin Independent School District
Austin, Texas

Carol J. Valenta
Senior Vice President
St. Louis Science Center
St. Louis, Missouri

Barry A. Van Deman
President and CEO
Museum of Life and Science
Durham, North Carolina

Senior Editorial Advisors

Napoleon Adebola Bryant, Jr.
Professor Emeritus of Education
Xavier University
Cincinnati, Ohio

Robert M. Jones
Professor of Educational Foundations
University of Houston-Clear Lake
Houston, Texas

Mozell P. Lang
Former Science Consultant
Michigan Department of Education
Science Consultant,
Highland Park Schools
Highland Park, Michigan

LIFE SCIENCE

Ready, Set, Science!   **1**

Lesson 1 What Inquiry Skills Will We Use?   **2**

Lesson 2 What Science Tools Will We Use?   **10**

Lesson 3 How Do Scientists Work?   **18**

Chapter Review and Test Preparation   **24**

UNIT A: A World of Living Things

Chapter 1   **Living and Nonliving Things**   **28**

Lesson 1 What Are Living and Nonliving Things?   **30**

Lesson 2 What Do Animals Need?   **36**

Lesson 3 What Do Plants Need?   **42**

Activities for Home or School   **51**

Chapter Review and Test Preparation   **52**

Science Spin Weekly Reader

Technology
Tomato Says, "Pass the Salt!" **48**

People
How Much Rain? **50**

Chapter 2   **Animals**   **54**

Lesson 1 What Are Mammals and Birds?   **56**

Lesson 2 What Are Reptiles, Amphibians, and Fish?   **64**

Lesson 3 What Are Some Animal Life Cycles?   **72**

Activities for Home or School   **83**

Chapter Review and Test Preparation   **84**

Science Spin Weekly Reader

Technology
Searching for the Giant Squid **80**

People
Working with Animals **82**

Chapter 3 — Plants — 86

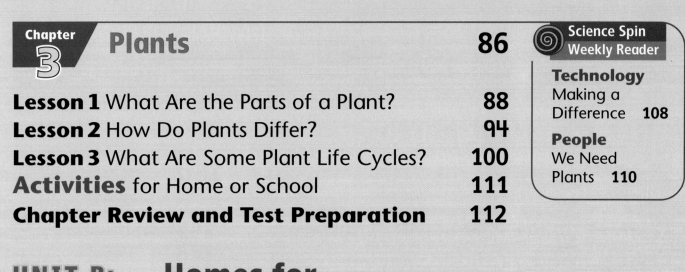

Lesson 1 What Are the Parts of a Plant? — 88
Lesson 2 How Do Plants Differ? — 94
Lesson 3 What Are Some Plant Life Cycles? — 100
Activities for Home or School — 111
Chapter Review and Test Preparation — 112

Science Spin Weekly Reader
Technology Making a Difference — 108
People We Need Plants — 110

UNIT B: Homes for Living Things

Chapter 4 — Living Things in Their Environments — 116

Lesson 1 What Is an Environment? — 118
Lesson 2 How Do Living Things Survive in Different Places? — 126
Lesson 3 What Are Food Chains and Food Webs? — 136
Activities for Home or School — 145
Chapter Review and Test Preparation — 146

Science Spin Weekly Reader
Technology Helping Hawai`i's Reefs — 142
People Pal to the Panda — 144

EARTH SCIENCE

UNIT C: Our Earth

Chapter 5 Exploring Earth's Surface **150**

Lesson 1 What Changes Earth's Surface? **152**
Lesson 2 What Are Rocks, Sand, and Soil? **160**
Lesson 3 What Can We Learn from Fossils? **168**
Activities for Home or School **179**
Chapter Review and Test Preparation **180**

Science Spin
Weekly Reader

Technology
Wild Waves **176**

People
Looking for
Change **178**

Chapter 6 Natural Resources **182**

Lesson 1 How Can People Use
Natural Resources? **184**
Lesson 2 How Can People Harm
Natural Resources? **194**
Lesson 3 How Can People Protect
Natural Resources? **202**
Activities for Home or School **213**
Chapter Review and Test Preparation **214**

Science Spin
Weekly Reader

Technology
Solar Car Crosses
Canada **210**

People
Planting a
Tree **212**

UNIT D: Weather and Space

Chapter 7 Weather **218**

Lesson 1 How Does Weather Change? **220**
Lesson 2 Why Do We Measure Weather? **228**
Lesson 3 What Is the Water Cycle? **236**
Activities for Home or School **247**
Chapter Review and Test Preparation **248**

Science Spin
Weekly Reader

Technology
The Coldest
Place on
Earth **244**

People
What's the
Weather? **246**

Chapter 8 **The Solar System** **250**

Lesson 1 What Are Stars and Planets? **252**
Lesson 2 What Causes Day and Night? **258**
Lesson 3 Why Does the Moon Seem
to Change? **264**
Lesson 4 What Causes the Seasons? **270**
Activities for Home or School **281**
Chapter Review and Test Preparation **282**

Science Spin
Weekly Reader

Technology
An Assistant in
Space **278**

People
A First into
Space **280**

PHYSICAL SCIENCE

UNIT E: Exploring Matter

 **Chapter 9** **Observing and
Classifying Matter** **286**

Lesson 1 What Is Matter? **288**
Lesson 2 What Are Solids? **296**
Lesson 3 What Are Liquids? **304**
Lesson 4 What Are Gases? **310**
Activities for Home or School **319**
Chapter Review and Test Preparation **320**

Science Spin
Weekly Reader

Technology
Up, Up, and
Away **316**

People
What's in a
Bubble? **318**

Chapter 10 **Changes in Matter** 322

Lesson 1 How Can Matter Change? 324
Lesson 2 How Can Water Change? 332
Lesson 3 What Are Other Changes
to Matter? 340
Activities for Home or School 349
Chapter Review and Test Preparation 350

Science Spin
Weekly Reader
Technology
The Future of
Bandages 346
People
A Famous
Scientist 348

UNIT F: Energy in Motion

Chapter 11 **Light and Heat** 354

Lesson 1 What Is Energy? 356
Lesson 2 What Is Light? 366
Lesson 3 What Is Heat? 372
Activities for Home or School 385
Chapter Review and Test Preparation 386

Science Spin
Weekly Reader
Technology
Liar, Liar, Face
on Fire! 382
People
A Hot Idea 384

Chapter 12 **Sound** 388

Lesson 1 What Causes Sound? 390
Lesson 2 How Does Sound Travel? 396
Lesson 3 How Do We Make
Different Sounds? 404
Activities for Home or School 413
Chapter Review and Test Preparation 414

Science Spin
Weekly Reader
Technology
The Sounds
Spring
Brings 410
People
A Call to
Invent 412

Chapter 13 Motion	416
Lesson 1 What Are Ways Things Move?	418
Lesson 2 What Makes Things Move?	424
Lesson 3 How Do Magnets Move Things?	432
Activities for Home or School	443
Chapter Review and Test Preparation	444

Science Spin Weekly Reader

Technology Swimmers Glide Like Sharks 440

People Playing with Magnets 442

References	446
Health Handbook	R1
Reading in Science Handbook	R14
Math in Science Handbook	R20
Safety in Science	R26
Glossary	R27
Index	R46

Ready, Set, Science!

Lesson 1 **What Inquiry Skills Will We Use?**

Lesson 2 **What Science Tools Will We Use?**

Lesson 3 **How Do Scientists Work?**

Vocabulary
inquiry skills
science tools
investigate

I wonder...

How can kids be scientists?

What do you wonder?

What Inquiry Skills Will We Use?

Fast Fact

A penny is like a sandwich made of metal. The inside layer is made of a metal called zinc. The outside layers are made of a metal called copper. You can observe coins to learn about them.

How Many Pennies?

You need

● pennies ● plastic jar

Step 1

Observe some pennies and a jar. Predict and write the number of pennies that will fill the jar.

Step 2

Fill the jar with pennies. Count and write the number of pennies that fit.

Step 3

Compare the number of pennies in the jar with the number you predicted.

Inquiry Skill

When you observe, you can use your senses of sight and touch.

READING FOCUS SKILL

MAIN IDEA AND DETAILS Look for details about the inquiry skills that scientists use.

Inquiry Skills

Scientists use inquiry skills when they do tests. **Inquiry skills** help people find out information.

Observe

Use your five senses to learn.

Compare

Observe ways things are alike and ways they are different.

Classify

Classify by sorting things into groups to show ways they are alike.

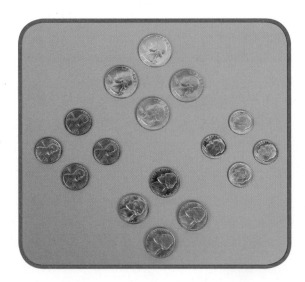

◀ sequence of size

◀ sequence of value

Sequence

Put things in order to show changes.

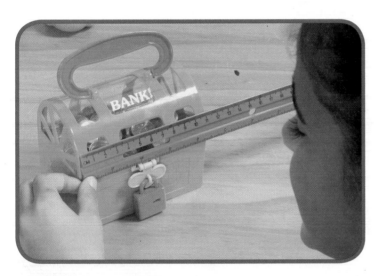

Measure

Use tools to find out how much.

Make a Model

Make a model to show what something is like or how it works.

Focus Skill **MAIN IDEA AND DETAILS**

What are some inquiry skills?

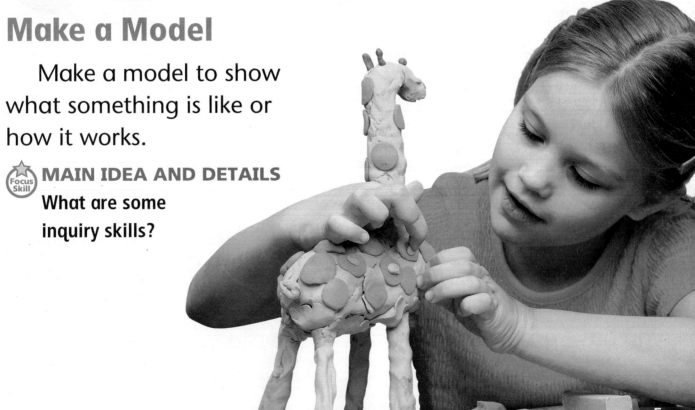

5

Hypothesize

Think of a scientific explanation that you can test.

A magnet attracts things made of iron.

The ball went really far! I must have thrown it hard.

Infer

Use what you know to make a good guess about what is happening.

Draw Conclusions

Use all the information you have gathered to make decisions.

I think this plant needs water.

Predict

Use what you know to make a good guess about what will happen.

MAIN IDEA AND DETAILS

Focus Skill

Why are drawing conclusions and predicting inquiry skills?

Insta-Lab

Stacking Pennies

Set a tray on a table. Predict what will happen if you try to stack 50 pennies. Stack the pennies. What happens? Was your prediction correct?

Plan an Investigation

Figure out what you will do to find out what you want to know.

Communicate

Share what you know by showing or telling others.

⭐ **Focus Skill** **MAIN IDEA AND DETAILS** Why is communicating an inquiry skill?

1. MAIN IDEA AND DETAILS Copy and complete this chart. Tell details about the main idea.

Main Idea and Details

Inquiry skills help people find out information.

You **A** ____ two things when you observe ways they are alike and ways they are different.

You **B** ____ when you put things in order.

You **C** ____ when you use what you know to make a good guess about what will happen.

2. SUMMARIZE Write two sentences that tell what the lesson is about.

3. VOCABULARY Use the term **inquiry skills** to tell about this picture.

Test Prep

4. What should you do if you want to find out how wide a box is?

Writing

Sentences to Compare
Observe a penny and a nickel. Write a few sentences. Tell ways the penny and the nickel are alike and ways they are different.

For more links and activities, go to www.hspscience.com

9

What Science Tools Will We Use?

Fast Fact

If you want to measure an object and you do not have a ruler or a tape measure, you can use your hand to see how many hands long the object is. You can predict a measurement and then measure to see if the prediction is correct.

Drops of Water on a Penny

You need

- dropper
- cup of water
- coin

Step 1

Predict the number of water drops you can put on a coin before the water runs off. Write your prediction.

Step 2

Use the dropper to drop water on the coin. Count the drops. Stop when the water starts to run off the coin.

Step 3

Compare your prediction with the number of drops you were able to put on the coin.

Inquiry Skill

When you predict, you tell what you think will happen.

READING FOCUS SKILL

MAIN IDEA AND DETAILS Look for details about science tools.

Science Tools

When scientists want to find out about things, they use different tools. These **science tools** are used to help people find out information.

Hand Lens

Use a hand lens to make objects look larger. Hold the hand lens near your face. Move the object until you see it clearly.

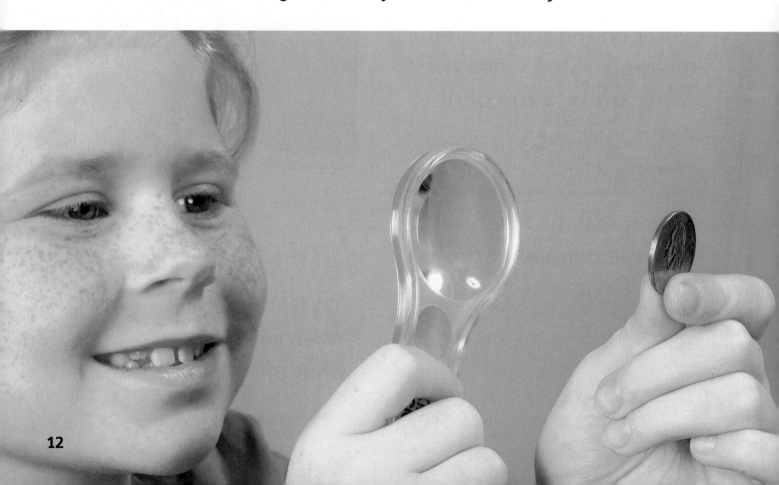

Magnifying Box

Use a magnifying box to make objects look larger. Place the object in the box, and look through the box.

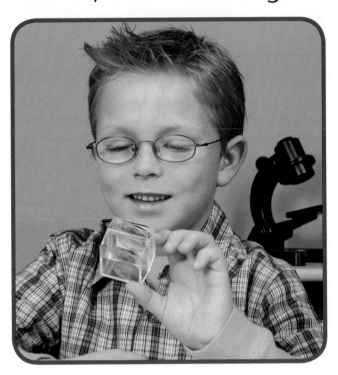

Forceps

Use forceps to hold small objects so you can see them better or separate them.

⭐ **Focus Skill** **MAIN IDEA AND DETAILS** What are some objects you might want to use a hand lens to observe?

13

Ruler

Use a ruler to measure length, width, and height. Put the first mark of the ruler at the end of the object. Read the number at the other end of the object.

Tape Measure

Use a tape measure to measure length, width, and height. Use a tape measure to measure around an object.

Dropper

Use a dropper to place small amounts of a liquid. Squeeze the bulb of the dropper. Then put the dropper in the liquid and slowly stop squeezing. To drop the liquid, slowly squeeze the bulb again.

Measuring Cup

Use a measuring cup to measure a liquid. Pour the liquid into the cup. Place the cup on a table. When the liquid stops moving, read the mark on the cup.

 **MAIN IDEA AND DETAILS**

Why is a measuring cup a useful science tool?

Balance

Use a balance to measure the mass of an object. Place the object on one side of the balance. Place masses on the other side. Add or remove masses until the two sides of the balance are even.

Thermometer

Use a thermometer to measure temperature. Place the thermometer where you want to measure the temperature. On the thermometer, read the number next to the top of the liquid.

MAIN IDEA AND DETAILS Why is a thermometer a science tool?

1. MAIN IDEA AND DETAILS Copy and complete this chart. Tell details about the main idea.

Main Idea and Details

Scientists use science tools.

A **A** _____ and a **B** _____ help you see small objects.

A **C** _____ holds small objects.

A **D** _____ and a **E** _____ measure length.

A **F** _____ and a **G** _____ measure liquids.

A **H** _____ measures temperature.

2. DRAW CONCLUSIONS How are a ruler and a tape measure alike? How are they different?

3. VOCABULARY Use the term **science tools** to tell about the lesson.

Test Prep

4. Which one would you use to look at something very small?
   A. a hand lens
   B. a measuring cup
   C. a ruler
   D. a thermometer

Links

Math

Estimate and Count

Estimate the number of pennies you need to make a row as long as a ruler. Then lay the pennies beside the ruler. Count the pennies. How many pennies did you need? Was the number of pennies more than, less than, or the same as your estimate?

 For more links and activities, go to **www.hspscience.com**

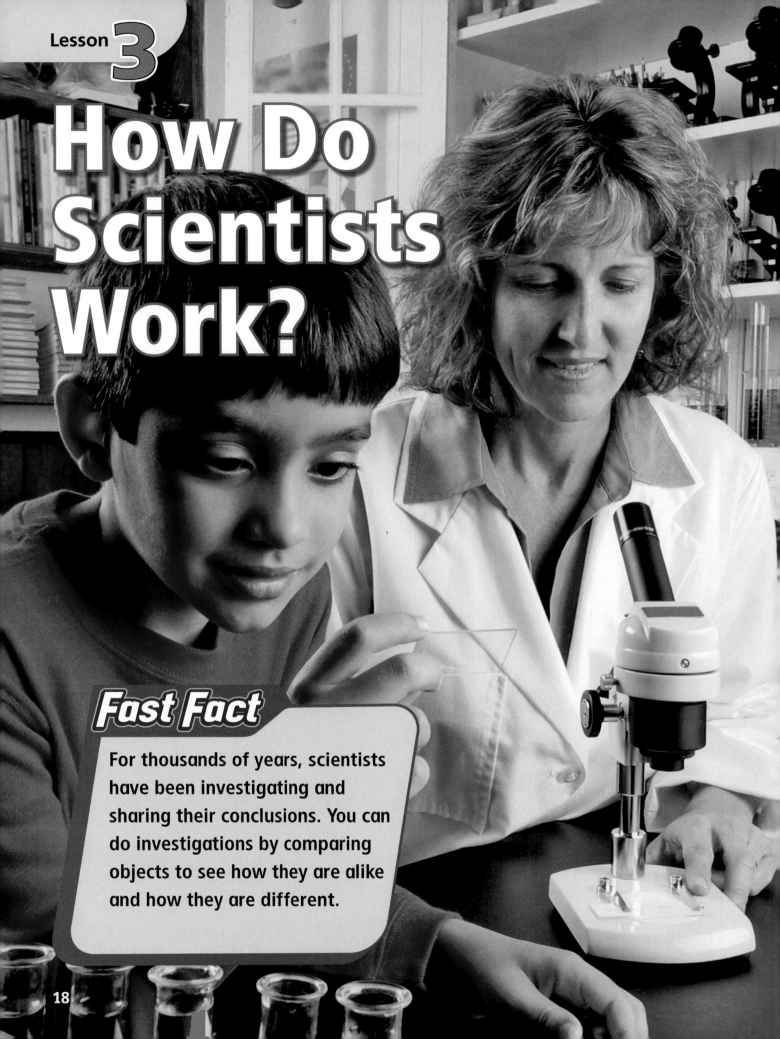

How Do Scientists Work?

Fast Fact

For thousands of years, scientists have been investigating and sharing their conclusions. You can do investigations by comparing objects to see how they are alike and how they are different.

Equal Coins

You need

- quarter
- 5 nickels
- balance

Step 1

A quarter and 5 nickels both equal 25 cents. Does a quarter have the same mass as 5 nickels? **Compare** to find out.

Step 2

Make sure the balance is even. Then place the quarter on one side of the balance and the 5 nickels on the other side.

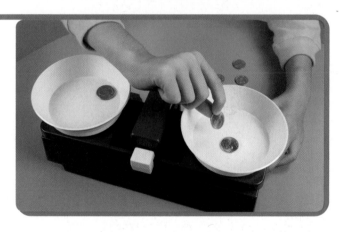

Step 3

Compare the two sides of the balance. Are they even?

Inquiry Skill

When you **compare**, you observe ways things are alike and ways they are different.

19

VOCABULARY

investigate

 READING FOCUS SKILL

SEQUENCE Look for the order of the steps scientists use when they are investigating.

Investigating

When scientists want to answer a question or solve a problem, they **investigate**, or plan and do a test. When you investigate, you use a plan like this.

1. Observe, and ask a question.

Think of a question you want to answer. Write what you already know about the topic of your question. Figure out what information you need.

2. Form a hypothesis.

Write a hypothesis, or a scientific explanation that you can test.

Does the mass of a real quarter equal the mass of a play quarter?

The mass of a real quarter is greater than the mass of a play quarter.

3. Plan a fair test.

A fair test will help you answer your question. List things you will need and steps you will follow to do the test. Decide what you want to learn from the test.

4. Do the test.

Follow the steps of your plan. Observe carefully. Record everything that happens.

SEQUENCE What should you do after you form a hypothesis?

Insta-Lab

Wet Quarters

Place a wet quarter on a glass bottle. Wrap your hands around the bottle. What do you observe?

5. Draw conclusions, and communicate results.

Think about what you found out. Was your hypothesis correct? Use what you found out to draw conclusions. Then communicate your results with others.

Investigate more.

If your hypothesis was correct, ask another question about your topic to test. If your hypothesis was not correct, form another hypothesis and change the test.

SEQUENCE What do you do before you draw conclusions?

My hypothesis was correct!

Will a real dime have the same mass as a play dime?

Focus Skill

1. SEQUENCE Copy and complete this chart. Tell about the way to investigate.

How to Investigate

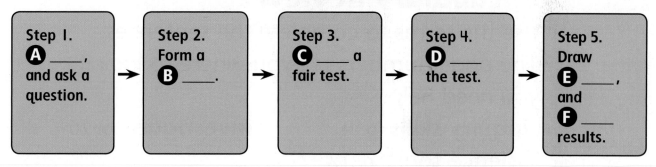

Step 1.
A ____, and ask a question.

→

Step 2.
Form a **B** ____.

→

Step 3.
C ____ a fair test.

→

Step 4.
D ____ the test.

→

Step 5.
Draw **E** ____, and **F** ____ results.

2. SUMMARIZE Write two sentences that tell what the lesson is about.

3. VOCABULARY Use the term **investigate** to tell about this lesson.

Test Prep

4. What is a hypothesis?

Art

Coin Rubbings

Place coins under a sheet of paper. Use crayons of different colors to make rubbings of the coins. Label each coin with its name. Why can you make rubbings of coins?

 For more links and activities, go to www.hspscience.com

Review and Test Preparation

Vocabulary Review

Use the terms to complete the sentences. The page numbers tell you where to look if you need help.

inquiry skills p. 4   **investigate** p. 20

science tools p. 12

1. Comparing and measuring are two

_____.

2. If you want to find out something, you can _____.

3. Scientists use _____ to find out information.

Check Understanding

4. Which one of the following details is

(Focus Skill) correct?

   A. A hand lens is an inquiry skill.

   B. Classifying is an inquiry skill.

   C. A dropper is an inquiry skill.

   D. A coin is an inquiry skill.

5. What is the next step you should do after

you ask a question?

    F. Investigate more.

    G. Draw conclusions.

    H. Plan a fair test.

    J. Form a hypothesis.

Critical Thinking

6. Look at the picture.

    Why are these things science tools?

7. Why must Miguel do a fair test if he wants
to find out information?

A World of Living Things

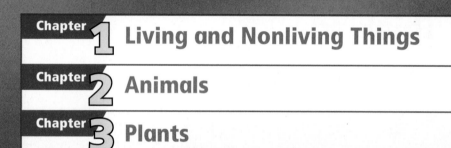

Chapter 1 Living and Nonliving Things

Chapter 2 Animals

Chapter 3 Plants

LIFE SCIENCE

Riddle's Elephant and Wildlife Sanctuary

TO: jack@hspscience.com

FROM: juan@hspscience.com

RE: Greenbrier, Arkansas

Dear Jack,

We went to a place that was made just for elephants. It is like their habitat, or their home. People who visit learn more about elephants.

Your friend,

Juan

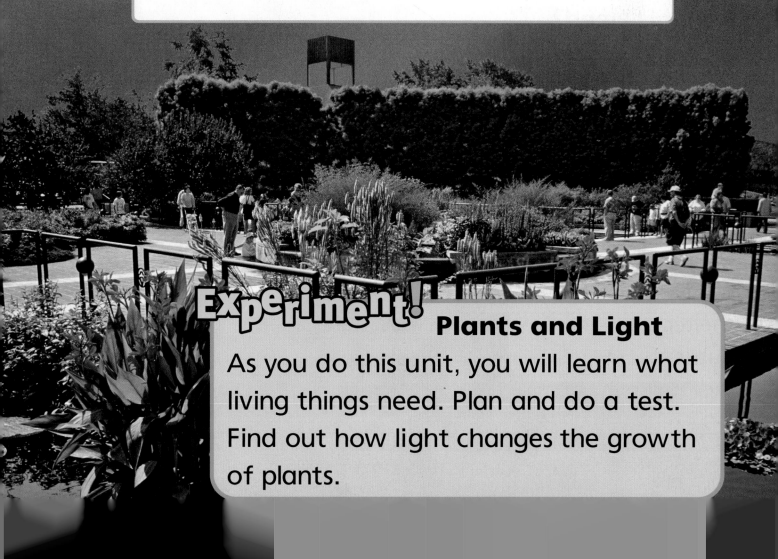

Chicago Botanic Garden

TO: brian@hspscience.com

FROM: lily@hspscience.com

RE: Chicago, Illinois

Dear Brian,

I like to help my grandma when she works in her garden. Just for fun, she took me to the Chicago Botanic Garden. It is really 26 gardens in one! I got to look for bugs.

Talk to you soon,

Lily

Experiment!

Plants and Light

As you do this unit, you will learn what living things need. Plan and do a test. Find out how light changes the growth of plants.

Living and Nonliving Things

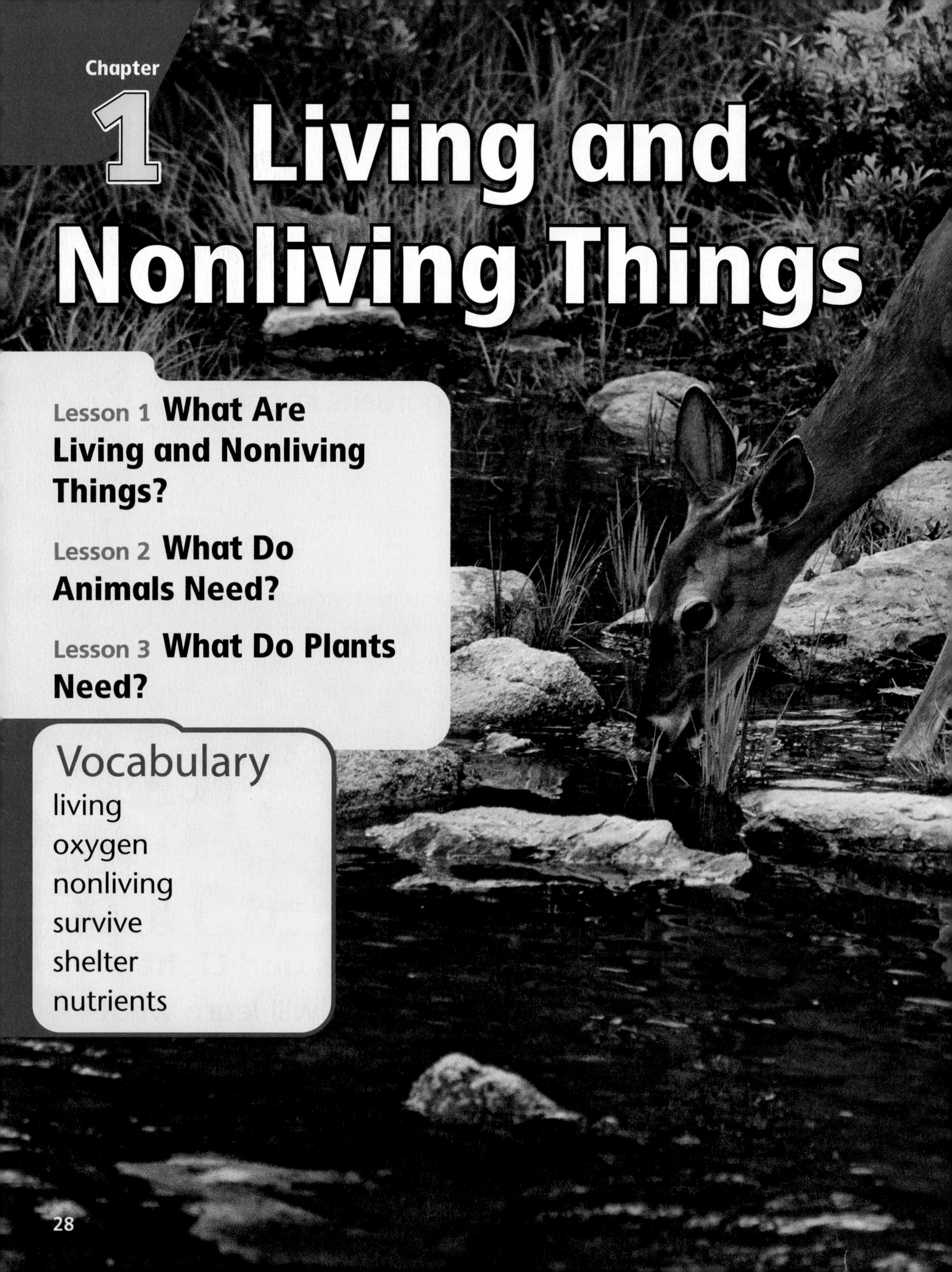

Lesson 1 What Are Living and Nonliving Things?

Lesson 2 What Do Animals Need?

Lesson 3 What Do Plants Need?

Vocabulary

living

oxygen

nonliving

survive

shelter

nutrients

I wonder...

How do you know whether something is living or nonliving?

What do you wonder?

What Are Living and Nonliving Things?

Fast Fact

A live frog has a sticky tongue that helps it get food. A model of a frog, such as a garden statue, is not alive, so it does not need food. You can classify things to see how they are alike and different.

Living or Nonliving

You need

● paper and pencil

Step 1

Go outside with your class. Draw pictures to record some of the things you see.

Step 2

Classify your pictures. Make a chart like this one.

Living and Nonliving	
Living	Nonliving

Step 3

Use the chart to talk about what you saw. Which things are living? Which things are not living?

Inquiry Skill

Classifying things helps you see how they are alike and how they are different.

4000004476

31

VOCABULARY

living
oxygen
nonliving

 READING FOCUS SKILL

COMPARE AND CONTRAST Look for ways living and nonliving things are alike and different.

Living Things

Living things need food, water, and **oxygen**, a gas in air and in water. Living things grow and change. They can also make new living things like themselves.

All animals are living things. Animals need food, water, and oxygen. Over time, animals grow bigger and change. Adult animals can make new animals.

Plants are also living things. Like animals, they need food and water. They also need oxygen and other gases. Plants grow and change. They can make new plants.

You can see living things everywhere on Earth. What living things are in this picture?

 COMPARE AND CONTRAST

How are animals and plants alike?

Nonliving Things

Nonliving things do not need food, water, and gases. They can not make new things like themselves. Water, air, and rocks are nonliving things.

COMPARE AND CONTRAST What living and nonliving things are in the picture below? How are they different?

1. COMPARE AND CONTRAST Copy and complete this chart. Tell how living and nonliving things are different.

Living Things

A Living things _____ food and water.

C Living things need _____.

E Living things make new _____.

Nonliving Things

B Nonliving things do not _____ food and water.

D Nonliving things do not need _____.

F _____ things can not make new things like themselves.

2. SUMMARIZE Use the chart to write a lesson summary.

3. VOCABULARY Explain the meanings of the terms **living** and **nonliving**.

Test Prep

4. If something needs water, what must it be?
   A. an animal
   B. a living thing
   C. a nonliving thing
   D. a plant

Links

Writing

Description of How I Am Changing

You are a living thing. Draw a picture that shows how you looked as a baby and how you look today. Write sentences that tell how you have grown and changed.

I'm taller and I have more teeth.

 For more links and activities, go to www.hspscience.com

What Do Animals Need?

Fast Fact

Birds build nests that hold their eggs and keep their chicks safe. You can find out what animals need when you observe them.

What Birds Eat

You need

- dish of birdseed   • dish of berries   • dish of breadcrumbs

Step 1

With your teacher, place three kinds of bird food outside where birds can find them.

Step 2

Observe the bird food in the morning, at noon, and in the afternoon. Record your **observations** in a chart.

What Birds Eat			
	birdseed	berries	bread crumbs
morning			
noon			
afternoon			

Step 3

Use your chart to tell what you **observed** about what birds outside your school like to eat.

Inquiry Skill

Observing animals can help you understand the kinds of food they like to eat.

VOCABULARY
survive
shelter

 READING FOCUS SKILL

MAIN IDEA AND DETAILS Look for details about the things animals need to live.

Food and Water

Animals need food and water to **survive**, or stay alive. Bigger animals need more food than smaller ones. Whales and bears need more food than rabbits and owls.

As an animal grows, it needs more food and water. An adult bird needs more food than a young bird.

 MAIN IDEA AND DETAILS What do animals need to survive?

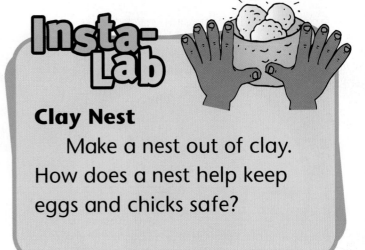

Space and Shelter

Animals need space. They need room to move around, find food, and care for their young.

Animals also need shelter. **Shelter** is a safe place to live. Prairie dogs dig holes for shelter. There they hide from animals that could eat them. The holes also keep them safe from bad weather. Owls and squirrels use trees for shelter. Some tigers and bears use caves.

Insta-Lab

Clay Nest

Make a nest out of clay. How does a nest help keep eggs and chicks safe?

★ **Focus Skill** **MAIN IDEA AND DETAILS**

Why do animals need space?

How Fish Get Oxygen

All animals need oxygen, but they get it in different ways. People and many animals use lungs to get oxygen from air. Fish use gills to take in oxygen from water.

gills

For more links and activities, go to www.hspscience.com

1. MAIN IDEA AND DETAILS Copy and complete this chart. Tell what animals need to survive.

Main Idea and Details

Animals need many things to survive.

Animals need space to move around.	**A** Animals need _____ to eat.	**B** Animals need _____ to drink.	**C** Animals need _____ to stay safe.	**D** Animals need _____ from air or from water.

2. DRAW CONCLUSIONS Why do different kinds of animals need different kinds of shelter?

3. VOCABULARY Use the term **survive** to tell about this picture.

Test Prep

4. Why do most small animals need less food and water than larger animals?

Links

Math

Compare Amounts

Different animals need different amounts of food. Use the chart to compare how much food three dogs eat each day. Which eats the most? The least? How much would each dog eat in 3 days?

Dog	Amount of Food
Sandy	1 cup
Rosey	2 cups
Bo	3 cups

For more links and activities, go to www.hspscience.com

What Do Plants Need?

Fast Fact

There are more than 300,000 kinds of plants. They all need the same things to live. Knowing the things all plants need helps you predict what will happen to plants that do not get them.

What Plants Need to Grow

You need

- 2 plants
- cup of water

Step 1

Put both plants in a sunny place. Water only one plant. **Predict** what will happen.

Step 2

Make a chart like this one.

Plant with water	Plant with no water

Step 3

Observe both plants every day. Water only one plant. Record any changes. Was your **prediction** correct?

Inquiry Skill

When you **predict**, you use what you know to say what you think will happen.

43

VOCABULARY
nutrients

 READING FOCUS SKILL

MAIN IDEA AND DETAILS Look for details about what plants need to live.

Water, Light, and Air

Plants need water, light, and gases in air to live and grow. They also need **nutrients**, or substances that help them grow, from soil. Plants use all these things to make the food they need.

Different plants need different amounts of water. A cactus grows in a dry desert. A bald-cypress tree grows in a wet swamp. Big trees need much more water than tiny plants do.

Some plants need more light than others. Sunflowers need a lot of sun. Their stems get weak if they do not get enough light. Ferns need only a little sun. They can grow well in the shade.

⭐ **MAIN IDEA AND DETAILS**

What do plants need to live?

Water in Soil

Put moist soil on a paper towel. Put another paper towel on top. Press down. Then remove the soil. What do you see on the paper towels? Wash your hands when you finish.

Room to Grow

As plants grow, they need more space. The roots and stems get bigger and longer. The plants have more leaves. A plant in a small container may need to be moved to a larger one to give it more room to grow.

MAIN IDEA AND DETAILS Why does a plant need room to grow?

1. MAIN IDEA AND DETAILS Copy and complete this chart. Tell what a plant needs to grow.

Main Idea and Details

Plants need many things to grow and stay healthy.

A Plants need water, _____, and _____ to make food.

B Plants need _____ from the soil.

C Plants need _____ to grow bigger.

2. SUMMARIZE Write two sentences that tell what this lesson is about.

3. VOCABULARY Why do plants need **nutrients**?

Test Prep

4. What do all plants need?
  A. water and no light
  B. water and light
  C. a lot of water
  D. a lot of light

Links

Writing

Sweet Potato Journal
Stick toothpicks in a sweet potato to hold it partly in a jar of water. Put the jar in a sunny place. Observe the sweet potato for a month. Draw pictures and write sentences about how it changes.

 For more links and activities, go to **www.hspscience.com**

Tomato Says, "Pass the Salt!"

According to experts, a large amount of U.S. farmland is too salty. They say each year about 101,000 square kilometers (38,000 square miles) of U.S. farmland can not be used. The soil has too much salt.

Most plants can't grow in soil that has too much salt. But scientists have made a new kind of tomato that grows well in salty soil. The plant can even be watered with salty water.

A New Kind of Plant

Scientists have figured out a way to change how a tomato plant grows. The change allows the tomato plant to absorb salty water. The plant stores salt in its leaves, where it will not harm the plant or the fruit.

The scientists who grew the special tomatoes are also working on making other plants that can live in salty soil.

Think About It

How might plants that can grow in salty soil help farmers?

Salt of the Earth

Scientists say that plants such as corn, wheat, and peas could all be changed to be able to grow in salty soil.

Find out more! Log on to **www.hspscience.com**

How Much Rain?

Brian Kessler knows plants need water. He has learned that plants get water when it rains.

Water comes from the water cycle. "I like how the water cycle works," says Brian. In the water cycle, water becomes a gas in the air, forms clouds, and comes back to Earth as rain or snow.

At home, Brian uses a weather tool. It is called a rain gauge. The rain gauge measures how much rain falls. Brian uses his rain gauge to keep track of how much rain falls at his home.

You Can Do It!

What Seeds Need

You need
- bean seeds
- 2 zip-top bags
- dry paper towel
- very wet paper towel

What to Do

1. Put a few seeds and a very wet paper towel in one bag. Close the bag tightly.
2. Put a few seeds and a dry paper towel in the other bag. Close the bag tightly.
3. Observe the seeds each day for a week.

Draw Conclusions

What happened to the seeds in each bag? What do seeds need to grow?

Plants, Pets, Both, or Neither?

Ask ten people if they take care of plants, pets, both, or neither. Record their answers with tally marks. Use the answers to make a bar graph.

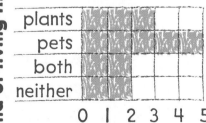

People Who Care for Living Things

kind of living thing

plants
pets
both
neither

0 1 2 3 4 5

number of people

Review and Test Preparation

Vocabulary Review

Use the terms below to complete the sentences. The page numbers tell you where to look if you need help.

living p. 32   **survive** p. 38

nonliving p. 34   **shelter** p. 39

1. A _____ thing does not need food, water, and air.

2. A cave may be a kind of _____.

3. Plants are _____ things.

4. Animals need food, water, and oxygen to _____.

Check Understanding

5. How are these things the same?

    A. They both need oxygen.
    B. They both need food.
    C. They are both living things.
    D. They are both nonliving things.

6. How are these animals

alike?

F. They both use gills to take in oxygen.

G. They both use lungs to take in oxygen.

H. They both need to take in oxygen.

J. Neither of them needs to take in oxygen.

Critical Thinking

7. How are these plants different from nonliving things?

8. Think about what animals need to live. How will the needs of a rabbit change as it grows?

2 Animals

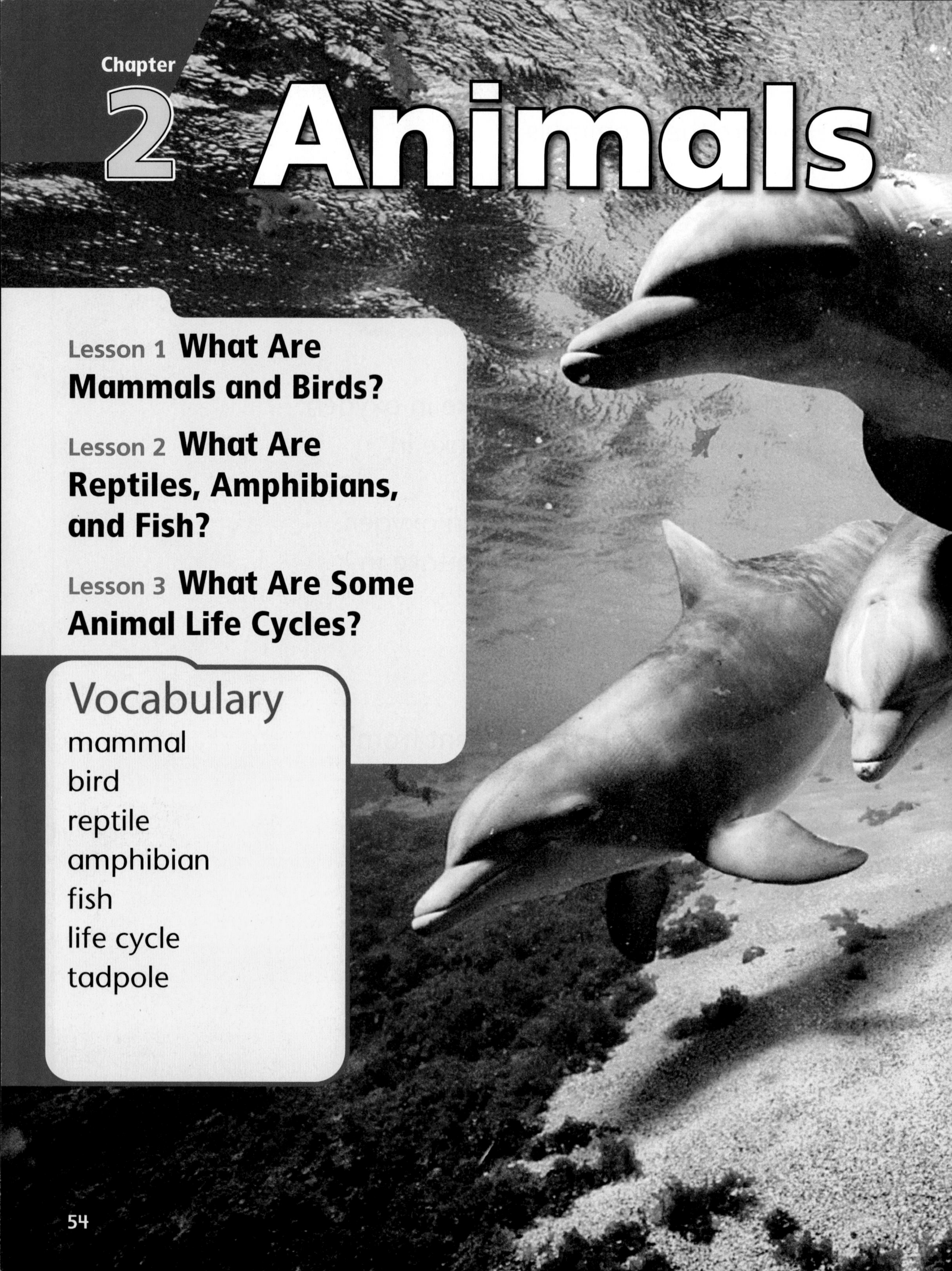

Lesson 1 What Are Mammals and Birds?

Lesson 2 What Are Reptiles, Amphibians, and Fish?

Lesson 3 What Are Some Animal Life Cycles?

Vocabulary

mammal
bird
reptile
amphibian
fish
life cycle
tadpole

I wonder...

How do dolphins breathe?

What do **you** wonder?

What Are Mammals and Birds?

No two zebras have exactly the same markings. You can compare animals in many ways.

Compare Hair and Feathers

You need

● feather

● hand lens

Step 1

Observe the feather with the hand lens. What does it look like and feel like?

Step 2

Observe the hair on your arm. **Compare** the hair with the feather.

Step 3

Draw pictures of what you observed. Write about how the feather and hair are alike and different.

Inquiry Skill

Comparing hair and a feather helps you understand how birds and mammals are alike and different.

57

VOCABULARY

mammal
bird

 READING FOCUS SKILL

COMPARE AND CONTRAST Look for ways mammals and birds are alike and different.

Mammals

Scientists look at animals' body parts when they group animals. A **mammal** has fur or hair that covers the skin on its body. Most mammal mothers give birth to live young. The young drink milk from their mothers' bodies.

A lion and a chipmunk are mammals. They have fur on their bodies. Their young are born live and drink milk from their mothers' bodies.

▲ chipmunk

◀ lion and cub

A manatee is also a mammal. A manatee does not have fur. But it does have some hair on its skin. A manatee mother gives birth to live young. The young drink milk from their mother's body. A manatee lives in water, but it has lungs, like other mammals. A manatee must rise to the top of the water to breathe in oxygen from the air.

▼ dolphin

A dolphin is a mammal, too. A dolphin mother gives birth to live young. The young drink milk from their mother's body. A dolphin uses its lungs to breathe in oxygen from the air.

COMPARE AND CONTRAST **How are mammals alike?**

Focus Skill

▲ heron

Birds

Birds are another group of animals. A heron is a bird. A **bird** has feathers that cover the skin on its body. A bird also has wings. A heron mother lays eggs. Chicks hatch from the eggs.

Insta-Lab

Make a Model

Use chenille sticks to make a model of a bird or a mammal. Ask a classmate to guess which animal you made. Tell why you made the model as you did.

◀ blue jays

A blue jay is a bird, too. It has feathers and wings that it uses to fly. A blue jay mother lays eggs.

penguins ▼

A penguin is also a bird. It has feathers and wings, but it cannot fly. It uses its wings as flippers to swim. A penguin mother lays one egg. The father keeps the egg warm until the new penguin hatches.

Birds are the only animals that have feathers. Birds have wings, and they lay eggs to have young.

COMPARE AND CONTRAST
How are birds alike?

Mammals and Birds Are Different

This chart lists some details about four animals. Talk about the information it shows.

Mammals and Birds

animal	body covering	how it has its young	what it feeds its young	where it lives
	fur	live	milk from mother's body	land
	feathers	eggs	food that parents find	land
	some hair	live	milk from mother's body	water
	feathers	eggs	food that parents find	land

COMPARE AND CONTRAST How are mammals and birds different?

1. COMPARE AND CONTRAST Draw and complete this chart. Tell how the animals are different.

Mammals and Birds

alike	different
Both have body coverings.	Mammals have fur or **A** ____. Birds have **B** ____.
Both have young.	Mammals have **C** ____ young. Birds lay **D** ____.

2. SUMMARIZE Use the chart to write a summary of the lesson.

3. VOCABULARY Use the word **mammal** to tell about this picture.

Test Prep

4. You see an animal that flies. It also has feathers. What can you tell about this animal?

A. It is a mammal.

B. It is a bird.

C. It drinks milk.

D. It lives in water.

Links

Writing

Animal Information

Draw a picture of a mammal or a bird. Write its name, whether it is a mammal or a bird, what its body covering is, and where it lives. Share your work with your classmates.

animal	robin
kind of animal	bird
body covering	feathers
where it lives	park

 For more links and activities, go to **www.hspscience.com**

What Are Reptiles, Amphibians, and Fish?

Fast Fact

There are more kinds of fish than there are kinds of mammals, birds, reptiles, and amphibians all put together. You can classify, or sort, animals to better understand all the kinds there are.

Classify Animals

You need

● animal picture cards

● index cards

Step 1

Observe the animals. How are they alike? How are they different?

Step 2

Classify the animals into groups. The animals in each group should be alike in some way.

Step 3

Write a label for each group. Tell how the animals in the group are alike.

Inquiry Skill

Classifying animals helps you see how they are alike and how they are different.

Reading in Science

VOCABULARY

reptile
amphibian
fish

 READING FOCUS SKILL

COMPARE AND CONTRAST Look for ways in which reptiles, amphibians, and fish are alike. Look for ways in which they are different.

Reptiles

A lizard is a reptile. A **reptile** has dry skin covered with scales. Most reptiles walk on four legs. Most reptile mothers lay eggs.

◄ **lizard**

corn snake ▶

A snake is a reptile. Like a lizard, it has dry, scaly skin. Unlike a lizard, a snake has no legs. Most snake mothers lay eggs, but some give birth to live young.

A turtle is a reptile. It has dry, scaly skin. A turtle is the only reptile that has a shell. Some turtles live on land and have legs and feet. Other turtles live in the water. Many water turtles have flippers instead of feet. Turtle mothers lay eggs on land.

Reptiles are the only animals with dry, scaly skin. What other reptiles can you name?

▲ turtle

COMPARE AND CONTRAST How are reptiles alike?

Insta-Lab

Snake Skin

Different kinds of snakes have different colors and markings on their skins. Use a hand lens to look at the skin of the snake shown on this page. Draw what you see.

Amphibians

A frog is an amphibian. An **amphibian** has smooth, wet skin. The young hatch from eggs. They live in water. Most adult amphibians live on land.

A salamander is an amphibian. Its skin is smooth and wet. Most salamander mothers lay their eggs in water. Most adult salamanders live on land.

Most amphibians have smooth, wet skin. Young amphibians live in water and take in oxygen through gills. Most adult amphibians live on land and breathe with lungs.

▲ frog

salamander ▼

COMPARE AND CONTRAST How are amphibians alike?

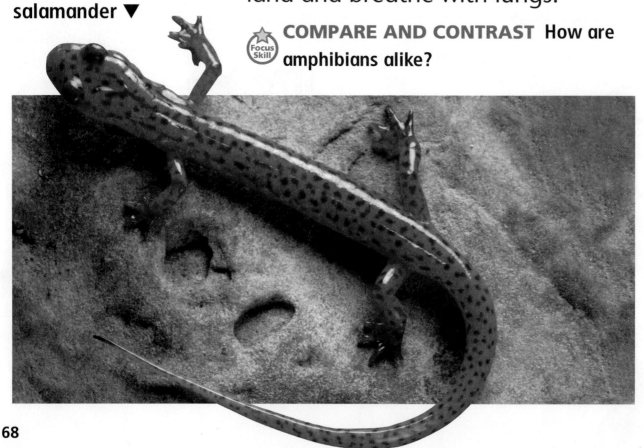

▲ shark

angelfish ▶

Fish

An angelfish is a fish. A **fish** lives in water and takes in oxygen through gills. It has scales that cover its body. It uses its fins to swim. An angelfish mother lays many eggs.

A shark is a fish. It takes in oxygen through gills and has scales. Its large, strong fins help it swim fast. A shark mother gives birth to live young.

All fish live in water and take in oxygen through gills. Most fish have scales and fins.

⭐ Focus Skill **COMPARE AND CONTRAST How are fish alike?**

Reptiles, Amphibians, and Fish Are Different

This chart lists some details about four animals. Talk about the information it shows.

animal	body covering	how it has its young	where it lives	how it takes in oxygen
	dry, scaly skin	eggs or live	land	lungs
	dry, scaly skin; shell	eggs	land or water	lungs
	smooth, wet skin	eggs	water when young, land as adult	gills when young, lungs as adult
	skin and scales	eggs	water	gills

Reptiles, Amphibians, and Fish

 COMPARE AND CONTRAST How are reptiles, amphibians, and fish different?

1. COMPARE AND CONTRAST Copy and complete this chart. Tell how the animals are different.

Reptiles, Amphibians, and Fish

alike

All have body coverings.

All have a place to live.

different

Reptiles have dry, scaly skin.
Amphibians have **A** ____, wet skin.
Fish have **B** ____.

Reptiles live on land or in **C** ____.
Young amphibians live in **D** ____.
Adult amphibians live on **E** ____.
Fish live in **F** ____.

2. DRAW CONCLUSIONS Are reptiles more like fish or more like amphibians? Explain.

3. VOCABULARY Tell about **reptiles**, **amphibians**, and **fish**.

Test Prep

4. How can you tell whether an animal is a reptile or an amphibian?

Links

Math

Make a Bar Graph
The length of an animal's life is called its life span. The giant tortoise has the longest life span of any animal. The chart shows some animal life spans. Use the data to make a bar graph.

Animal Life Spans

animal	life span
giant tortoise	150 years
alligator	70 years
elephant	70 years
cat	20 years
goldfish	10 years

For more links and activities, go to www.hspscience.com

What Are Some Animal Life Cycles?

Fast Fact

A newborn bison weighs about as much as a seven-year-old child. Animals grow and change. To see how, you can sequence, or put in order, pictures of their lives.

Sequence Animals' Lives

You need

● **picture cards**

Step 1

Sort the pictures. Put all the pictures of the same animal in a group.

Step 2

Sequence, or put in order, each group of picture cards. Show how each animal changes as it grows.

Step 3

Tell why you put your cards in the **sequence** you did.

Inquiry Skill
Sequencing helps you see how things happen in order.

VOCABULARY

life cycle
tadpole

 READING FOCUS SKILL

SEQUENCE Look for what happens first, next, then, and last in each animal's life cycle.

The Life Cycle of a Cat

Every animal has a life cycle. A **life cycle** is all the parts of an animal's life. It begins with a new living thing. When the living thing has its own young, a new life cycle begins.

Young mammals start growing inside their mothers' bodies. Kittens grow inside the mother cat. When the kittens are big enough, they are born.

A newborn kitten is helpless. Its mother must care for it. The mother keeps the kitten safe and clean.

2 kitten about 3 weeks old

1 cat and kittens

Like all mammal mothers, the mother cat feeds her kittens with milk from her body. The milk helps the kittens grow.

The kittens get bigger and stronger. As a kitten grows up, it begins to look more like its parents.

After about one year, the cat is fully grown. It can have kittens of its own.

 SEQUENCE What happens first, next, then, and last as a cat grows?

3 young cat about 6 months old

4 adult cat

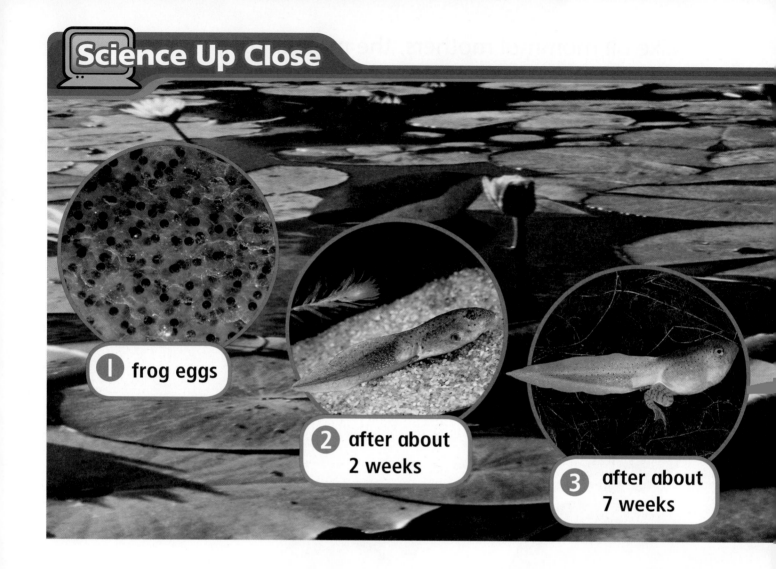

1 frog eggs

2 after about 2 weeks

3 after about 7 weeks

The Life Cycle of a Frog

The life cycle of a frog is different from the life cycles of most other animals. First, a **tadpole**, or young frog, hatches from an egg. A tadpole lives in water. It uses its gills to take in oxygen and its tail to swim. It does not yet look like its parents.

Next, the tadpole eats water plants and insects. It gets bigger and grows two back legs.

5 after about 14 weeks

4 after about
9 weeks

For more links and activities, go to
www.hspscience.com

Then, the tadpole starts
to look more like a frog. It
still has a tail, and now it also
has four legs. It uses lungs to
breathe.

Last, the frog is fully grown
and has no tail. The frog looks
like its parents. It lives on land
most of the time. It can have
its own young.

SEQUENCE What happens first,
next, then, and last as a frog grows?

Insta-Lab

A Dragonfly's Life Cycle

Look at the three picture
cards that show a dragonfly's
life cycle. Put them in the
sequence in which they
happen. Why did you put the
cards in the order you did?

The Life Cycle of a Sea Turtle

A sea turtle is a reptile. A sea turtle mother comes out of the ocean at night. She crawls up the beach alone.

The sea turtle digs a hole. She lays her eggs in the hole and buries them to keep them safe. Then she goes back to the ocean.

In about 60 days, the young turtles hatch. They dig their way out of the sand. Then they hurry into the ocean. They will grow to be like their parents.

SEQUENCE **What happens after a turtle hatches?**

Focus Skill

1. SEQUENCE Draw and complete this chart. Tell what happens first, next, then, and last in the life cycle of the frog.

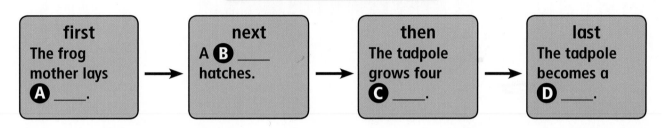

Frog Life Cycle

first	next	then	last
The frog mother lays **A** ____.	A **B** ____ hatches.	The tadpole grows four **C** ____.	The tadpole becomes a **D** ____.

2. SUMMARIZE Use the chart to write a summary of the lesson.

3. VOCABULARY Explain the meanings of the terms **life cycle** and **tadpole**.

Test Prep

4. Which is the correct sequence of a life cycle?
   A. tadpole, frog, egg
   B. one-month-old puppy, newborn puppy, dog
   C. egg, young sea turtle, adult sea turtle
   D. egg, frog, tadpole

Art

Model an Animal's Life Cycle
Choose an animal. Use clay to model the stages of that animal's life cycle.

 For more links and activities, go to www.hspscience.com

Searching for the Giant Squid

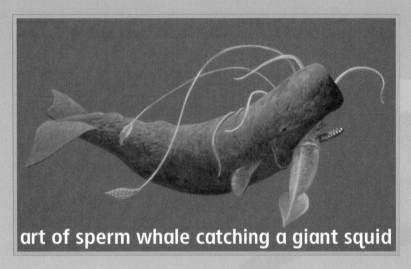

art of sperm whale catching a giant squid

There is a giant creature lurking in the depths of Earth's oceans. It can grow up to 18 meters (60 feet) long. This giant is not some monster, however. It is the giant squid.

But scientists have never seen the giant alive. They want to learn more about this huge animal that lives deep in the ocean.

Scientists believe giant squid live about a mile down in the ocean. They live in the coldest, darkest part of the ocean. What little scientists know about this giant is from dead animals that have washed up on a beach or been caught in fishing nets.

Down in the Deep

Recently, scientists traveled in small submarines to look for the giant squid. Even with the light from the submarine, they could not find a giant squid.

The sperm whale is the giant squid's main enemy. Scientists attached video cameras to the heads of some sperm whales with suction cups. They hoped the cameras would take pictures of giant squid swimming. The cameras filmed other types of squids, but not the giant squid. For now, the giant squid remains a mystery.

Think About It

Why have scientists attached video cameras to the heads of sperm whales?

What Does a Giant Squid Look Like?

A giant squid has eight arms and two tentacles. A tentacle is like an arm, except it is much longer.

A giant squid can be 60 feet long and weigh 1,000 pounds.

A giant squid has huge eyes, as big as a kid's head.

A giant squid has a beak that looks somewhat like a parrot's beak.

Spin-In

Find out more! Log on to
www.hspscience.com

WORKING WITH ANIMALS

To some people, JoAnne Simerson has the greatest job in the world. Simerson works in a zoo. She is an expert on animal behavior.

Simerson works with many kinds of animals. Her favorites are big mammals like polar bears. In the wild, polar bears play games with one another. In the zoo, Simerson encourages the bears to do the same thing. She gives the bears different toys. The bears need to play so they stay active and learn new things.

You Can Do It!

How Body Coverings Help Animals

You need
- 2 thermometers
- mitten

What to Do

1. Make sure the thermometers show the same temperature. Record the temperature.

2. Put one thermometer in the mitten. Put both of the thermometers in the freezer. Wait 10 minutes.

3. Take the thermometers out of the freezer. Record the temperatures.

Draw Conclusions

How is the mitten like an animal's body covering? How does a body covering help an animal?

Animal Group Survey

Think of a question about animals. For example, you might ask which animal group is the most interesting. Ask 10 people your question. Record their answers. Show their answers in a graph. Share your graph.

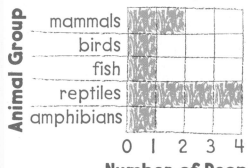

Most Interesting Animal Group

Animal Group: mammals, birds, fish, reptiles, amphibians

Number of People: 0 1 2 3 4

Review and Test Preparation

Vocabulary Review

Use the terms to complete the sentences. The page numbers tell you where to look if you need help.

mammal p. 58   **amphibian** p. 68

bird p. 60   **life cycle** p. 74

reptile p. 66   **tadpole** p. 76

1. An animal with fur or hair is a _____.

2. A young frog is a _____.

3. An animal with dry, scaly skin is a _____.

4. An animal with smooth, wet skin is an _____.

5. All the stages of an animal's life are its _____.

6. An animal that has feathers and lays eggs is a _____.

Check Understanding

7. Write **first**, **next**, **then**, and **last** to show the sequence.

_____ _____ _____ _____

8. How are these animals alike?

   A. Both lay eggs.
   B. Both have shells.
   C. Both are reptiles.
   D. Both care for their young.

Critical Thinking

Adam observes some birds in a tree.

9. What is happening in each picture?

10. Write about and draw another animal's life cycle.

Lesson 1 What Are the Parts of a Plant?

Lesson 2 How Do Plants Differ?

Lesson 3 What Are Some Plant Life Cycles?

Vocabulary

roots
stems
leaves
flowers
trunk
shrub
life cycle
germinate

I wonder...

What will happen to these dandelion seeds after they reach the ground?

What do **you** wonder?

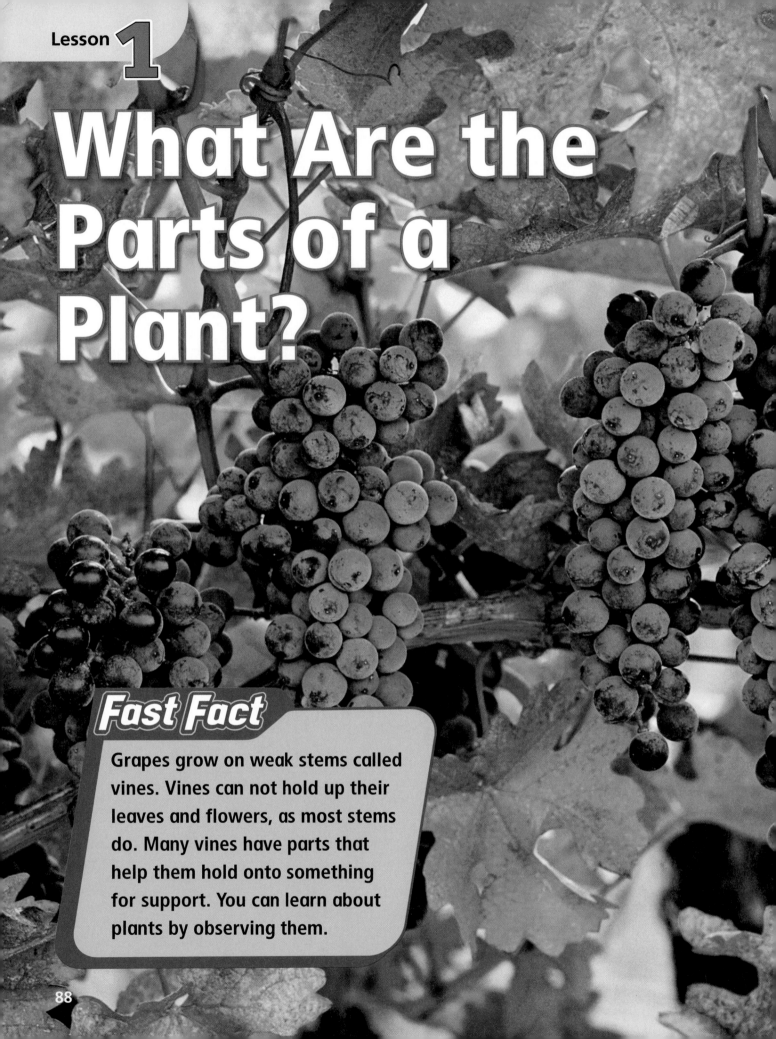

What Are the Parts of a Plant?

Fast Fact

Grapes grow on weak stems called vines. Vines can not hold up their leaves and flowers, as most stems do. Many vines have parts that help them hold onto something for support. You can learn about plants by observing them.

Parts of a Plant

You need

- **2 carnations**
- **2 clear cups of colored water**

Step 1

Bend the stem of one carnation.

Step 2

Put each carnation in a cup of colored water.

Step 3

Observe the carnations for two days. What changes do you see?

Inquiry Skill

You can use your senses of sight, smell, and touch to **observe** plants.

VOCABULARY

roots
stems
leaves
flowers

 READING FOCUS SKILL

MAIN IDEA AND DETAILS Look for details about each part of a plant.

Parts of a Plant

Plants need sunlight, air, water, and nutrients from the soil to grow. Each part of a plant helps the plant get the things it needs.

Roots take in water and nutrients from the soil. Some roots also store food for plants. Most plants, such as this rose plant, have roots that grow underground. They help hold the plant in the ground.

Stems carry water and nutrients from the roots to the leaves. Most stems also help hold up the plant so it can get light.

rose plant ▶

stem

roots

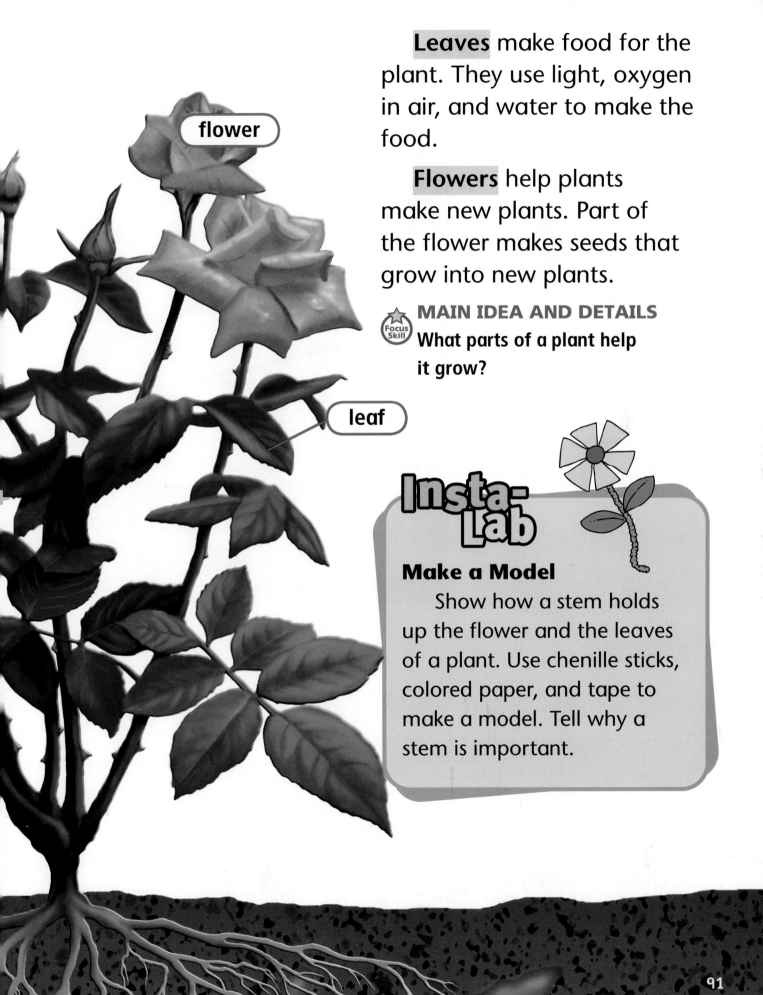

flower

leaf

Leaves make food for the plant. They use light, oxygen in air, and water to make the food.

Flowers help plants make new plants. Part of the flower makes seeds that grow into new plants.

⭐ (Focus Skill) **MAIN IDEA AND DETAILS**
What parts of a plant help it grow?

Insta-Lab

Make a Model

Show how a stem holds up the flower and the leaves of a plant. Use chenille sticks, colored paper, and tape to make a model. Tell why a stem is important.

Parts of a Flower

▲ petals with pollen

▲ fruit with seeds

Flowers are made up of many parts. The petals are usually the colorful parts. The pollen is like a powder. Pollen helps the plant make seeds. A fruit grows around the seeds to hold and protect them.

MAIN IDEA AND DETAILS What are some parts of a flower?

For more links and activities, go to **www.hspscience.com**

1. MAIN IDEA AND DETAILS Copy and complete this chart. Write details about each plant part.

Main Idea and Details

> Each part of a plant helps the plant get the things it needs to live.

Roots take in **A** _____ and nutrients from soil.	A **B** _____ carries water to the leaves.	Leaves make **C** _____ for the plant.	**D** _____ help plants make new plants.

2. DRAW CONCLUSIONS What would happen to a plant if an animal ate all its leaves?

3. VOCABULARY Use the terms **roots**, **stem**, and **leaves** to tell how this plant gets and uses water.

Test Prep

4. How do flowers help make new plants?

Links

Plant Riddles

Use four index cards. On each card, write a riddle about a plant part. Write the answer on the back. Trade cards with a partner. Read each riddle, and name the plant part.

> I carry water to the leaves. What am I?

> I help hold the plant in the ground. What am I?

> I help make new plants. What am I?

> I make food for the plant. What am I?

For more links and activities, go to www.hspscience.com

How Do Plants Differ?

Fast Fact

Some plants have stems that grow partly underground. You can classify plants by looking at their parts.

Classify Leaves

You need

● leaves   ● index cards

Step 1

Observe the leaves. How are they alike? How are they different?

Step 2

Classify the leaves by grouping leaves that are alike.

Step 3

Write a label for each group of leaves. Tell how they are alike. Then tell about leaves you see where you live.

Inquiry Skill

When you **classify** things, you show how they are alike and how they are different.

VOCABULARY

trunk
shrub

 READING FOCUS SKILL

COMPARE AND CONTRAST Look for ways plants are alike and ways they are different.

Kinds of Leaves

Plants have leaves that are different shapes and sizes. Leaves can be long, short, wide, or narrow. They can be shaped like needles. Some leaves have smooth edges. Others have wavy or pointed edges. Some are divided into parts.

plant ▼

 COMPARE AND CONTRAST How are the fern, spruce, and maple leaves different?

| **Fern** | **Spruce** | **Maple** |

| Tulip | Cactus | Tree | Shrub |

Kinds of Stems

Plants have different kinds of stems. A tree has one main stem called a **trunk**. It is hard and woody. A **shrub**, or bush, is a plant with many woody stems. Other plants, such as tulips, have soft stems. A cactus has a thick stem that stores water.

 COMPARE AND CONTRAST
How are stems different?

What Kind of Stem?
Look outside and choose a plant. Does it have a woody stem or a soft stem? Does it have one stem or many stems? Draw a picture of the stem or stems. Describe the plant to a classmate.

Kinds of Roots

Most plants have either one thick main root or many thin roots. The thin roots are usually about the same size.

Carrot plants have one thick root. Tiny, thin roots grow out from it. Corn plants have many thin roots. Smaller roots grow out from them.

 **COMPARE AND CONTRAST** How are the roots of carrot plants different from the roots of corn plants?

carrot plant ▶

roots

◀ corn plant

roots

1. COMPARE AND CONTRAST Copy and complete this chart. Tell how plants are alike and how they are different.

Plants

alike

Plants have leaves.

Plants have stems.

Plants have roots.

different

Some leaves have smooth edges.
Some leaves have edges that are wavy or **A** _____.

Some stems are hard and woody.
Some stems are **B** _____.

Some plants have one **C** _____ root.
Some plants have many **D** _____ roots.

2. SUMMARIZE Write a sentence that tells the most important idea of this lesson.

3. VOCABULARY Use the term **trunk** to tell about a tree.

Test Prep

4. Which kind of plant has many woody stems?

A. flower
B. shrub
C. tree
D. tulip

Links

Math

Measure Lengths of Leaves
Leaves from different kinds of plants are different lengths. Gather leaves from five kinds of plants. Use a ruler to measure the length of each one. Record the information in a chart.

Lengths of Leaves

plant	leaf length
ivy vine	2 inches
maple tree	
pine tree	
lilac bush	

 For more links and activities, go to www.hspscience.com

What Are Some Plant Life Cycles?

Fast Fact

When pinecones first grow on a tree, they are soft and green. As pinecones grow, you can see that they become hard and brown. You can communicate what you observe about how plants change.

Life Cycle of a Bean Plant

You need

- cup filled with soil
- pencil
- beans
- water

Step 1

Use the pencil to make holes in the soil. Put a bean in each hole. Cover the beans with soil.

Step 2

Water the soil. Put the cup in a warm, sunny place.

Step 3

Observe the cup each day for two weeks. Water the soil when it is dry. Draw what you observe. **Communicate** what is happening.

Inquiry Skill

You can use pictures to help you **communicate**.

VOCABULARY
life cycle
germinate

 READING FOCUS SKILL

SEQUENCE Look for the order of the stages of a plant's life cycle.

Life Cycle of a Bean Plant

All the stages of a plant's life make up its **life cycle**. A plant's life cycle begins with a seed. First, the seed **germinates**, or begins to grow. Next, the seed grows into a mature, or adult, plant. Then, the plant makes seeds that may grow into new plants.

Inside each bean seed is a tiny plant and some stored food. The plant uses the food when it begins to grow.

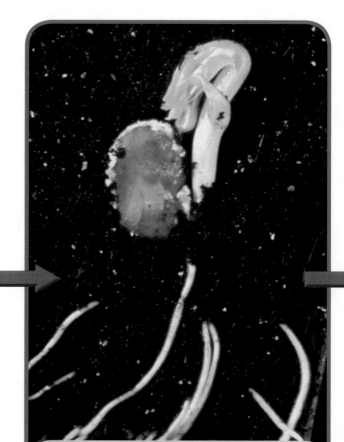

When a seed gets water, warmth, and oxygen from the air, it may germinate, or start to grow. The root grows down.

Last, a new life cycle begins. Different kinds of plants have different life cycles.

⭐ **Focus Skill** **SEQUENCE** What happens after a bean seed germinates?

The stem of the tiny plant breaks through the ground. It grows up toward the light. It starts making food that the plant uses to keep growing.

More leaves and stems grow. Flowers will grow on the bean plant and make seeds.

Life Cycle of a Pine Tree

A pine tree's life cycle begins with a seed. But pine trees do not have flowers and fruits that hold seeds. Instead, they make seeds in cones.

⭐ **SEQUENCE** **What happens after a pinecone makes seeds?**

Next, the seeds germinate. After the new plants grow a little, they look like small pine trees.

Pinecones hold and protect the pine seeds until they are ready to grow. Then, the pinecones open up. The wind blows the seeds, and they fall to the ground.

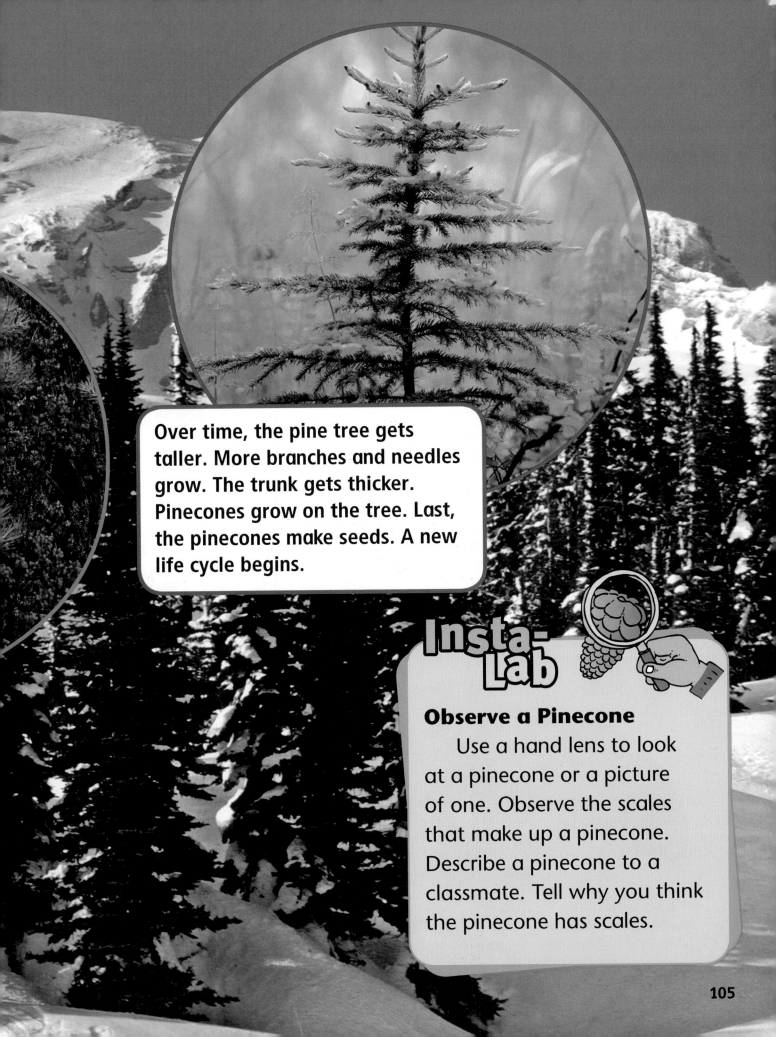

Over time, the pine tree gets taller. More branches and needles grow. The trunk gets thicker. Pinecones grow on the tree. Last, the pinecones make seeds. A new life cycle begins.

Insta-Lab

Observe a Pinecone

Use a hand lens to look at a pinecone or a picture of one. Observe the scales that make up a pinecone. Describe a pinecone to a classmate. Tell why you think the pinecone has scales.

Plants Look Like Their Parents

Plants make new plants that look very much like them. At first, the new plant may look different. Later, it grows the same kind of leaves, stems, and flowers or cones as the plant it came from.

An oak tree grows from a seed inside an acorn. The seed grows into a small plant. The plant grows and changes until it looks like an oak tree.

Even though the new tree is like its parent, the new tree can look a little different. When the new tree is grown, it may be taller or shorter than the parent tree. The new tree may have more or fewer branches and smaller or larger leaves.

SEQUENCE What happens as young plants grow and change?

oak tree ▼

acorn

106

Focus Skill

1. SEQUENCE Copy and complete this chart to tell about the life cycle of a bean plant.

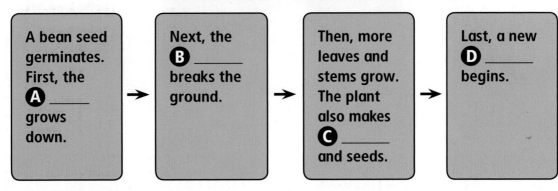

Life Cycle of a Bean Plant

A bean seed germinates. First, the **A** _____ grows down. → Next, the **B** _____ breaks the ground. → Then, more leaves and stems grow. The plant also makes **C** _____ and seeds. → Last, a new **D** _____ begins.

2. DRAW CONCLUSIONS How are flowers and pinecones alike?

3. VOCABULARY Explain the meanings of the terms **life cycle** and **germinate**.

Test Prep

4. What will a seed grow into? How do you know?

Links

Physical Education

A Germinating Seed

Pretend you are the tiny plant inside a seed. Use your body to show how the seed opens and the tiny plant begins to grow.

 For more links and activities, go to www.hspscience.com

Making a Difference

Children in Clarksville, Tennessee, have green thumbs. But they did not paint their thumbs green. We say they have green thumbs because they planted more than 100 trees.

The kids planted the trees as part of Make a Difference Day. The newspaper *USA Today* started Make a Difference Day more than 14 years ago.

On Make a Difference Day, millions of people do something nice for their communities. Three million people took part in a recent Make a Difference Day.

Planting Trees

The children in Clarksville had to work hard to plant 125 trees. The trees were about 10 to 12 inches tall when they were planted.

The trees will be good for the community. They will give lots of shade to block the sun. People will enjoy the shade in the summer because it can get very hot in Tennessee.

The trees will also become homes for birds and help keep the air clean.

Think About It

Can you think of other ways that trees help a community?

Idea Generator

If kids and their families want to help but do not know what to do, they can turn to the Idea Generator. This is a Website run by *USA Today*. After a person answers three questions, the Idea Generator comes up with ideas for Make a Difference projects.

Find out more! Log on to
www.hspscience.com

We Need Plants

Kevin Sykes and his classmates like plants. What did they do? They learned how to plant shrubs. After they dug a hole, they placed the plant in the ground and filled the hole with soil. Then they gave the plant plenty of water.

The kids think plants do all kinds of good things for Earth. Scientists agree. The roots of plants hold the soil in place so it does not wash away. Seeds and other plant parts give animals and people food to eat. Plants, such as trees, give us shade and wood to build things.

You Can Do It!

Which Grow First?

What to Do

1. Plant a few seeds from two kinds of plants in a cup filled with soil. Plant more seeds from the two plants in another cup filled with soil.

2. Make sure the seeds in both cups get water and sunlight.

3. Observe to see which seeds start to grow first.

Materials
- seeds from two kinds of plants
- 2 cups   • soil   • water

Draw Conclusions

Did all the seeds start to grow at the same time? Why do you think this happened?

The Parts of Plants You Eat

Find pictures of plant parts you eat. Then make a chart to show which part of the plant you eat.

The Plant Parts I Eat

plant parts	stem	leaf	root	flower	seed	fruit

Review and Test Preparation

Vocabulary Review

Match each term with the picture that shows its meaning. The page numbers tell where to look if you need help.

roots p. 90   **leaves** p. 91

stems p. 90   **flowers** p. 91

1. _____

2. _____

3. _____

4. _____

Check Understanding

5. Write **first, next, then,** and **last** to show the sequence.

_____   _____   _____   _____

6. Which sentence gives a correct detail about plants?

A. Flowers make seeds.

B. Stems make pollen.

C. Roots make food for the plant.

D. Leaves grow underground.

Critical Thinking

7. Why is the root the first part of a plant to grow?

8. Jeanie has a plant that does not look healthy. The soil around the plant looks very dry. What should Jeanie do? Why?

Homes for Living Things

Chapter 4 Living Things in Their Environments

Thistle Dew Farm

TO: raven@hspscience.com

FROM: tyler@hspscience.com

RE: New Martinsville, West Virginia

Dear Raven,

Would you want to be covered in bees? The beekeeper at this honeybee farm thought it was fun. I'm glad he did not ask me to touch a bee! We got to taste the honey.

Tyler

TO: rosa@hspscience.com

FROM: hector@hspscience.com

RE: Awendaw, South Carolina

Dear Rosa,

I saw the coolest thing this weekend. A sea turtle dug a hole in the sand. She used her flippers. Then she placed her eggs inside the hole. Soon young turtles will hatch and make their way to the water.

See you soon,

Hector

Experiment!

Water Pollution

As you do this unit, you will learn about homes that are safe for living things. Plan and do a test. See what happens when you pollute the water needed by a plant.

Living Things in Their Environments

Lesson 1 **What Is an Environment?**

Lesson 2 **How Do Living Things Survive in Different Places?**

Lesson 3 **What Are Food Chains and Food Webs?**

Vocabulary

environment
habitat
adapt
desert
rain forest
grassland
tundra
ocean

pond
food chain
food web

I wonder...

In what kind of environment do elephants live?

What do **you** wonder?

What Is an Environment?

Alligators live in lakes, ponds, and rivers. They can hide in the water while they hunt for food. You can draw conclusions to figure out why animals live in certain places.

Energy Flow

You need

- glass tank with pebbles and soil

- water

- small plants and worms

Step 1

Make a model to show how living things get energy. Put pebbles in the bottom of a glass tank. Put soil on top of the pebbles.

Step 2

Add plants. Water the soil. Place worms in the tank.

Step 3

Observe the tank each day. What changes do you see? How do the living things get energy?

Inquiry Skill

You can make a model to show how plants and animals get energy.

119

READING FOCUS SKILL

MAIN IDEA AND DETAILS Look for details about where animals and plants live.

Environments and Habitats

An **environment** is made up of all the living and nonliving things in a place. Animals and plants are the living things. Water, weather, and rocks are some of the nonliving things. Environments can be hot or cold. They can be wet or dry. Animals and plants from one environment often can not live in another one.

An environment is made up of different habitats. A **habitat** is a place where living things have food and water and the kind of shelter they need. In a forest environment, a pond is a habitat for fish. Part of the forest may be a habitat for birds. What habitats do you see in this picture?

MAIN IDEA AND DETAILS
What do animals and plants need in a habitat?

People and Environments

People can change environments. They may cut down trees and clear away other plants to build houses. When they do this, animals can lose their habitats.

Environments also change when people bring in new plants or animals. People brought water hyacinths to Florida.

The water hyacinths grew quickly and covered the water. They shut out air and light. The other plants began to die. The hyacinths used all the oxygen in the water. Then the fish died.

MAIN IDEA AND DETAILS **What can happen when people change environments?**

water hyacinths

▲ sea otters

red pigfish ▶

How Animals and Plants Adapt

Over time, animals and plants **adapt**, or change, to be able to live in their environment. They adapt in different ways to meet their needs. A fish has gills to take in oxygen from water. An otter has fur to keep it warm.

 MAIN IDEA AND DETAILS

Why do plants and animals adapt?

Insta-Lab

How Feathers Help Ducks

Cut out two paper feathers. Cover both sides of one feather with margarine. Dip both feathers into a bowl of water. Which one does not soak up water? Why do you think ducks have an oily coating on their feathers?

Beaks and Teeth

Animals' beaks and teeth are adapted to help them get food.

You can tell what kind of food a bird eats by looking at the shape of its beak.

▲ eats insects

▲ eats small seeds

▲ eats big seeds

You can tell what kind of food a mammal eats by looking at its teeth.

▲ horse—eats plants

▲ tiger—eats meat

▲ bear—eats plants and meat

For more links and activities, go to www.hspscience.com

1. MAIN IDEA AND DETAILS Copy and complete this chart. Tell about environments.

Main Idea and Details

An environment is made up of living and nonliving things.

| Plants and **A** _____ live in environments. | An environment can be hot, **B** _____, **C** _____, or dry. | There are many habitats in an **D** _____. | Animals have **E** _____ for survival in an environment. |

2. SUMMARIZE Use the chart to write a summary of the lesson.

3. VOCABULARY Use the term **adapt** to tell about this picture.

Test Prep

4. Which are nonliving things in an environment?
   A. air and plants
   B. animals and air
   C. plants and water
   D. water and rocks

Links

Writing

Description of an Environment
Choose an animal. Describe its environment. Then draw a picture of the animal in its environment. Share your work with a classmate.

For more links and activities, go to
www.hspscience.com

How Do Living Things Survive in Different Places?

Fast Fact

Some butterflies stay safe by blending in with their environment. Making inferences will help you figure out how animals stay safe.

How Color Helps a Butterfly

You need

- paper squares
- orange paper
- clock

Step 1

Scatter equal numbers of purple, orange, and yellow squares on the sheet of paper.

Step 2

Count the purple squares for five seconds. Record the number. Repeat for the orange and yellow squares.

Step 3

Which color squares were hardest to count? What can you **infer** about how color helps a butterfly?

Inquiry Skill

When you **infer**, you use what you see to figure out why something happened.

127

Reading in Science

VOCABULARY
desert
rain forest
grassland
tundra
ocean
pond

READING FOCUS SKILL

MAIN IDEA AND DETAILS Look for ways animals and plants have adapted to their environments.

Desert

Animals and plants have adapted to the environments they live in.

A **desert** is a dry environment that gets little rain. Few kinds of plants and animals are adapted to living there. A cactus stores water that it can use later. Lizards hide under rocks during the day, when it is hot. They come out to find food at night, when it is cool.

▲ The veiled chameleon eats fruits, flowers, and leaves to get water.

MAIN IDEA AND DETAILS How have plants and animals adapted to living in deserts?

The sharp needles on a saguaro cactus keep away animals that want to eat it.

Rain Forest

A **rain forest** is a wet environment that gets rain almost every day. Many rain forests are also hot all year. They have many tall trees that block the sunlight. Some plants grow high on the trees to reach the light.

Some monkeys live high in the trees, too. They can hold onto branches with their tails. This lets them grab food with their hands. Bats hunt at night, when they can catch flying insects and other small animals.

The green tree frog has sticky feet that help it climb. ▼

Focus Skill **MAIN IDEA AND DETAILS** How have plants and animals adapted to living in rain forests?

▲ Cheetahs are the fastest animals on land. The color of gazelles helps them hide from cheetahs. The cheetahs can not see the gazelles in the grass.

Grassland

A **grassland** is an open environment that is covered with grass. Few trees grow there, so it is hard for large animals to hide. Elephants and other animals travel in groups of their own kind to stay safe. Some animals are able to run fast. This helps them stay safe.

MAIN IDEA AND DETAILS How have animals adapted to living in the grassland?

Insta-Lab

Keeping Warm

Does fat keep animals warm? Place shortening in a plastic bag. Put another plastic bag over each hand. Then put one hand in the bag with the shortening and the other hand in an empty bag. Put both hands in a bowl of cold water. Which hand stays warm longer?

Tundra

A **tundra** is a cold, snowy environment. Plants do not grow very tall, and they grow close together. This helps protect them from the very cold temperatures. Many tundra animals have thick fur to keep them warm. Some animals have fur that changes with the seasons. In spring, new brown fur grows in to help them hide in summer. In fall, white fur grows in to help them hide in winter.

▲ Polar bears stay warm because of their fat and their thick fur.

 MAIN IDEA AND DETAILS

How have plants and animals adapted to living in the tundra?

Caribou travel from place to place to find the plants they eat.

Ocean

An **ocean** is a large body of salt water. Most ocean plants and animals live in the top layer of the ocean. There, the plants can get the sunlight they need, and the animals can find food.

Ocean animals stay safe in many ways. Some fish change colors to help them hide. Others swim fast or hide in small cracks. A jellyfish stings other animals that come too close to it.

MAIN IDEA AND DETAILS How do ocean animals stay safe?

Fish have scales to protect their bodies.

A shark's sharp teeth help it catch food. Its scales and body shape help it swim quickly.

An octopus uses its eight long arms to catch food.

Pond

A **pond** is a small freshwater environment. Water lilies may grow on the surface of a pond. There, they can get the sunlight they need. Many animals, such as beavers, live in ponds. Beavers have webbed feet to help them swim. They use their sharp teeth to cut down trees to build their homes.

 MAIN IDEA AND DETAILS How have plants and animals adapted to living in ponds?

Water striders can walk on the surface of the pond without sinking.

water lilies

1. MAIN IDEA AND DETAILS Copy and complete this chart. Tell how plants and animals have adapted to living in their environments.

Main Idea and Details

Plants and animals have adapted to living in many environments.

| A cactus in the desert can store water. | Grassland animals travel **A** _____. | Animals that live in a tundra have thick **B** _____. | Some ocean animals change their color to **C** _____. | Plants in a pond grow where they can get **D** _____. |

2. DRAW CONCLUSIONS Why would it be hard for a rain-forest animal to live in a grassland environment?

3. VOCABULARY Use the terms **desert** and **tundra** to tell about environments.

Test Prep

4. What kind of environment does an animal with webbed feet probably live in?
   A. cold
   B. warm
   C. dry
   D. wet

Links

Math

Solve a Problem
Use this chart to find out how much more rain falls in a rain forest than in a desert. How could you solve the problem without measuring the difference? Write a math sentence that shows how.

Average Rainfall in One Month	
desert	2 cm
rain forest	20 cm

For more links and activities, go to www.hspscience.com

What Are Food Chains and Food Webs?

Fast Fact

This blue heron eats fish. You can communicate what you learn about what animals eat.

What Animals Eat

You need

- animal cards
- books about animals
- markers

Step 1

Choose a picture of an animal. Find out what that animal eats.

Step 2

Draw and label a picture of the food.

Step 3

Use your pictures and cards to **communicate** your ideas.

Inquiry Skill

When you **communicate** your ideas, you tell what you know.

137

READING FOCUS SKILL

SEQUENCE Look for the order in which animals eat other living things.

Food Chains

Living things need one another to survive. A **food chain** shows the order in which animals eat plants and other animals.

Food chains start with sunlight and plants. In this food chain, first, the grass uses sunlight to make its food. Second, a grasshopper eats the grass. Third, a frog eats the grasshopper. Fourth, a snake eats the frog. Last, a hawk eats the snake.

 SEQUENCE What happens after a grasshopper eats grass?

Insta-Lab

Food Chain Mix-Up

On three index cards, draw a plant and two animals that all belong in the same food chain. Mix up the cards, and ask a partner to put them in the right order. Have your partner explain how the food chain works.

Food Webs

Most animals eat more than one kind of food. So an animal may be part of more than one food chain. Connected food chains are called a **food web**. Look at this food web. Use the arrows to find out the foods each animal eats.

 SEQUENCE What happens after the frog eats the grasshopper?

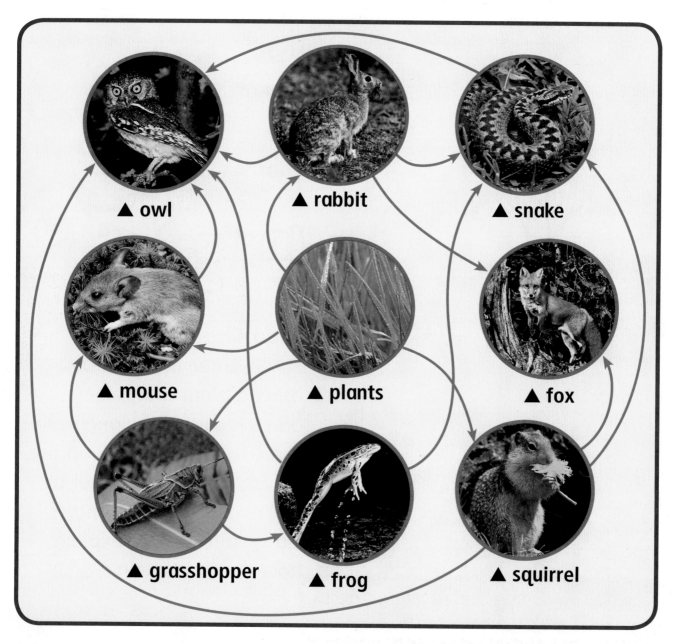

▲ owl ▲ rabbit ▲ snake

▲ mouse ▲ plants ▲ fox

▲ grasshopper ▲ frog ▲ squirrel

1. SEQUENCE Copy and complete this chart to show a food chain.

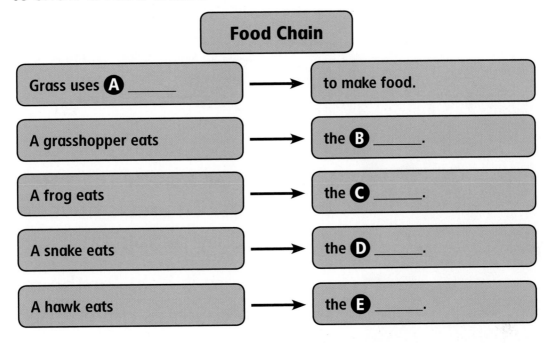

Food Chain

Grass uses **A** _____ → to make food.

A grasshopper eats → the **B** _____.

A frog eats → the **C** _____.

A snake eats → the **D** _____.

A hawk eats → the **E** _____.

2. SUMMARIZE Write two sentences that tell what this lesson is about.

3. VOCABULARY Explain the difference between a **food chain** and a **food web**.

Test Prep

4. Which is a food chain?
   A. plant, fox, mouse
   B. seeds, squirrel, fox
   C. snake, seeds, frog
   D. grasshopper, frog, plant

Links

Art

Food Web Mobile
On index cards, draw and label plants and animals that make up a food web. Punch a hole in the top, the bottom, and both sides of each card. Connect the cards with yarn to show how the food web works. Then hang the cards from a hanger.

For more links and activities, go to **www.hspscience.com**

Helping Hawai'i's Reefs

In Hawai`i, coral reefs surround the islands. The reefs have been damaged by people and ships.

But there is help for the reefs. The United States government has passed laws to help protect the reefs around Hawai`i.

What Are Coral Reefs?

A coral reef is made up of the skeletons of tiny sea animals. A reef is often found in warm, shallow waters. More than half the United States' coral reefs are located in the waters around Hawai`i.

Coral reefs provide homes for other sea animals. Reefs also protect coastlines from dangerous waves. When waves pass over reefs, they slow down and get smaller.

How Are Reefs Formed?

A coral reef is built by tiny sea creatures called coral polyps. When coral polyps die, their hard outer skeletons stay and other polyps grow on top of the skeletons. After a long time, the coral skeletons build up, forming a reef.

A reef can also be formed by people. For example, people have made several reefs by sinking ships or even subway cars. These reefs then provide shelter for fish and a place for underwater plants to grow.

Think About It

How do coral reefs help fish to survive?

Find out more! Log on to
www.hspscience.com

PAL TO THE PANDA

Lu Zhi is a wildlife biologist. A wildlife biologist is a scientist who studies wild animals. Lu works to protect pandas.

Lu has studied giant pandas in China for most of her life. She was one of the first scientists to go into a den with a wild panda. A den is a panda's home. Panda dens are usually in a cave made of rock or in the bottom of a hollow tree.

Pandas live in forest areas where a plant called bamboo is found. Bamboo is a type of grass that pandas eat. Lu works to protect these forest areas.

You Can Do It!

Make a Worm Habitat

Materials
- clear jar
- soil
- water
- leaves
- earthworms

What to Do

1. Nearly fill a clear jar with soil. Sprinkle water on the soil.

2. Place earthworms on the soil. Sprinkle soil and leaves over the earthworms.

3. Observe the habitat for several days. Return the earthworms outdoors.

Draw Conclusions

How did the worms use their habitat? Why do you think earthworms need soil, leaves, and water?

Observe Animals

On a nature walk, list the animals you observe. Tell how the animals might meet their needs for food, water, and shelter.

grass   duck   fly

fish   frog

Review and Test Preparation

Vocabulary Review

Match each term with the picture that shows its meaning. The page numbers tell you where to look if you need help.

desert p. 128	**tundra** p. 131
rain forest p. 129	**ocean** p. 132
grassland p. 130	**pond** p. 134

1. _____

2. _____

3. _____

4. _____

5. _____

6. _____

Check Understanding

7. What is always at the beginning of a
(Focus Skill) food chain?

    A. fish

    B. sunlight and plants

    C. owls

    D. trees and birds

8. In which kind of environment do caribou
and polar bears live?

    F. cold

    G. dry

    H. hot

    J. wet

Critical Thinking

9. These pictures show what an arctic fox
looks like in winter and in summer.

Tell how the fox has adapted to living in
its environment.

10. What might happen to a food web if a
new kind of animal came to live in an
environment?

Our Earth

| Chapter 5 | Exploring Earth's Surface |
| Chapter 6 | Natural Resources |

EARTH SCIENCE

Lexington Children's Museum

TO:	megan@hspscience.com
FROM:	cole@hspscience.com
RE:	Lexington, Kentucky

Dear Megan,
Most of the materials used to build houses come from the earth. I learned about houses around the world when I went to this children's museum. I got to carve a window through a cave wall. That was fun.
Cole

Soda Dam

TO: marcus@hspscience.com
FROM: crystal@hspscience.com
RE: Santa Fe, New Mexico

Dear Marcus,

My family went to Soda Dam. Bubbles rise off the river just like soda bubbles. The water came from deep inside the earth. Mixed with it is white stuff that used to be rocks. It piled up to form the dam. It is really cool!

Crystal

Experiment!

Plants and Erosion

As you do this unit, you will find out about the earth. Plan and do a test. See how plants change the way soil is washed away by water.

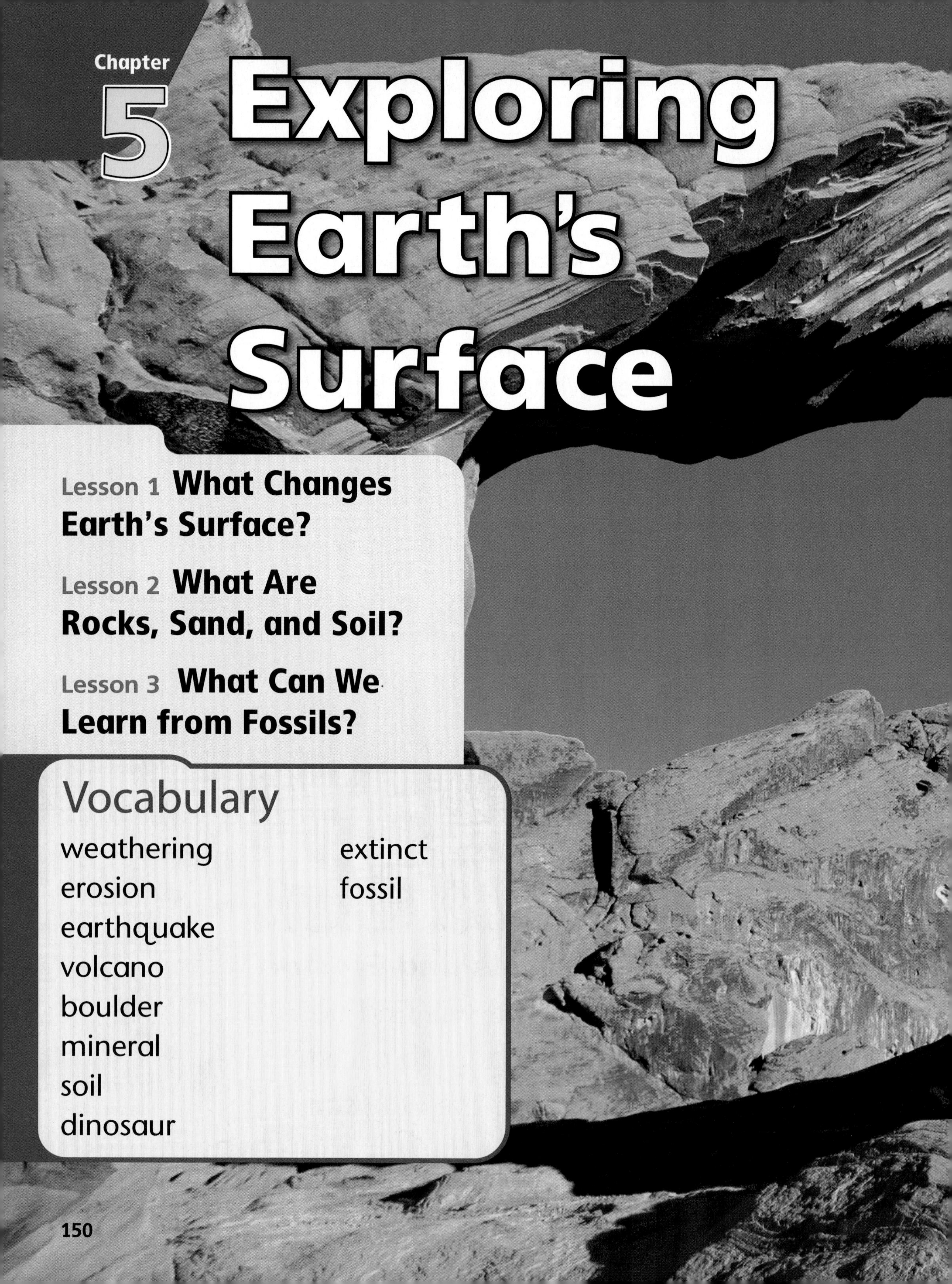

Chapter 5

Exploring Earth's Surface

Lesson 1 **What Changes Earth's Surface?**

Lesson 2 **What Are Rocks, Sand, and Soil?**

Lesson 3 **What Can We Learn from Fossils?**

Vocabulary

weathering
erosion
earthquake
volcano
boulder
mineral
soil
dinosaur
extinct
fossil

I wonder...

Why do some rocks have such odd shapes?

What do you wonder?

What Changes Earth's Surface?

How Land Shapes Change

You need

- rock salt
- hand lens
- jar, sand, and water
- forceps and spoon

Step 1

Hold a grain of rock salt with forceps. **Observe** the size and shape of rock salt with a hand lens.

Step 2

Put a layer of the rock salt in a jar. Add a layer of sand and a few spoonfuls of water. Shake the jar for five minutes.

Step 3

Use forceps to remove the rock salt. **Observe.** How has the rock salt changed?

Inquiry Skill

You can use a hand lens to **observe** more closely changes in small objects.

VOCABULARY

weathering
erosion
earthquake
volcano

READING FOCUS SKILL

CAUSE AND EFFECT Look for the causes and effects of changes to Earth's surface.

Weathering and Erosion

Earth is made up of rock. Often the rock is under water or soil. This rock is Earth's crust. Earth's crust is always changing. One kind of change is caused by weathering. **Weathering** happens when wind and water break down rock into smaller pieces.

Weathering can happen when water freezes in the cracks of rocks. When the water freezes, it takes up more space. It makes the cracks bigger. It can break the rock into pieces.

Strong winds can blow away dry, loose soil and small rocks or sand.

Wind and water may cause erosion. **Erosion** happens when wind or moving water moves sand and small rocks, or pebbles. This movement can cause more weathering and erosion. It changes the shapes of rocks.

 CAUSE AND EFFECT What are the effects of weathering and erosion?

▲ Water can change the shape of rocks. It can make sharp edges smooth.

◄ The rushing waters of a river wore away rock and formed this canyon.

Earthquakes and Volcanoes

Earthquakes and volcanoes can change Earth's surface quickly.

An **earthquake** is a shaking of Earth's surface. It can cause land to fall or rise. An earthquake may form lakes or cause mudslides. If an earthquake happens in the ocean, it can cause a huge wave to form.

▼ volcano

An earthquake caused this change to Earth's surface.

A **volcano** is a place where hot melted rock called lava comes out of the ground onto Earth's surface. The lava builds up to form a mountain.

⭐ *Focus Skill* **CAUSE AND EFFECT** What are some of the effects of earthquakes and volcanoes?

Make a Model

Use clay of different colors to make a model of a volcano. Use your model to tell about volcanoes.

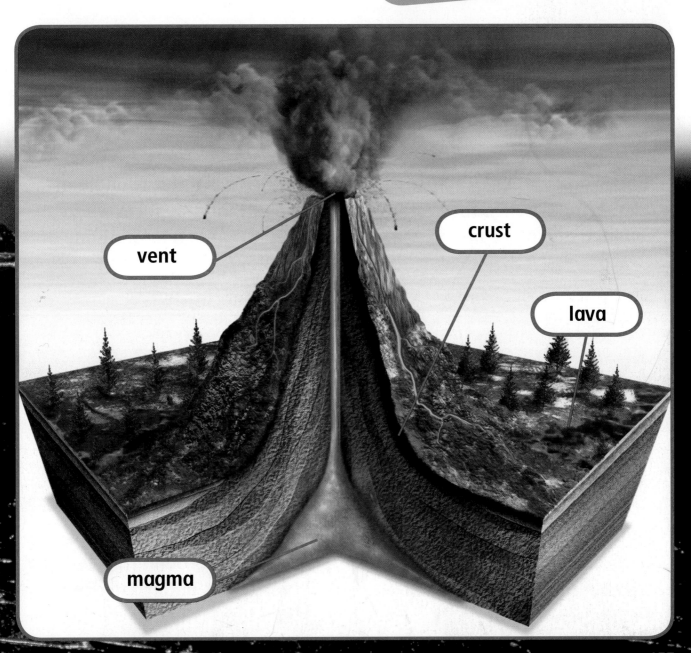

vent

crust

lava

magma

Landforms

Earth's surface has many kinds of landforms. Each kind has a different shape. Some are tall, and some are flat. Each one is formed in a different way.

 CAUSE AND EFFECT What can cause islands to form?

A bay is part of an ocean or a lake. It forms when the water covers a low place on the shore.

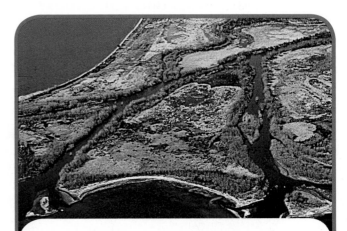

A delta is a flat triangle of land that may form where a river meets a larger body of water.

Mountains are tall landforms that can form when the plates of Earth's crust push against each other.

An island is land that has water all around it. Lava from volcanoes under the oceans can form islands.

Focus Skill

1. CAUSE AND EFFECT Copy and complete the chart. Tell the causes and the effects.

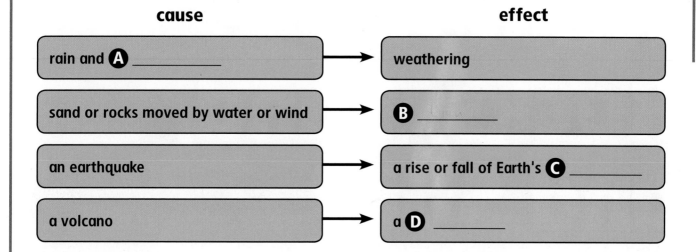

cause		effect
rain and **A** _____	→	weathering
sand or rocks moved by water or wind	→	**B** _____
an earthquake	→	a rise or fall of Earth's **C** _____
a volcano	→	a **D** _____

2. SUMMARIZE Write a summary of this lesson. Begin with the sentence **Earth's surface changes.**

3. VOCABULARY Use the term **weathering** to tell about this picture.

Test Prep

4. What can happen when water or wind moves sand or small pieces of rock?
   A. Earthquakes can happen.
   B. Erosion takes place.
   C. Islands form.
   D. Volcanoes form.

Links

Writing

Description of a Change
Find a picture in this lesson that shows how Earth is changing. Write a few sentences about the picture. Ask a classmate to read the sentences and find the picture you wrote about.

A volcano

 For more links and activities, go to **www.hspscience.com**

What Are Rocks, Sand, and Soil?

Fast Fact

Tiny grains of sand were once part of large rocks. You can use what you know to draw conclusions about how this change happened.

Hardness of Rocks

You need

● rocks ● copper penny ● steel paper clip

Scratch each rock with your fingernail, a penny, and a paper clip.

Make a chart like this one to record which objects leave marks on which rocks.

Which Objects Leave Marks on Rocks?			
	fingernail	penny	paper clip
rock 1			
rock 2			
rock 3			

Objects harder than a rock leave a mark. Look at your chart. **Draw conclusions** about which materials are harder than each rock.

Inquiry Skill

You can **draw conclusions** by using your observations and what you already know.

Reading in Science

VOCABULARY
boulder
mineral
soil

READING FOCUS SKILL

COMPARE AND CONTRAST Look for ways rocks are alike and ways they are different.

Rocks and Sand

Rocks are parts of Earth's crust. Some rocks are so large that you can climb them. A **boulder** is a very large rock. Some rocks are so small that you need a microscope to see them. Pebbles and tiny grains of sand are small rocks.

boulder ▶

Rocks are made up of minerals. A **mineral** is solid matter found in nature. A mineral was never living. Not all rocks look and feel the same because rocks are made in different ways and have different minerals. Rocks can have many colors. Some are rough, and some are smooth. Some rocks are harder than others.

▲ sand

 COMPARE AND CONTRAST How are the rocks below alike? How are they different?

limestone

marble

slate

sandstone

granite

obsidian

163

Soil

Soil is made of small bits of rock mixed with matter that was once living, such as dead plant parts.

There are many kinds of soil. Each kind is made up of different matter, so soils have different properties. A soil may be dark or light. It may feel powdery or sticky. It may have a strong smell.

Some of the things in soil are silt, clay, sand, and humus.

COMPARE AND CONTRAST
How are soils alike? How are they different?

Clay

Clay is smooth when it is dry. It is sticky when it is wet.

Silt

Silt is smooth and powdery.

Insta-Lab

A Closer Look at Soil

Use a hand lens to look at some soil. What do you see? Work with a classmate to compare observations.

Humus	Sand

Humus is brown and soft. It holds water well. Humus is made up of dead plant parts and other things that were once living.	Sand grains are rough. They are larger than grains of silt or clay.

Soil for Growing Things

Plants need soil to grow. Soil holds a plant's roots in place. The roots keep the soil from blowing away. A plant's roots take in water and nutrients, or minerals, from the soil. Nutrients help the plant grow and stay healthy.

Soils hold different amounts of water and have different nutrients. Different soils are good for different kinds of plants.

 COMPARE AND CONTRAST How can one soil be better for growing plants than another soil?

Focus Skill

1. COMPARE AND CONTRAST Copy and complete the chart. Tell how rocks are alike and how they are different.

Rocks

alike

| All are pieces of the **A** _____ crust. |

| All are made up of **B** _____. |

different

| They can be different colors. |

| They can be large or **C** _____. |

| They can be rough or **D** _____. |

2. DRAW CONCLUSIONS Why is humus a good soil to use to grow plants?

3. VOCABULARY Tell how **soil** helps this plant grow.

Test Prep

4. Why do different kinds of soil look, smell, and feel different?

Links

Math

Compare Masses

Choose four rocks. Place two masses on one side of a balance. Place a rock on the other side. Compare the rock's mass to the masses. Which mass is greater? Record the results for each rock.

For more links and activities, go to www.hspscience.com

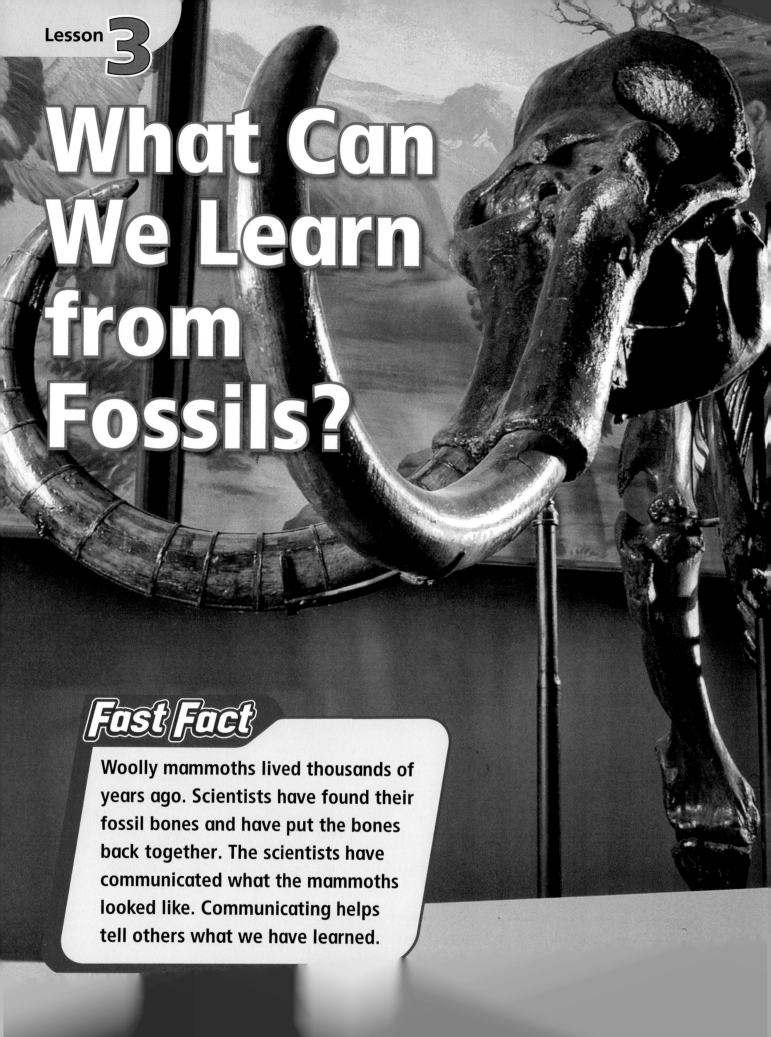

What Can We Learn from Fossils?

Fast Fact

Woolly mammoths lived thousands of years ago. Scientists have found their fossil bones and have put the bones back together. The scientists have communicated what the mammoths looked like. Communicating helps tell others what we have learned.

Uncovering Fossils

You need

- small objects
- clay
- tools

Step 1

Place a small object inside a ball of clay. Let the clay get hard.

Step 2

Trade balls of clay with a classmate. Use the tools to gently uncover the object in the clay.

Step 3

Communicate to a classmate what you discover.

Inquiry Skill

You can **communicate** by telling or showing others what you discover.

VOCABULARY
dinosaur
extinct
fossil

 READING FOCUS SKILL

SEQUENCE What happened to some plants and animals that lived long ago?

Fossils

Dinosaurs were animals that lived millions of years ago on Earth. No dinosaurs live on Earth now. They have all become **extinct**, or died out. They were not able to survive in their environment.

Scientists have learned about dinosaurs from their fossils. A **fossil** is what is left of an animal or a plant that lived long ago. A fossil can be a footprint or an impression in rock. Fossils can also be shells, teeth, and bones that have turned to rock.

picture of extinct fern

living fern today

fern fossil impression in rock

Scientists compare fossils with plants and animals that live today. This helps the scientists learn about the extinct plants and animals.

Fossils can show the sizes of animals. They can give clues about how the animals moved. Fossils may also give clues about where the animals lived and what they ate.

▲ Florida panther

 SEQUENCE What happened to some plants and animals of long ago after they died?

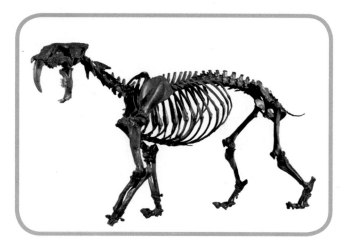

▲ fossil of saber-toothed cat

picture of saber-toothed cat ▶

171

A Trilobite Fossil Forms

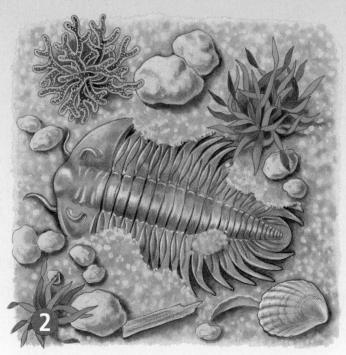

1 First, a trilobite died. Mud and sand covered the trilobite.

2 Next, the trilobite's soft parts rotted away. Its shell and other hard parts remained.

How Fossils Form

Fossils form when plants and animals are buried under mud, clay, or sand. The soft parts of the plant or animal rot away. The hard parts turn to rock. The fossils may be found millions of years later.

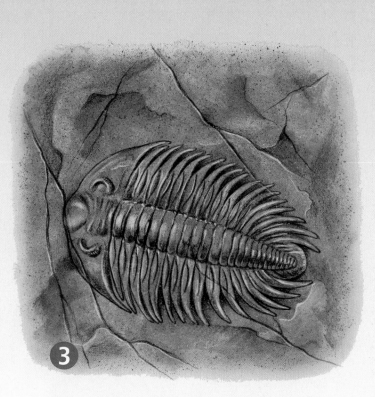

3

Then, the mud, the sand, and the hard parts of the trilobite slowly turned to rock.

4

Last, after millions of years, erosion removed the rock covering the fossil, and the fossil was found.

 For more links and activities, go to **www.hspscience.com**

A trilobite was an animal that lived in the sea. A shell covered its soft body. The pictures show how its fossil formed.

Insta-Lab

Make a Print in Clay

Flatten four pieces of clay. Press a different object into each one. Remove the objects. Trade prints with a classmate. Guess what object made each print fossil.

What We Find Out from Fossils

Fossils may be found broken into many pieces. Scientists put the pieces together. They use the fossils to infer what plants and animals of long ago looked like.

Observe each animal and its fossil.

SEQUENCE What do scientists do after they find fossil pieces?

pterodactyl

stegosaurus

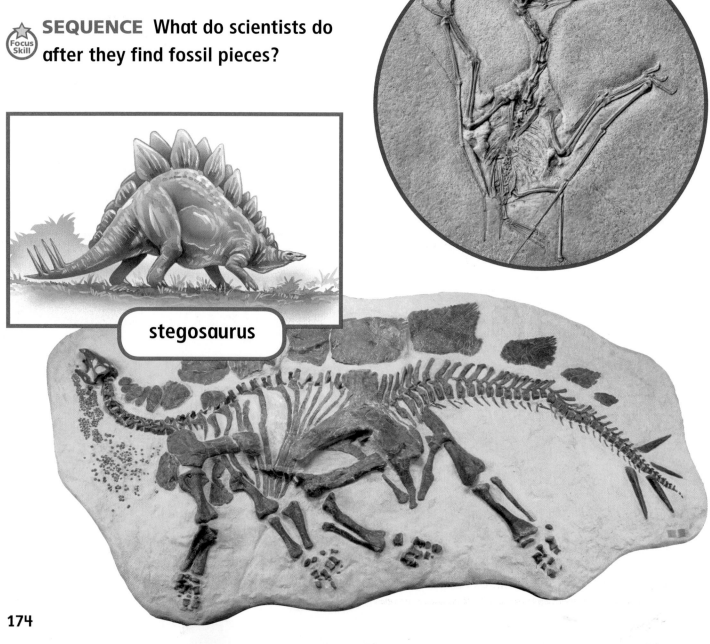

1. SEQUENCE Copy and complete the chart.
Tell how a trilobite became a fossil.

How a Trilobite Fossil Forms

First, a trilobite **A** _____ . Mud and sand covered it.

→

Next, its **B** _____ parts rotted away and its **C** _____ parts remained.

→

Then, the mud, the sand, and the hard parts of the trilobite slowly turned to **D** _____ .

2. SUMMARIZE Use the vocabulary terms to write a summary of this lesson.

3. VOCABULARY Use the terms **extinct** and **fossil** to tell about this picture.

Test Prep

4. Which animal is extinct?
- **A.** alligator
- **B.** dinosaur
- **C.** elephant
- **D.** giraffe

Links

Social Studies

Then and Now

Observe fossils found in your state. Compare them with animals and plants that live today. Draw a picture of a fossil and a picture of a plant or animal that lives today. Tell how they are alike and how they are different.

elephant   mammoth fossil

For more links and activities, go to
www.hspscience.com

Wild Waves

Cortes Bank is a great place to surf. But this area is different from other surfing spots. Cortes Bank is about 100 miles from land!

Ridge Makes Rough Waters

Cortes Bank is an undersea mountain range that is, in some places, only three feet below the surface. It has some of the biggest waves in the world.

Predicting Waves

Ocean experts use different tools to measure ocean waves. They use information from satellites in space and weather maps. The information is then put into a computer, which can predict how fast and how high waves will be.

Think About It

Why do you think surfers like to surf at Cortes Bank?

Surf's Up

According to experts, waves at Cortes Bank can reach more than 70 feet high. That's as tall as a seven-story building! Some waves move at speeds of more than 50 kilometers (30 miles) per hour.

Seven Story Tall Building

Find out more! Log on to **www.hspscience.com**

Looking for Change

Marguerite Thomas Williams spent many years working hard in school. She studied an area of science called geology. Geology is the study of rocks and landforms on Earth.

Williams was interested in how water changes the shape of Earth. In 1942, Williams earned a Ph.D. in geology. A Ph.D. is the highest award a college can give a student. Williams was the first African American to earn a Ph.D. in geology in the United States.

Dr. Williams studied areas changed by water. ▼

SCIENCE Projects
for Home or School

You Can Do It!

Soil Study

What to Do

1. Collect plant parts that once were living, such as berries, leaves, and sticks.

2. Bury each thing outside in its own hole about four inches deep. Mark each hole with a craft stick.

3. Uncover the matter once a week for four weeks.

4. Record what you observe.

Materials
- plastic gloves
- craft sticks
- parts of plants

Draw Conclusions
How did the matter change? How do plant parts that once were living become part of the soil?

Rock Collection

Collect some small rocks. Observe how they are alike and how they are different. Look at their colors, shapes, and textures. Then decide how you want to classify the rocks.

rough rocks

smooth rocks

Review and Test Preparation

Vocabulary Review

Match each term with the picture that shows its meaning. The page numbers tell you where to look if you need help.

volcano p. 157   soil p. 164

boulder p. 162   fossil p. 170

1. _____

2. _____

3. _____

4. _____

Check Understanding

5. 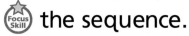 Write **first**, **next**, and **then** to show the sequence.

  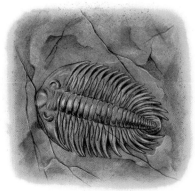

6. Which two things can change Earth's surface quickly?

A. boulders and soil

B. dinosaurs and fossils

C. earthquakes and volcanoes

D. weathering and erosion

Critical Thinking

7. Tell how this rock shows the effects of erosion.

8. What can fossils tell about animals that lived long ago?

Chapter 6

Natural Resources

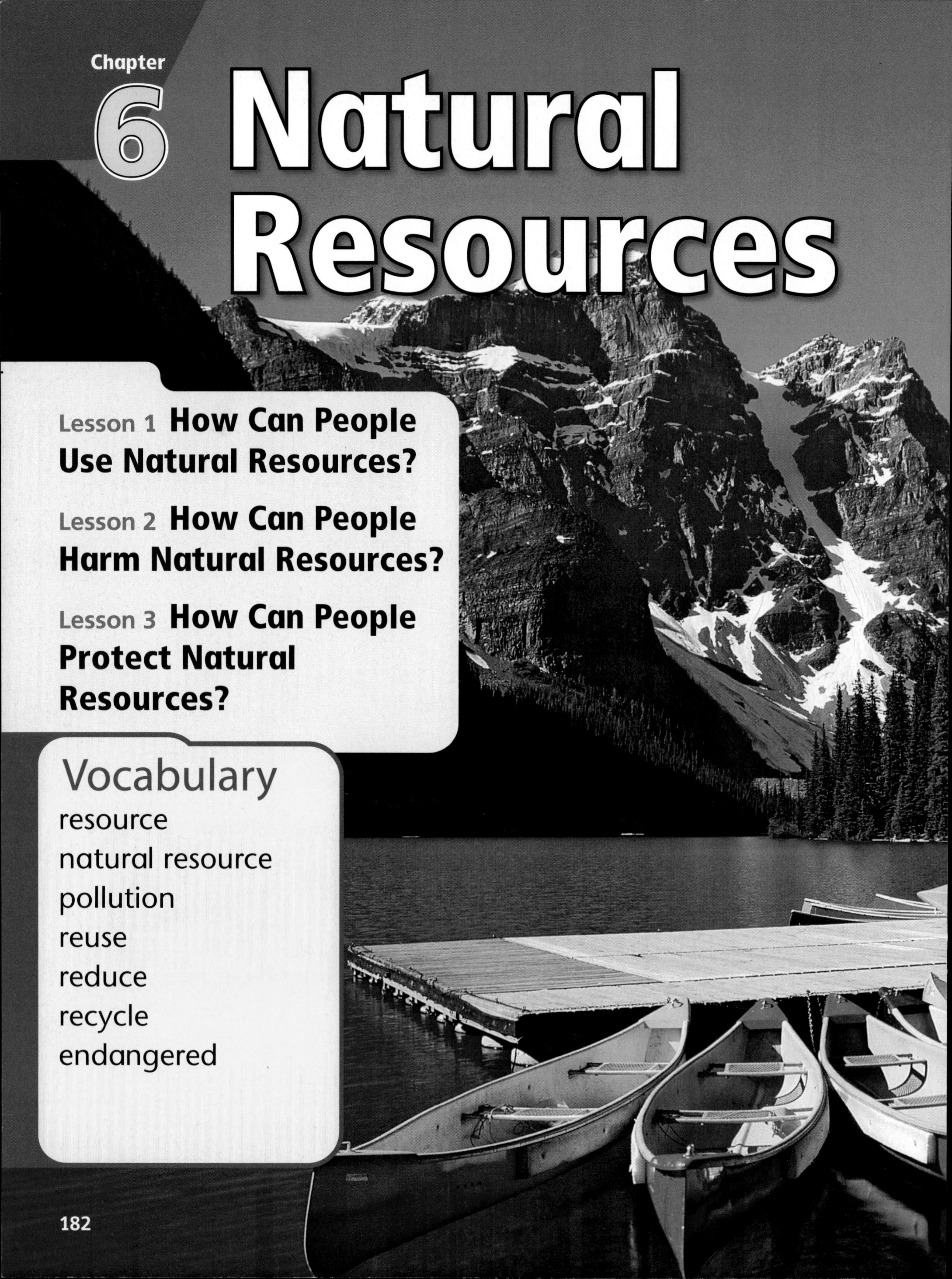

Lesson 1 **How Can People Use Natural Resources?**

Lesson 2 **How Can People Harm Natural Resources?**

Lesson 3 **How Can People Protect Natural Resources?**

Vocabulary

resource
natural resource
pollution
reuse
reduce
recycle
endangered

I wonder...

What natural resources do people use every day?

What do YOU wonder?

How Can People Use Natural Resources?

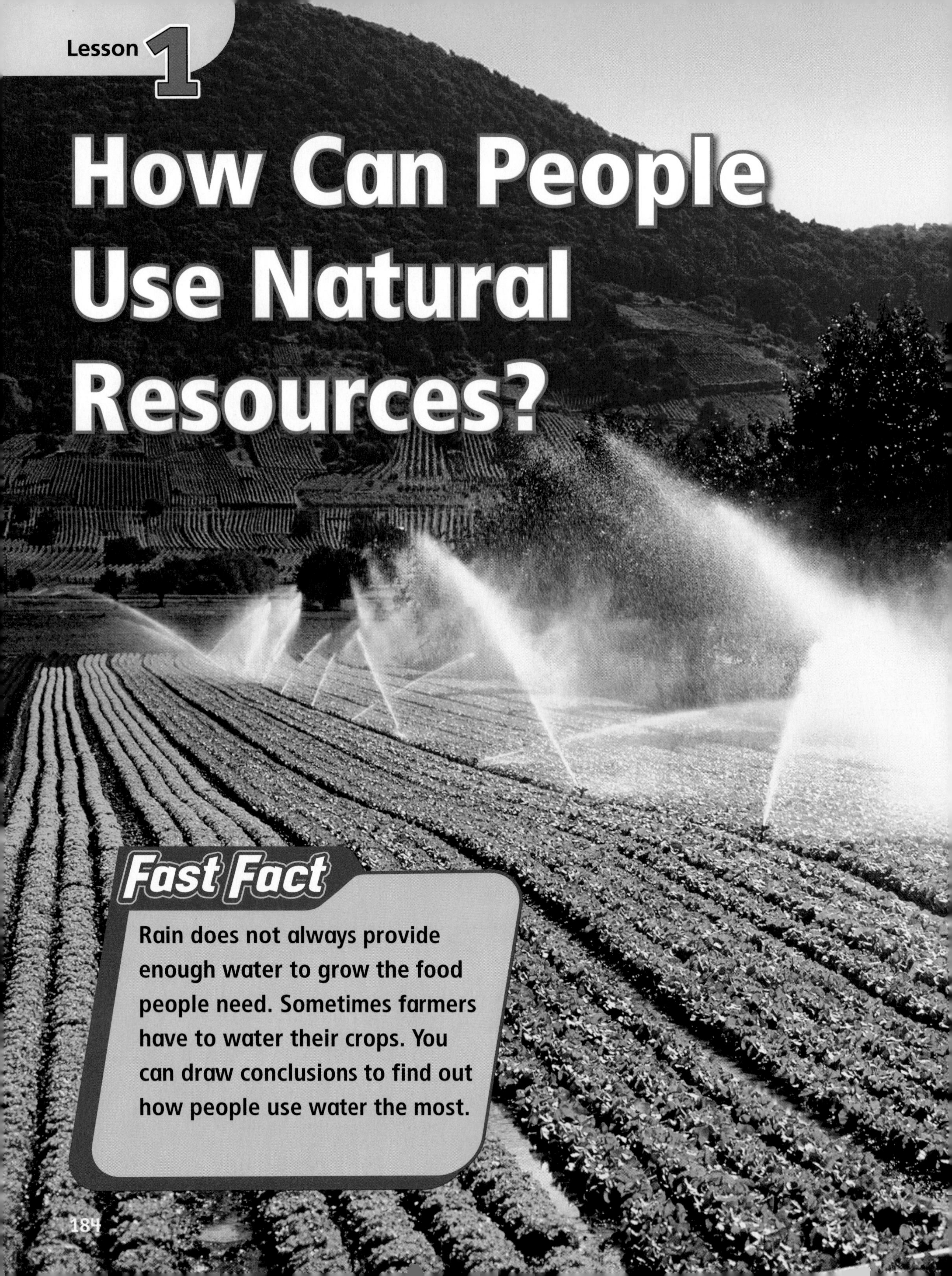

Fast Fact

Rain does not always provide enough water to grow the food people need. Sometimes farmers have to water their crops. You can draw conclusions to find out how people use water the most.

Ways We Use Water

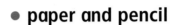

You need

- **paper and pencil**

Step 1

List the ways you and your classmates use water in one day.

Step 2

Record the data in a chart like this one. Make a mark each time someone uses water. Count the marks at the end of the day.

Ways Our Class Uses Water in One Day	
way	times
washing hands	

Step 3

Draw conclusions. For what did your class use water most often?

Inquiry Skill

To **draw conclusions** about something, you use your observations and what you know.

READING FOCUS SKILL

MAIN IDEA AND DETAILS Look for details about how people use natural resources.

Air and Water

Air and water are natural resources. A **resource** is anything that people can use to meet their needs. A **natural resource** is a resource that comes from nature.

People breathe air. They use moving air, or wind, as a source of energy. When wind pushes on a boat's sails, the boat moves across the water.

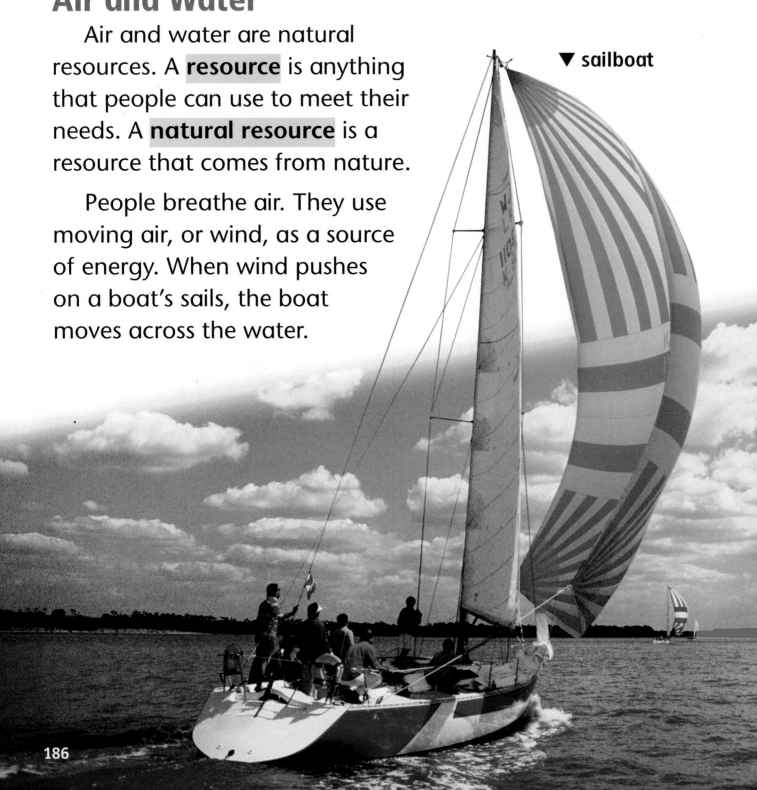

▼ **sailboat**

▲ Swimmers can breathe air through a tube called a snorkel.

People use water in many ways. They drink it and use it to bathe, cook, and clean. They use it to grow plants and raise animals. People also enjoy doing water activities for fun.

People travel and ship goods over water in boats. They also use moving water as a source of energy to help them produce electricity.

 MAIN IDEA AND DETAILS How do people use air and water?

Rocks and Soil

Rocks and soil are two important natural resources. Rocks are pieces of Earth's crust. People use them to make things such as buildings and roads.

People get metals, such as copper, from rocks called ores. Ores may be found near Earth's surface or deep below ground. People dig out an ore and then get the metal out of it. Metal is used to make things such as pots, bikes, and cars.

▲ copper ore

copper pots ▶

copper mine

▲ Soil helps strawberry plants grow.

▲ laying clay bricks

People use soil to grow plants. Soil holds plants in place. It also has nutrients and water that plants need to grow.

Clay is made up of tiny bits of rock. People use clay for building. The clay is formed into bricks or blocks. The clay blocks are dried until they are hard. Then they are used to make buildings and other things.

 MAIN IDEA AND DETAILS How do **Focus Skill** people use rocks and soil?

Plants

Plants are another important natural resource. People use plants to make and build things. They use cotton to make cloth. They use wood from trees to build houses and to make furniture and paper.

People also use plants for fuel. They may burn tree branches or logs cut from trees. Burning dried plants releases energy stored in the plants.

▲ cotton plant

cotton shirt and socks ▶

wooden bookshelves, floor, and chair

▲ Plants from an herb garden are used in cooking.

People also use plants for food. They eat some plant parts. They use other plant parts to make foods such as bread.

 MAIN IDEA AND DETAILS
How do people use plants?

Make a List
Which things in your classroom are made from natural resources? Make a list. Then share it with a classmate. Tell what natural resources were used to make each thing.

Animals

Some people use animals to meet their needs for food and clothing. They drink milk from cows or use it to make foods such as cheese. They eat eggs from chickens and use wool from sheep to make warm clothes.

 MAIN IDEA AND DETAILS

How do some people use animals?

1. MAIN IDEA AND DETAILS Copy and complete this chart. Tell how people use natural resources.

Main Idea and Details

People use natural resources to meet their needs.

| People breathe **A** _____. | People use **B** _____ to clean. | People use **C** _____ to get metal. | People use **D** _____ to make bricks to build with. | People use **E** _____ to make clothing and paper. |

2. SUMMARIZE Use the chart to write a lesson summary.

3. VOCABULARY Use the term **natural resources** to tell about this picture.

Test Prep

4. Which natural resource is used for fuel?
   A. plants
   B. rocks
   C. soil
   D. water

Links

Writing

Facts About a Natural Resource

Draw and label a picture of a plant from your state. Then write a few facts about how people use it. Share your facts with classmates.

The mangrove tree grows in salty water.

For more links and activities, go to www.hspscience.com

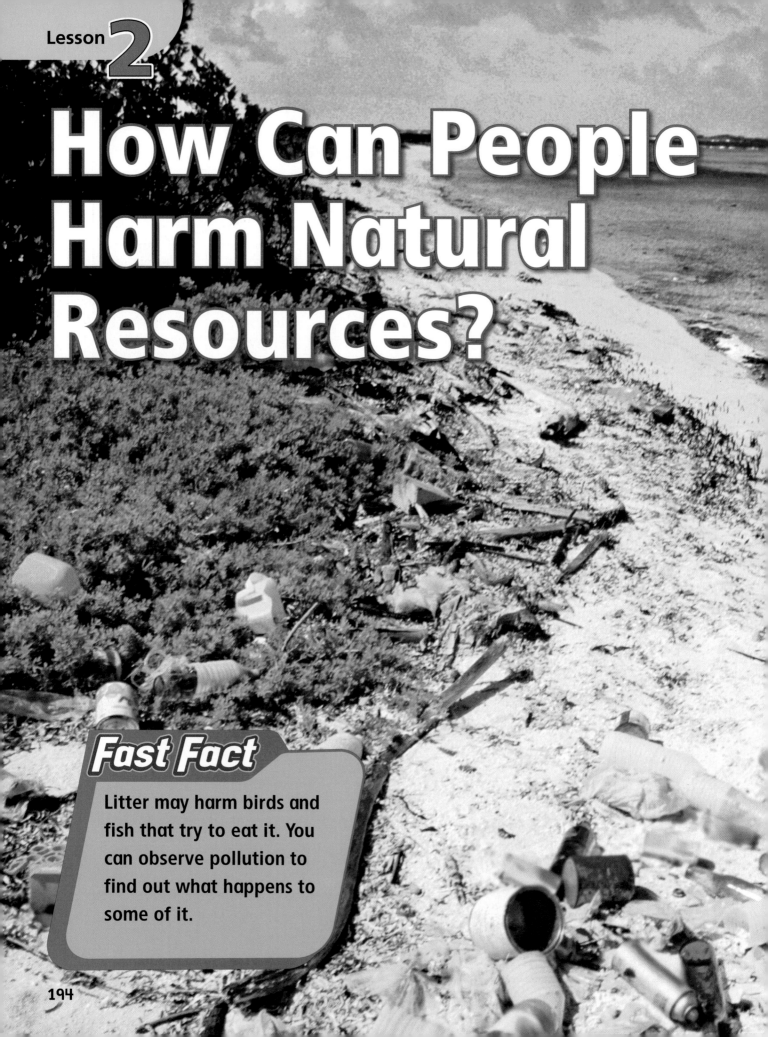

How Can People Harm Natural Resources?

Fast Fact

Litter may harm birds and fish that try to eat it. You can observe pollution to find out what happens to some of it.

What Happens to Pollution

You need

● shoe box and soil   ● trash objects   ● trowel or shovel   ● water

Step 1

Use a trowel or shovel to put soil in a box. Add trash and more soil. Put the box in a sunny place. Wash your hands if you touch the soil.

Step 2

Water the soil three times each week for one month. At the end of each week, uncover the objects and record what you **observe**.

Step 3

Communicate to your classmates what you observe each week.

Inquiry Skill

You can **observe** things to see how they change over time.

VOCABULARY
pollution

 READING FOCUS SKILL

CAUSE AND EFFECT Look for the causes and effects of pollution.

Pollution

Waste that harms air, water, or land is called **pollution**. When people make pollution, they harm natural resources.

Smoke and fumes from factories and cars cause air pollution. Dirty air can harm your lungs and make it hard for you to breathe. It harms plants and animals, too.

Trash, oil spills, and waste from factories cause water pollution. Dirty water can make people and animals ill. It can also harm plants.

Water can become polluted. ▼

▲ Car fumes are one kind of air pollution.

DANGER BEACH CLOSED

landfill

Trash that people do not put in trash cans is called litter. Litter can harm plants and animals. Plants covered by litter can not get the light they need to make food. Animals can get trapped by litter. If animals eat litter, they may get sick.

When people put trash in trash cans, it can be taken to landfills. Putting trash in landfills keeps it from making water and land polluted.

▲ If trash is not placed in a trash can, it becomes litter.

CAUSE AND EFFECT What are some effects of air and water pollution?

Insta-Lab

Model an Oil Spill
Put some water in a jar, and add a little oil. Dip a real feather or a paper feather into the oily water. Then feel the feather. How do you think oil spills harm birds?

197

Wasting Resources

When people use natural resources that they do not need, they waste the resources. Sometimes people want to use land on which trees are growing. They cut all the trees down. They can then use the land, but the trees are wasted.

Building

People need buildings, but they also need to protect natural resources. They may need to cut down some trees to make space for buildings. However, they should not cut down all the trees.

Animals use trees for homes and for food. When trees are cut down, animals must find new homes and new ways to get food. If they cannot do these things, they will die.

CAUSE AND EFFECT What can cause an animal to need a new home?

People Can Avoid Wasting

People waste resources when they do not turn off water or lights when they are not using them. They also waste resources by throwing away things that can be made into new things. What resources are being wasted in these photographs?

For more links and activities, go to
www.hspscience.com

1. CAUSE AND EFFECT Copy and complete this chart. Tell the effect of each cause.

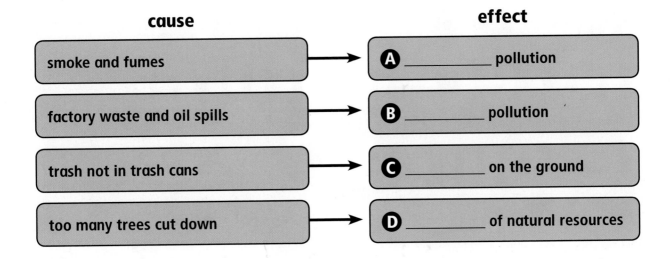

cause

| smoke and fumes |
| factory waste and oil spills |
| trash not in trash cans |
| too many trees cut down |

effect

Ⓐ _____ pollution

Ⓑ _____ pollution

Ⓒ _____ on the ground

Ⓓ _____ of natural resources

2. DRAW CONCLUSIONS Why is it important not to waste natural resources?

3. VOCABULARY Tell how **pollution** can harm people, plants, and animals.

Test Prep

4. How do some people protect resources?

Links

Math

Make a Bar Graph

Ask ten people a question about saving water. For example, "How often do you turn off the water while you brush your teeth?" Show the answers in a bar graph.

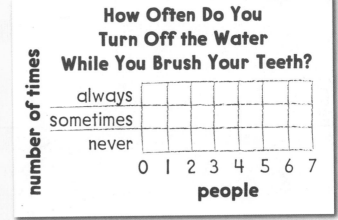

How Often Do You Turn Off the Water While You Brush Your Teeth?

number of times

always
sometimes
never

0 1 2 3 4 5 6 7
people

 For more links and activities, go to www.hspscience.com

How Can People Protect Natural Resources?

Fast Fact

Paper, bottles, and even playground equipment can be made from old materials. You can plan an investigation to find out how to use things in new ways.

RECYCLE

How to Reuse Things

You need

● used things ● colored markers ● glue ● newspaper

Step 1

How can you make something useful from used things? **Plan an investigation** to find out.

Step 2

Write the steps you need to take.

Step 3

Follow your steps to make a useful object. Then communicate to classmates how you made your object.

Inquiry Skill

When you **plan an investigation**, you ask a question and find a way to answer the question.

VOCABULARY

reuse
reduce
recycle
endangered

 READING FOCUS SKILL

CAUSE AND EFFECT Look for the effects of protecting natural resources.

Reuse, Reduce, and Recycle

People protect natural resources when they use less of them. One way to do this is to **reuse** things, or use them again. When you reuse things, you need fewer new things made from natural resources. You make less trash, too.

You also save natural resources when you **reduce**, or lessen, the amount you use. Walking or riding a bike reduces the amount of gas that is used. It also keeps the air cleaner.

Reusing a lunchbox makes less trash and saves resources. ▼

This woman is saving gasoline by not driving her car. ▶

 recycling

Recycling is another way to save natural resources. When people **recycle**, they use the materials in old things to make new things. This makes less trash, too. Some things made of glass, plastic, metal, and paper can be recycled. What things do you recycle?

⭐ **CAUSE AND EFFECT** What happens when people reuse things?

Insta-Lab

Reuse a Plastic Jar

How many ways can you and your classmates think of to reuse a plastic jar? Write your ideas on slips of paper, and put the slips in the jar. Then take turns reading the ideas.

Conserving

Most people use coal, gas, and oil for energy. In time, these natural resources will be used up. People must conserve them, or use them wisely to make them last longer. Using other energy sources can help.

Some people use the power of water and wind to produce electricity. Some use the energy of sunlight. Water, wind, and sunlight do not get used up as coal, gas, and oil do.

▲ **dam**

▼ **windmills**

▲ This park helps keep endangered animals safe.

In places where many trees are cut down, people can plant new trees. Trees provide homes for animals, and the roots hold the soil in place.

Some kinds of animals are **endangered**. This means that very few of these animals are left. If people do not protect them, they may all die. People can help by making sure the animals' homes are safe. They can also move the animals to places where they can get the things they need to live.

 CAUSE AND EFFECT What will happen to some natural resources in time if people keep using them?

Reducing Pollution

Cities and towns can reduce pollution by passing laws that protect natural resources. In many places, littering and burning trash are against the law. Companies must follow the laws, too. They may not dump harmful waste into water or onto the ground. Factories must reduce the amount of smoke and gases they make. This keeps the air cleaner.

These children are reducing pollution at their school by picking up litter. How can you help reduce pollution?

 CAUSE AND EFFECT What are the effects of laws that protect natural resources?

1. CAUSE AND EFFECT Copy and complete this chart. Tell the effect of each cause.

cause	effect
People reuse things.	They save **A** _____. They make less **B** _____.
People recycle things.	They use old things to make **C** _____ things. They make less **D** _____.

2. SUMMARIZE Write a lesson summary. Begin with the sentence **People can protect natural resources**.

3. VOCABULARY Tell how people can help **endangered** animals.

Test Prep

4. How do people reduce pollution?

   A. They cut down trees.

   B. They make more litter.

   C. They use less gasoline.

   D. They burn trash.

Links

Art

Poster

Make a poster to show some useful things you can make with an empty milk carton. Label each new thing you can make.

 For more links and activities, go to **www.hspscience.com**

Solar Car Crosses Canada

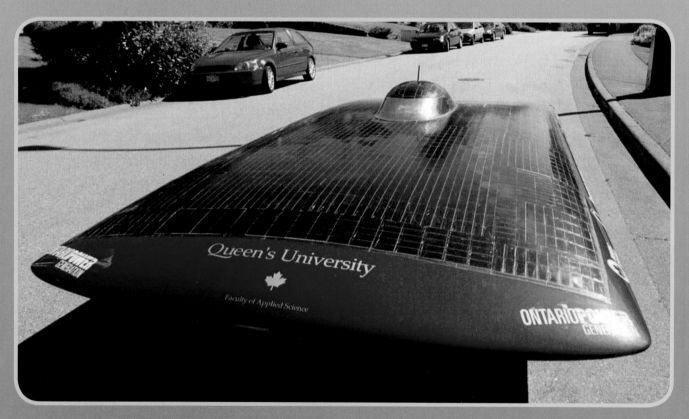

Students from Canada set a world record recently with a car powered by the sun. The car was called the Midnight Sun VII.

The students drove 9,368 miles in the solar-powered car. It took the team 41 days to drive across Canada and the United States.

Sun Is the Fuel

The car uses the sun for power, so it does not need gas for fuel. The car does not produce any harmful gases that pollute the air.

9,368 miles in 41 days

The team places special material, called solar cells, on top of the car. The solar cells collect sunlight and turn it into electricity. The electricity powers the car's motor. The energy can be stored in the car's batteries for days that are not sunny.

The students say that it will be a long time before people can buy solar cars. But the team hopes that the car will show people how solar power can be used.

Think About It

How might solar power help conserve our natural resources?

Spin-In

Find out more! Log on to
www.hspscience.com

Planting a Tree

Earth Day is a great day for people to help take care of the environment. That's why Nico Reyes wanted to pitch in. He wanted to help take care of the environment in the city where he lives.

What did Nico do? He, along with many other people, planted young trees along a river. The trees will grow up to be big and tall. Trees help to hold the soil so it does not wash away. The trees will also help keep the air clean.

Nico Reyes

212

You Can Do It!

Build a House

What to Do

1. Roll some clay flat. Use a craft stick to cut the clay into blocks.

2. Let the clay blocks dry in a warm place.

3. Arrange the blocks to make the walls of a house. Use craft sticks to make a roof.

Materials
- clay
- rolling pin
- craft sticks

Draw Conclusions
How can people use natural resources to build houses?

See What Is in the Air

Spread petroleum jelly on two numbered index cards. Place one card outside on a windowsill. Place the other card inside. The next day, observe each card with a hand lens. Draw and write about what you see. Share your results.

Review and Test Preparation

Vocabulary Review

Use the terms below to complete the sentences. The page numbers tell you where to look if you need help.

resource p. 186   **reuse** p. 204

natural resource p. 186   **recycle** p. 205

pollution p. 196   **endangered** p. 207

1. When very few animals of a certain kind are left, that kind of animal is _____.

2. When you use old things to make new things, you _____.

3. A resource that comes from nature is a ____.

4. When you use things again, you _____ them.

5. Anything people can use to meet their needs is a _____.

6. Waste that harms air, water, or land is _____.

Check Understanding

7. How can people harm natural resources?

    A. They can waste them.

    B. They can protect them.

    C. They can reuse them.

    D. They can save them.

8. Which tells an effect of recycling?

    F. It makes more trash.

    G. It makes more pollution.

    H. It saves natural resources.

    J. It wastes natural resources.

Critical Thinking

9. What natural resources do you need to grow a plant?

10. How can you conserve natural resources at home?

EARTH SCIENCE

Weather and Space

| Chapter 7 | Weather |
| Chapter 8 | The Solar System |

○○○ **International Snow Sculpture Championships**

TO:	jesse@hspscience.com
FROM:	amy@hspscience.com
RE:	Breckenridge, Colorado

Dear Jesse,
Remember last winter when we made a snowman together? Take a look at these snow sculptures. Wow! Write back soon!
Amy

TO: ruby@hspscience.com

FROM: joel@hspscience.com

RE: New York, New York

Dear Ruby,

My class went to the planetarium. We learned about the stars and planets. My mom and I got up really early today. We went outside and looked at the stars. I could not believe how bright they looked. We didn't even need a telescope!

Your friend,

Joel

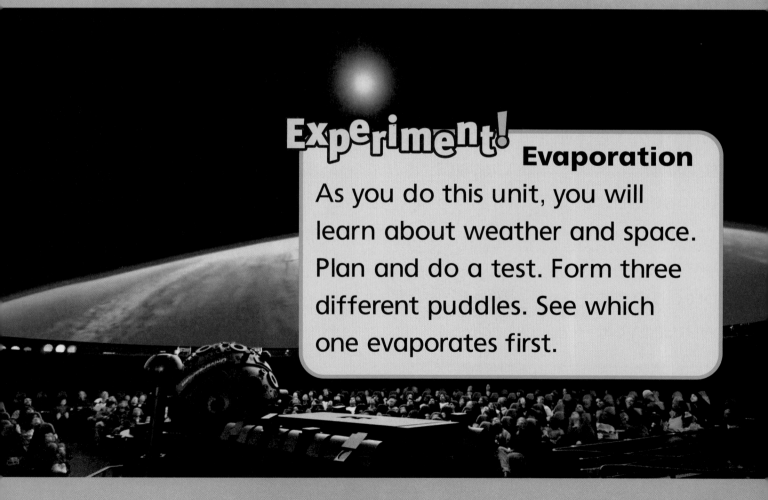

Experiment!

Evaporation

As you do this unit, you will learn about weather and space. Plan and do a test. Form three different puddles. See which one evaporates first.

Chapter 7 Weather

Lesson 1 How Does Weather Change?

Lesson 2 Why Do We Measure Weather?

Lesson 3 What Is the Water Cycle?

Vocabulary

weather
weather pattern
season
temperature
thermometer
wind
precipitation
water cycle

evaporate
condense
drought

I wonder...

How do people know what the weather is going to be?

What do YOU wonder?

How Does Weather Change?

Fast Fact

It takes both light and water to make a rainbow. You may see a rainbow if the sun shines during or right after a rain shower. By observing the weather, you can see its patterns.

Changes in Weather

You need

● poster board   ● markers

Step 1

Make up a symbol to stand for each kind of weather. Then draw a chart like this one.

Step 2

Observe the weather each day for 5 days. Record what you **observed**.

Step 3

What kinds of weather did you **observe**? Share your information.

Inquiry Skill

Observing weather helps you see how it changes. It also helps you see weather patterns.

READING FOCUS SKILL

SEQUENCE Look for the order of seasons and the ways the weather changes from one season to the next.

Weather

What is the weather like today? Is it hot or cold? Is it rainy, snowy, sunny, cloudy, or windy? **Weather** is what the air outside is like. It can change in just a few hours or over many months. A change in the weather that repeats is called a **weather pattern**.

 SEQUENCE What usually happens after it rains?

Spring

A **season** is a time of year that has a certain kind of weather. In many places, the weather changes with each season. In spring, the air gets warmer. In some places, it is very rainy in spring. As the weather gets warmer and wetter, plants begin to grow.

SEQUENCE How does the air change in spring?

Insta-Lab

Model a Rainbow

Place a mirror in a jar of water. Make the room dark. Shine a flashlight on the mirror. Move the light around. Shine it from different directions until you see rainbow colors.

Summer

Summer comes after spring. In most places, summer is the warmest time of year. The days are often hot and sunny. But storms can quickly change the weather. In summer, trees and other plants have a lot of leaves.

Focus Skill **SEQUENCE** **Which season comes before summer?**

Fall

Fall is the next season. In fall, the air gets cooler. Some fall days are sunny, while others are cloudy. In fall, the leaves of some trees change color and then drop off. Some plants stop growing and die.

⭐ Focus Skill **SEQUENCE** How may trees change from summer to fall?

Winter

After fall, winter comes. This is the coldest season. In some places, it gets cold enough to snow. In these places, many trees and bushes have no leaves until spring.

In other places, the air cools down just a little. It may never snow there. Many trees and plants keep their leaves. Many flowers keep growing.

Spring comes again after winter. The pattern of changing seasons goes on.

SEQUENCE What might happen to trees when winter ends?

1. SEQUENCE Copy and complete this chart. Tell about each season in order.

Sequence of Seasons

| **Spring** The air gets warmer, and it is rainy. | → | **A** _____ It is the warmest time of year. | → | **Fall** The air gets **B** _____. | → | **C** _____ It is the **D** _____ time of year. |

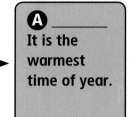

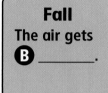

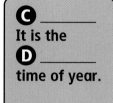

2. SUMMARIZE Write a summary of the lesson. Begin with the sentence **Weather can change with the seasons.**

3. VOCABULARY Describe how **weather patterns** change from summer to fall.

Test Prep

4. How can you tell it is spring?
   A. Trees have no leaves.
   B. Trees grow new leaves.
   C. Some leaves change color.
   D. Trees have lots of leaves.

Links

Weather Report
Choose a season. Write a short weather report for one day of that season where you live. Then present your weather report to the class. Use a map to point out your state.

For more links and activities, go to **www.hspscience.com**

227

Why Do We Measure Weather?

Fast Fact

The coldest temperature ever measured in the United States was recorded in Alaska on January 23, 1971. You can compare temperatures to see how the weather changes.

Measure Temperature

You need

- **thermometer**

Step 1

Make a chart like this one.

Temperature	
Morning	
Noon	
Late Afternoon	

Step 2

Read the thermometer in the morning, at noon, and in the late afternoon. Record each temperature.

Step 3

Compare the temperatures.

Inquiry Skill

Comparing temperatures helps you look for a pattern of temperature change.

VOCABULARY

temperature
thermometer
wind
precipitation

READING FOCUS SKILL

MAIN IDEA AND DETAILS Look for details that tell why and how weather is measured.

Measuring Weather

Scientists use tools to measure the weather. Some tools tell how warm the air is. Some tools tell how fast the wind is blowing. Other tools tell how much rain has fallen.

Measuring weather helps scientists see patterns. Patterns help the scientists predict the weather. Then they can warn people when a big storm is coming.

MAIN IDEA AND DETAILS What kinds of weather do scientists measure?

Measuring Temperature

Temperature is how warm something is. A tool called a **thermometer** measures temperature. Scientists use thermometers to record the temperature of the air. In some thermometers, warmer air makes the liquid in the thermometer go up. Cooler air makes the liquid go down.

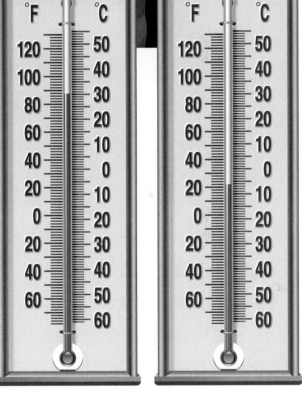

▲ **Which thermometer shows the temperature for a cold day?**

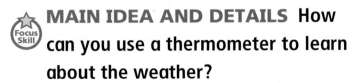 **MAIN IDEA AND DETAILS** How can you use a thermometer to learn about the weather?

Measuring Wind

Wind is moving air. It can move in different directions. Scientists use a weather vane to find out which way the wind is blowing. The wind turns the arrow on the vane. The arrow points to the direction the wind is coming from.

Insta-Lab

Draw and Compare

Look outside. Is the wind blowing? How can you tell? Draw a picture that shows what the wind is doing. Use your picture to tell about the wind's speed.

Scientists measure the speed of wind with a tool called an anemometer.

You can use the pictures on this page to estimate wind speed. They show the effects of wind at different speeds. The wind speeds are measured in miles per hour.

 MAIN IDEA AND DETAILS
What tools measure wind? What do they help you learn?

▲ anemometer

Effects of Wind at Different Speeds

0–1 mile

1–3 miles

8–12 miles

25–31 miles

32–38 miles

64–75 miles

Measuring Precipitation

Water that falls from the sky is called **precipitation**. Rain, snow, sleet, and hail are kinds of precipitation.

Scientists use a rain gauge to find out how much rain falls. This container catches rain. Then scientists can measure how many inches of rain fell. You can use a ruler and a jar to make your own rain gauge.

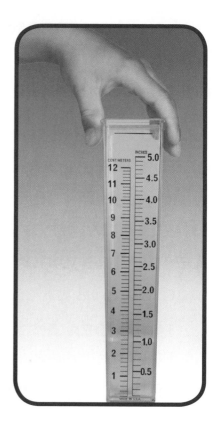

rain gauge ▲

 MAIN IDEA AND DETAILS What is precipitation? What are kinds of precipitation?

234

1. MAIN IDEA AND DETAILS Copy and complete this chart. Tell about the weather tools that scientists use.

Main Idea and Details

> **Scientists use tools to measure weather.**

> A **A** _____ measures how much rain falls.

> An anemometer measures the speed of the **B** _____.

> A **C** _____ measures the direction of the wind.

> A **D** _____ measures the temperature of the air.

2. DRAW CONCLUSIONS Why is it important to measure weather?

3. VOCABULARY Use the term **precipitation** to tell about this picture.

Test Prep

4. How do scientists learn about weather?

Links

Math 🕐②③

Make a Bar Graph

Rainfall changes from month to month. This chart shows the rainfall in Tampa, Florida, for four different months. Use the data to make a bar graph. What can you tell from your graph?

Tampa, Florida

Month	Rainfall
April	2 inches
May	3 inches
September	7 inches
October	2 inches

 For more links and activities, go to **www.hspscience.com**

What Is the Water Cycle?

Water in the Air

You need

- **2 zip-top bags**

- **colored water**

- **tape**

Step 1

Fill each bag halfway with water. Zip the bags closed.

Step 2

Tape one bag to a window in the sun. Tape the other bag to a window in the shade.

Step 3

Wait 30 minutes. Then observe both bags. Record what you observed. Which bag shows more change? **Infer** what caused the change.

Inquiry Skill

When you **infer**, you use what you see to figure out what happened.

Reading in Science

VOCABULARY

water cycle
evaporate
condense
drought

 READING FOCUS SKILL

CAUSE AND EFFECT Look for causes and effects as you read about the water cycle.

The Water Cycle

Water moves over and over from Earth's surface into the air and then back to Earth's surface. This movement of water is called the **water cycle**.

 CAUSE AND EFFECT What makes water move from Earth into the air?

What Happens During the Water Cycle

3 The water vapor cools and **condenses**, or changes into tiny drops of water.

2 The gas, called water vapor, is pushed upward and meets cool air.

1 The sun's heat makes water **evaporate**, or change to a gas.

4 The water droplets and dust particles in the cool air form clouds.

5 The water drops join into larger drops. These heavy drops fall as rain or snow.

6 Precipitation flows into streams, lakes, and oceans. Then the water cycle begins again.

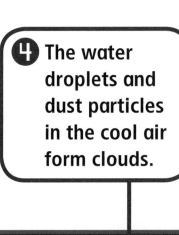

For more links and activities, go to **www.hspscience.com**

Droughts

Sometimes it does not rain for a long time. This time is called a **drought**. During a drought, it may be hotter than usual. The land may get very dry. Streams and ponds may dry up. Winds may blow away the soil.

Without water, plants and animals may die. People try to use very little water during a drought.

Focus Skill **CAUSE AND EFFECT** What can happen because of a drought?

▲ corn plants harmed by a drought

Floods

If a lot of rain falls, it can cause a flood. Rivers and streams overflow. Some land is covered with water.

Too much water can kill plants and animals. People must get to safe, dry places during a flood.

 CAUSE AND EFFECT What can happen because of a flood?

Insta-Lab

Model a Flood

Fill a shallow pan with soil. Shape some hills. Use a bowl of water for a lake. Add small objects to the scene. Sprinkle water until you model a flood. Share your results.

Storms

Storms are a kind of weather that can be harmful. A thunderstorm has rain, thunder, and lightning. The rain from the storm may cause a flood. Lightning may strike trees and other tall things.

When it is cold, a lot of snow may fall. A snowstorm with strong winds is called a blizzard. The blowing snow makes it hard to see. Stay indoors during thunderstorms and snowstorms to keep safe.

CAUSE AND EFFECT **Why are some storms harmful?**

242

1. CAUSE AND EFFECT Copy and complete this chart. Write an effect for each cause.

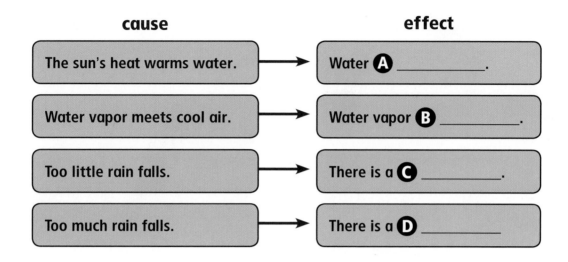

cause	effect
The sun's heat warms water.	→ Water **A** _____.
Water vapor meets cool air.	→ Water vapor **B** _____.
Too little rain falls.	→ There is a **C** _____.
Too much rain falls.	→ There is a **D** _____.

2. SUMMARIZE Use the vocabulary to write a summary of the lesson.

3. VOCABULARY Explain what happens during the **water cycle**.

Test Prep

4. It has not rained for a long time. It is hot, and the soil is dry. What is this time called?

A. a flood

B. a blizzard

C. a drought

D. a thunderstorm

Links

Art

Water Cycle Poster
Make a poster to show the water cycle. On your poster, label the parts of the water cycle.

For more links and activities, go to **www.hspscience.com**

The Coldest Place on Earth

Experts say that Antarctica is the coldest place on Earth. But if it's so cold, how do animals and people stay warm there?

Cold Weather, Warm Penguins

Penguins are birds that live in Antarctica. They stay warm because they have feathers that are very small and close together. The feathers have oil on them. Cold water can not get through the feathers to touch the penguins' skin.

Weddell seals also live in Antarctica. They swim in the cold ocean water to catch fish and other food. Weddell seals stay warm because they have a layer of blubber, or fat. A coat of thick fur keeps water from touching the seals' skin.

Playful Penguin FACTS

❄ Penguins can waddle faster than humans can walk.

❄ Penguins line up and dive into the water again and again.

❄ Penguins sometimes toboggan, or slide, on their bellies.

❄ Penguins surf waves to get back to shore.

Keeping People Warm

Scientists who work in Antarctica have learned how to stay warm as well. When they are outside, scientists wear layers of special clothing. The clothing helps people stay warm the same way animals do. It keeps the cold air from reaching their skin.

Think About It

What are some other things people have learned from observing animals?

Spin In

Find out more! Log on to
www.hspscience.com

What's the Weather?

Willow Wilaszek lives in Alaska. The Peninsula Winter Games are played in Alaska in the winter. The games are played mostly outdoors. Willow and other children enjoy playing the games.

What does Willow know about winter weather? She knows that she must wear extra clothes because of the very cold temperatures every winter. Before she plays outside in winter, she chooses the best clothes to keep her warm.

How Water Vapor Condenses

You need
- 2 metal cans
- ice water
- warm water

What to Do

1. Fill one can halfway with ice water.
2. Fill the other can halfway with warm water.
3. Wait five minutes. Then look at the outside of each can. Record changes you observe.

Draw Conclusions

Are the cans different on the outside? How? Why did the changes happen?

What Is the Temperature?

Does the temperature outside stay the same from day to day? Use a thermometer to check the temperature every day at the same time. Use your data to make a graph. What pattern do you see? Share the graph with your class.

Temperature at 10:00

Monday	
Tuesday	
Wednesday	
Thursday	
Friday	

Review and Test Preparation

Vocabulary Review

Use the terms to complete the sentences. The page numbers tell you where to look if you need help.

weather pattern p. 222   **precipitation** p. 234
thermometer p. 231   **water cycle** p. 238

1. Rain, snow, and sleet are kinds of _____.

2. The movement of water from Earth's surface into the air and back is the _____.

3. A weather change that repeats is a _____.

4. One tool that measures the weather is a _____.

Check Understanding

5. Put these seasons in the correct sequence.

spring   fall   summer   winter

6. Think about weather patterns. Write about the four seasons. Tell what each season's weather is like.

7. How are these tools alike?

A. Both measure rainfall.
B. Both measure temperature.
C. Both measure weather.
D. Both measure wind.

Critical Thinking

8. Think about the water cycle. Explain what will happen to a puddle when the sun comes out.

9. Write about three tools a scientist could use to learn about a thunderstorm.

Lesson 1 What Are Stars and Planets?

Lesson 2 What Causes Day and Night?

Lesson 3 Why Does the Moon Seem to Change?

Lesson 4 What Causes the Seasons?

Vocabulary

solar system	moon
planet	season
orbit	
star	
constellation	
rotate	

I wonder...

Why does the moon seem to move across the sky?

What do you wonder?

What Are Stars and Planets?

Fast Fact

Stars are always in the sky, even in the daytime. You can infer why we see most stars only at night.

Stars and Light

You need

- black paper
- tape

- "star" cup

- flashlight

Tape the paper to a wall. Point the bottom of the cup toward the paper. Shine the flashlight into the cup. What do you see?

Turn off the lights. Shine the flashlight again. What do you see now?

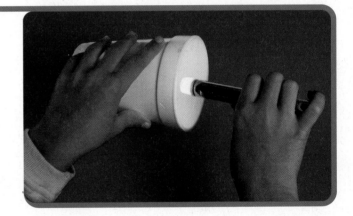

Infer why the "stars" look different with the lights on and with the lights off.

Inquiry Skill

When you **infer**, you use what you see to figure out why something happened.

253

VOCABULARY

solar system
planet
orbit
star
constellation

 READING FOCUS SKILL

MAIN IDEA AND DETAILS Look for details about the solar system.

The Solar System

The **solar system** is made up mainly of the sun, the planets, and the planets' moons. A **planet** is a large ball of rock or gas that moves around the sun. Earth is a planet in the solar system.

You can see a few parts of the solar system at night. In the daytime they are still there. You just can not see them when it is light outside.

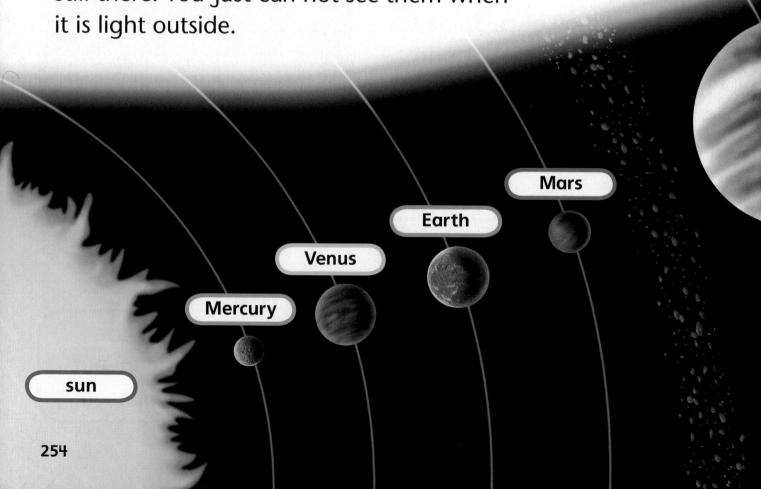

Mars

Earth

Venus

Mercury

sun

The sun is the center of the solar system. The nine planets move in paths around the sun. Each path is called an **orbit**.

The planets are different from one another. They look different. They are different sizes. They are at different distances from the sun, and they move in different orbits around it.

⭐ (Focus Skill) **MAIN IDEA AND DETAILS**
What are the parts of the solar system?

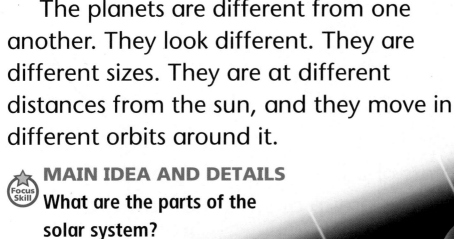

Pluto

Neptune

Uranus

Saturn

Jupiter

Insta-Lab

Change the Size You See
Find out why large planets look small from Earth. Hold a ball close to your eyes. Then slowly move it away from you. How does the ball's size seem to change? Tell why you think this happens.

Stars

A **star** is a huge ball of hot gases. The hot gases give off light and heat energy. The closest star to Earth is the sun.

You can see the sun in the daytime, but most stars can be seen only at night. Some stars are smaller than the sun. Others are bigger. They all look like tiny points of light because they are so far away. A group of stars that forms a pattern is called a **constellation**.

(Focus Skill) MAIN IDEA AND DETAILS What is a star?

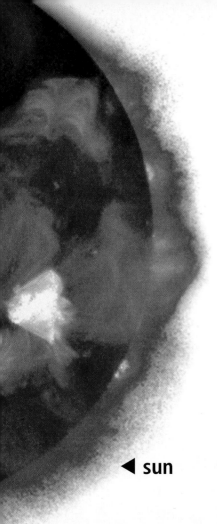

◄ sun

▲ Big Dipper, part of the constellation Ursa Major

▲ Orion

◄ Little Dipper, part of the constellation Ursa Minor

1. MAIN IDEA AND DETAILS Copy and complete this chart. Tell details about the solar system.

Main Idea and Details

> **The solar system is made up of the sun, planets, and moons.**

> Earth is a **A** _____ in the solar system.

> The **B** _____ is the center of the solar system.

> The planets move in **C** _____ around the sun.

2. SUMMARIZE Write a lesson summary that uses the vocabulary terms.

3. VOCABULARY Use the terms **constellation** and **star** to tell about this picture.

Test Prep

4. When is the only time you can see most stars?
  A. in the morning
  B. in the afternoon
  C. in the daytime
  D. at night

Links

Writing

Report About a Planet
Choose a planet. Find out four facts about it, and write a short report. Share your report with the class.

> Mars
> Mars is the fourth
> planet from the sun.
> It is very dry on Mars.
> Mars looks red from Earth.
> It has two moons.

For more links and activities, go to www.hspscience.com

What Causes Day and Night?

Fast Fact

Most parts of Earth have light and darkness each day because Earth is always spinning. You can observe the effects of Earth's movements.

Why Shadows Change

You need

- two pieces of chalk of different colors

Step 1

Stand outside in the morning. Have a partner trace your feet with chalk.

Step 2

Have your partner use chalk of a different color to trace your shadow.

Step 3

Wait two hours. Stand in the same place again. Have your partner trace your shadow again. Repeat two hours later. Communicate what you **observe**.

Inquiry Skill

When you **observe**, you use your senses to learn about things.

Reading in Science

VOCABULARY
rotate

 READING FOCUS SKILL

CAUSE AND EFFECT Look for the effects of Earth's rotation on day and night and on shadows.

Earth's Rotation

It looks as if the sun rises in one place in the morning and sets in another place at night. The sun does not really move across the sky. Earth is moving.

Earth spins around and around like a top. It takes about 24 hours for Earth to **rotate**, or spin all the way around. One rotation, or spin, of Earth takes one day.

day

Earth's rotation causes day and night. Sunlight shines on only the part of Earth that is facing the sun. This side of Earth has daytime. The other side is dark and has nighttime.

As Earth rotates, the part that was light turns away from the sun and gets dark. The part that was dark moves into the light. In most places this pattern of day and night repeats every 24 hours.

CAUSE AND EFFECT How does Earth's rotation cause day and night?

Model Day and Night

Put a piece of tape on a globe. Slowly spin the globe as you shine a flashlight on it. When is the tape in the light? When is it in the dark?

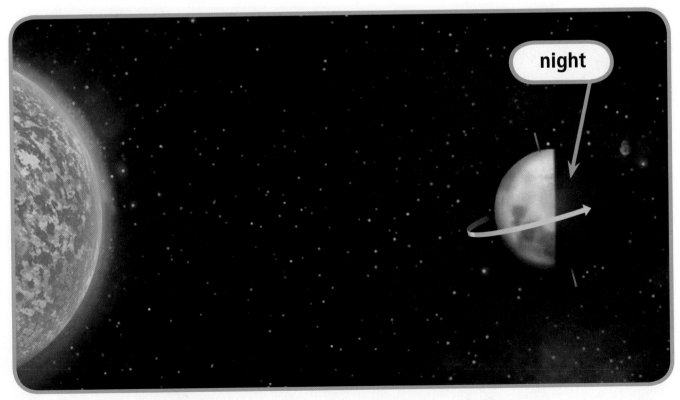

night

Changes in Shadows

When an object does not allow the sun's light to pass, it makes a shadow. As Earth rotates, the sun seems to move. The sun's light shines on objects from different directions as the day goes on. This causes the sizes and shapes of shadows to change.

Look at the pictures to see how a shadow changes. When is the shadow long? When is it short? How does the direction the sun shines from change the shadow?

CAURE Focus Skill **CAUSE AND EFFECT** What causes shadows to change?

noon

morning

evening

1. CAUSE AND EFFECT Copy and complete this chart. Tell the effect of each cause.

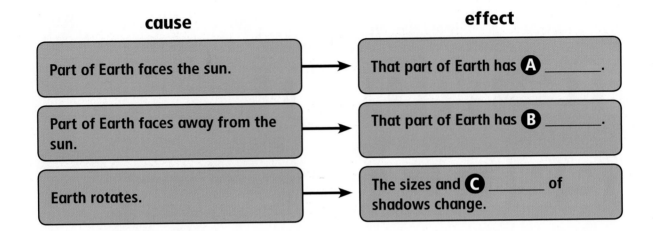

cause		effect
Part of Earth faces the sun.	→	That part of Earth has **A** _____.
Part of Earth faces away from the sun.	→	That part of Earth has **B** _____.
Earth rotates.	→	The sizes and **C** _____ of shadows change.

2. DRAW CONCLUSIONS How can you tell when the part of Earth where you live is facing away from the sun?

3. VOCABULARY Use the term **rotate** to tell why shadows change.

Test Prep

4. How does Earth's rotation cause day and night?

Links

Math

Make a Bar Graph
Different planets have different numbers of hours in their days. This is because they all rotate at different speeds. Make a bar graph that shows the number of hours in a day for each planet.

Number of Hours in a Day on Different Planets

Earth
Jupiter
Saturn
Neptune
Mars

0 5 10 15 20 25
number of hours

planet

 For more links and activities, go to www.hspscience.com

Why Does the Moon Seem to Change?

Fast Fact

The light we see from the moon really comes from the sun. You can make a model to show how this happens.

Why the Moon Seems to Shine

You need

- foam ball
- foil
- craft stick
- flashlight

Step 1

Work with a partner. Wrap foil around a ball to **make a model** of the moon. Use a craft stick to make a handle.

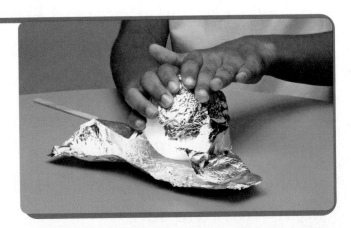

Step 2

Hold the handle. Look at the ball in the dark. What does it look like? Shine the flashlight on the ball. What does it look like now?

Step 3

Communicate the effect the light had on the ball.

Inquiry Skill

You can **make a model** to show how something happens.

Reading in Science

VOCABULARY

moon

 READING FOCUS SKILL

CAUSE AND EFFECT Look for the cause of the changes in the way you see the moon.

The Moon Shapes You See

The **moon** is a huge ball of rock that moves in an orbit around Earth. It takes nearly one month for the moon to orbit, or travel around, Earth.

On many nights, the moon seems to shine brightly. But the moon does not give off light of its own, as stars do. It reflects light from the sun.

full moon

first quarter moon

new moon

The moon is always orbiting Earth. So, the part you can see of the moon's lit side changes each night. This makes it seem as if the moon's shape changes.

The phases, or shapes you see, change as the moon moves. The changes follow a pattern that repeats about every 29 days.

Model Moon Phases

Wrap a ball in foil. Hold the ball while a partner shines a light onto it. Slowly turn in place, keeping the ball in front of you. When do you see the new moon, quarter moons, and full moon?

CAUSE AND EFFECT What happens because the moon moves around Earth?

last quarter moon

crescent moon

Phases of the Moon

The moon moves one-fourth of the way around Earth in a little more than 7 days. Use the pictures to see how the moon moves. About how long does it take the moon to move halfway around Earth? How does its shape seem to change? What happens after about 29 days?

crescent moon

first quarter moon

last quarter moon

full moon

For more links and activities, go to **www.hspscience.com**

Focus Skill

1. CAUSE AND EFFECT Copy and complete this chart. Tell the effect of each cause.

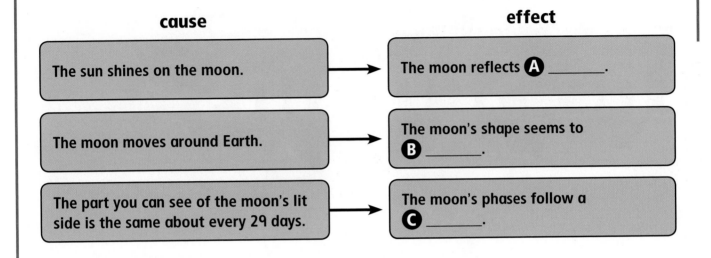

cause

The sun shines on the moon.

The moon moves around Earth.

The part you can see of the moon's lit side is the same about every 29 days.

effect

The moon reflects **A** _____.

The moon's shape seems to **B** _____.

The moon's phases follow a **C** _____.

2. SUMMARIZE Write two sentences that tell what this lesson is mostly about.

3. VOCABULARY Explain why the **moon** seems to give off light.

Test Prep

4. Which happens about every 29 days?

   A. The moon orbits Earth.

   B. The moon orbits the sun.

   C. The moon gets bigger.

   D. The moon gets smaller.

Links

Art

Make a Calendar

Make a blank calendar. Go outside each night for one month, and observe the moon. Draw what you see. Label the new, first quarter, full, and last quarter moon. How many days are there between the phases?

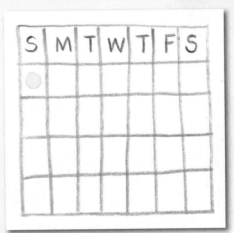

 For more links and activities, go to **www.hspscience.com**

What Causes the Seasons?

Fast Fact

When North America has summer, South America has winter. You can communicate other facts about the seasons.

Earth's Tilt

You need

- **foam ball and pencil**

- **lamp**

Step 1

Move the ball so that the pencil tip is tilted away from the lamp. Where on the ball does the light shine most brightly?

Step 2

Move the ball to the other side of the lamp. Do not change the pencil's direction or tilt. Where does the light shine most brightly?

Step 3

Communicate what you observe.

Inquiry Skill

When you **communicate** your ideas, you tell or show others what you know.

Reading in Science

Earth's Orbit Around the Sun

It takes about 365 days for Earth to complete one orbit around the sun. Those 365 days make up Earth's year.

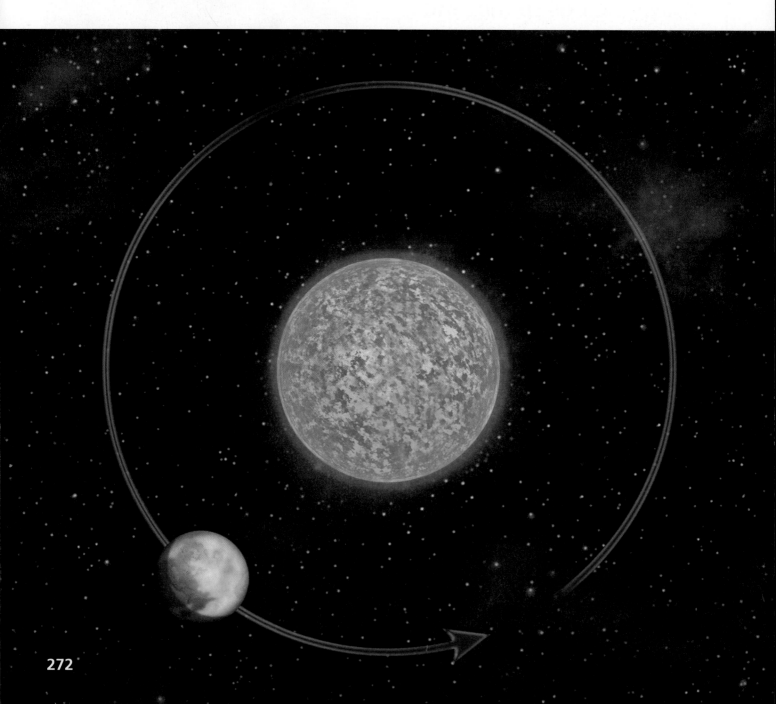

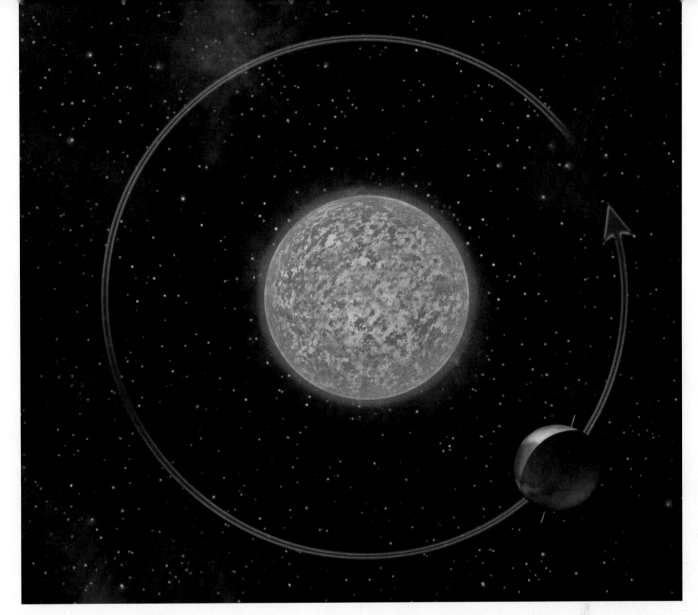

▲ Earth is tilted as it orbits the sun.

Earth is always tilted in the same direction. But the part that is tilted toward the sun changes as Earth orbits the sun. At one time of the year, the north part of Earth is tilted toward the sun. At other times of year, it is tilted away from the sun.

⭐ **CAUSE AND EFFECT** Why is one part of Earth sometimes tilted toward the sun and sometimes away from the sun?

Seasons Change

The part of Earth that is tilted toward the sun changes as Earth orbits the sun. This causes the seasons to change.

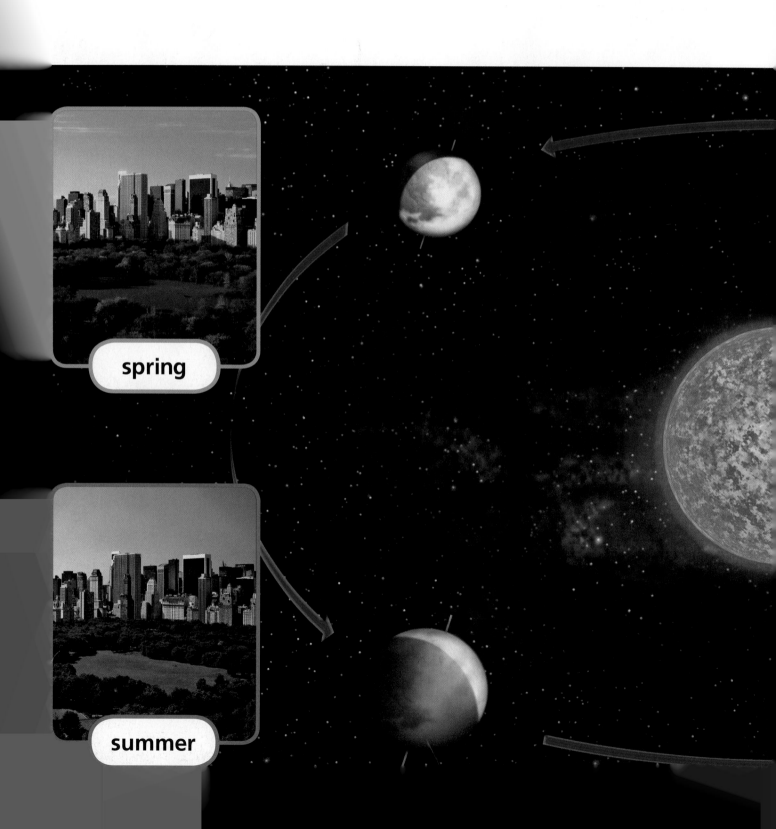

spring

summer

A **season** is a time of the year that has a certain kind of weather. Spring, summer, fall, and winter are seasons. They repeat in the same pattern each year.

⭐ (Focus Skill) **CAUSE AND EFFECT** What causes the seasons to change?

winter

fall

275

Why Seasons Change

When the part of Earth where you live is tilted toward the sun, it is summer. Sunlight hits that part of Earth directly. This causes warmer temperatures. There are more hours of daylight.

When the part of Earth where you live is tilted away from the sun, it is winter. Sunlight hits that part of Earth at a slant. This causes cooler temperatures. There are fewer hours of daylight.

CAUSE AND EFFECT What happens when a part of Earth is tilted toward the sun?

Insta-Lab

Slanting Light

Shine a flashlight directly onto a sheet of paper. Now tilt the paper so that the light hits it at a slant. Tell what looks different about the light on the page.

Which day has the most hours of daylight? Why?

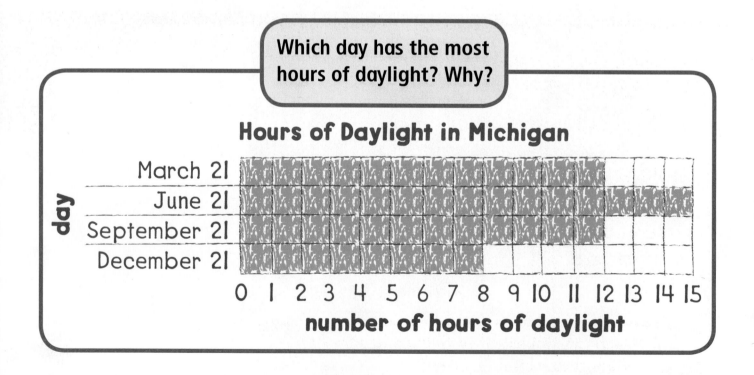

Hours of Daylight in Michigan

day: March 21, June 21, September 21, December 21

number of hours of daylight: 0 1 2 3 4 5 6 7 8 9 10 11 12 13 14 15

1. CAUSE AND EFFECT Copy and complete this chart. Tell the effect of each cause.

cause

Part of Earth is tilted toward the sun. → Temperatures are **A** _____. There are **B** _____ hours of daylight.

Part of Earth is tilted away from the sun. → That part has **C** _____. Temperatures are **D** _____. There are **E** _____ hours of daylight.

2. DRAW CONCLUSIONS As summer changes to fall, will there be more or fewer hours of daylight? How do you know?

3. VOCABULARY How do the **seasons** form a pattern?

Test Prep

4. Why do the seasons change?

Writing

Sentences About Seasons
Write about Earth's tilt at the beginning of each season where you live. Draw pictures to show the tilt in each season.

Seasons

 For more links and activities, go to www.hspscience.com

An Assistant in Space

Scientists are building a robot that talks and floats. It will help astronauts in space. The robot is called the Personal Satellite Assistant (PSA).

A Floating Clipboard

One scientist called the PSA "a floating, talking clipboard." The PSA will have taped information and play it for astronauts. It could tell astronauts how to complete a job.

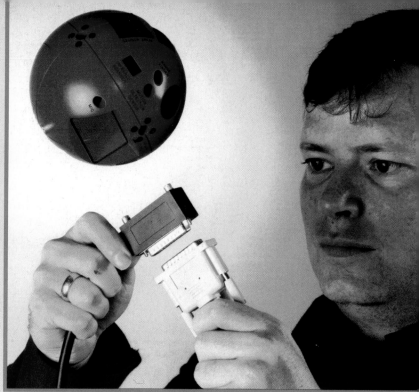

The robot comes with a light and a camera. It can talk to other computers aboard the International Space Station. The PSA may also help keep astronauts safe. The PSA could explore areas for astronauts. It could then tell astronauts the temperature of the area and what the air is like. That way, astronauts would know whether it would be safe for humans to explore an area.

Scientists plan to test the PSA aboard a future space shuttle flight. If the tests go well, the PSA might soon be used aboard the space station.

Think About It

If you had a PSA, how would you use it?

Coming Attractions

Scientists got the idea for the PSA from the movie *Star Wars*. Instead of training a Jedi knight, the softball-sized PSA will give astronauts a helping hand.

Find out more! Log on to
www.hspscience.com

A First Into Space

◀ Ellen Ochoa

In 1991, Ellen Ochoa became the first Latina astronaut. Since becoming an astronaut, Ochoa has been in space four times. She has spent almost 1,000 hours in space.

The longest trip for Ochoa was an 11-day trip to space in 1999. She and her crew delivered supplies for the first astronauts who were going to live in the International Space Station.

Make a Sundial

Materials
• stick   • small stones

What to Do

1. Place the end of the stick in the ground, pointing straight up.

2. When it is 1:00, place one stone at the end of the stick's shadow. Place two stones at 2:00, three stones at 3:00, and so on. Do not move the stones or the stick.

3. Use the stones and the stick's shadow to tell the time the next day.

Draw Conclusions
Why does the shadow move? How can the stones be used to tell time the next day?

Temperature Pattern

How do temperatures change from season to season? Find out the usual monthly temperatures where you live. Make a line graph. What patterns do you see? Communicate your observations.

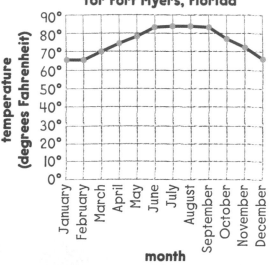

Usual Monthly Temperatures for Fort Myers, Florida

Review and Test Preparation

Vocabulary Review

Use the terms below to complete the sentences. The page numbers tell you where to look if you need help.

solar system p. 254   **star** p. 256

planet p. 254   **constellation** p. 256

orbit p. 255   **rotates** p. 260

1. A path around something is an _____.

2. A huge ball of hot gases is a _____.

3. When something spins around, it _____.

4. The sun, all its planets, and the planets' moons make up the _____.

5. A large ball of rock or gas that moves around the sun is a _____.

6. A group of stars that forms a pattern is a _____.

Check Understanding

7. When are the stars and planets in the sky?

  A. only in the morning
  B. only at night
  C. only in the afternoon
  D. all the time

8. Which detail about Earth's rotation is correct?

  F. It causes the sun to move.
  G. It causes winter to become spring.
  H. It causes Earth to have day and night.
  J. It causes summer to become fall.

Critical Thinking

9. What would happen if Earth were not tilted as it orbits?

10. Why do all parts of Earth not have light at the same time?

Exploring Matter

PHYSICAL SCIENCE

Chapter 9 Observing and Classifying Matter

Chapter 10 Changes in Matter

Gateway Arch

TO: casey@hspscience.com

FROM: blake@hspscience.com

RE: St. Louis, Missouri

Dear Casey,

This summer, my family and I took a trip to St. Louis. We had a great time. We got to ride on a riverboat. We also went up into the Gateway Arch. We were very high off the ground.
Your best friend,
Blake

TO: lamar@hspscience.com

FROM: mindy@hspscience.com

RE: Seminole, Oklahoma

Dear Lamar,

Visiting Aunt Susan has been so much fun. We went to a children's museum. My favorite part was riding around in Safety Town. I didn't know there was so much to do in a museum. Wish you could have come, too.

Love,

Mindy

Experiment!

Solids in Water

As you do this unit, you will learn about matter. Plan and do a test. Find out how water temperature changes the way solids dissolve.

Observing and Classifying Matter

Lesson 1 **What Is Matter?**

Lesson 2 **What Are Solids?**

Lesson 3 **What Are Liquids?**

Lesson 4 **What Are Gases?**

Vocabulary

matter	volume
property	milliliter
mass	gas
solid	
texture	
centimeter	
liquid	

I wonder...

What kinds of matter are the sand, the sea, and the air?

What do **you** wonder?

What Is Matter?

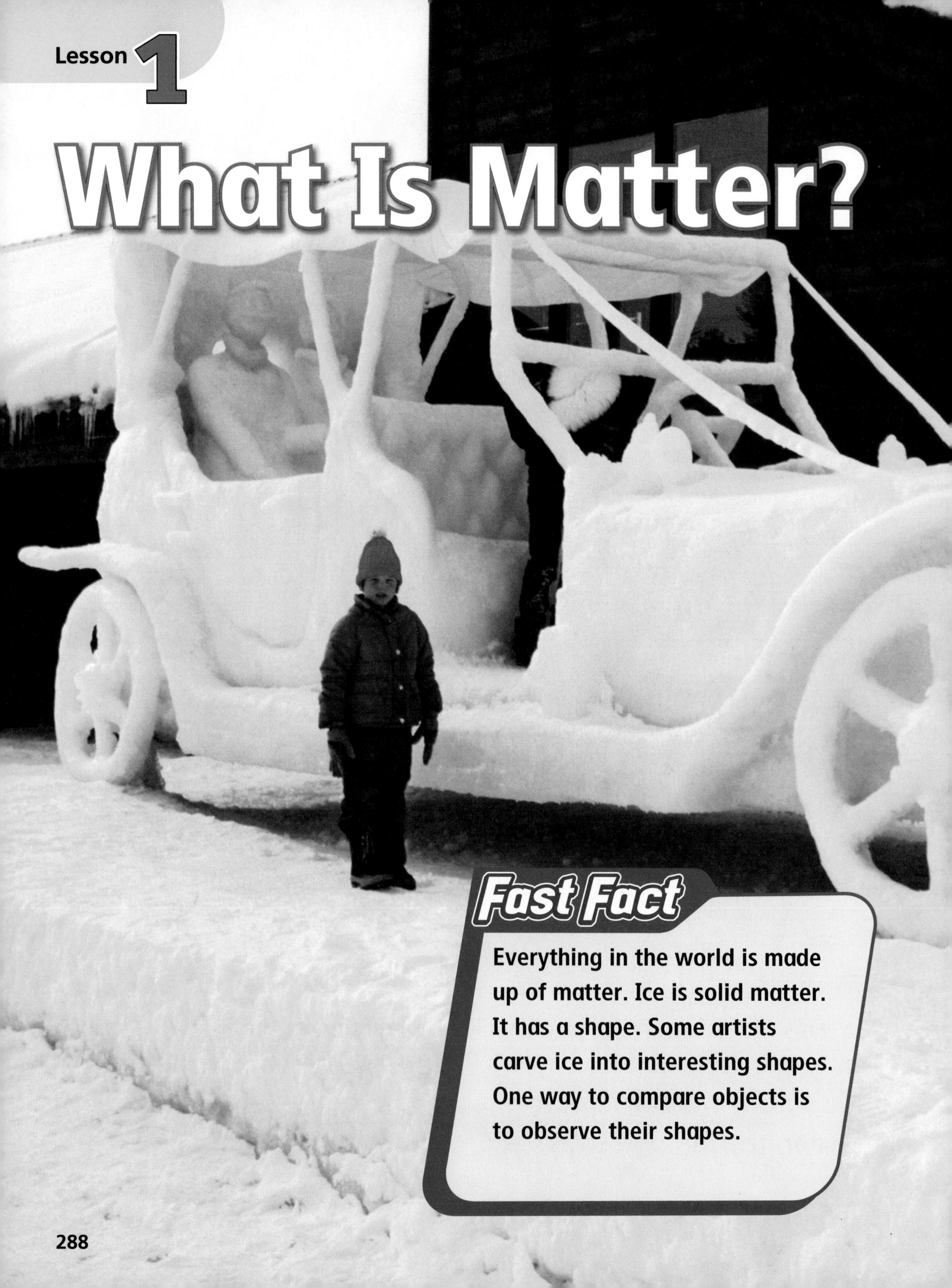

Fast Fact

Everything in the world is made up of matter. Ice is solid matter. It has a shape. Some artists carve ice into interesting shapes. One way to compare objects is to observe their shapes.

Kinds of Matter

You need

- jar of water with lid on   • zip-top bag filled with air   • block

Step 1

Gently shake the jar of water. Observe any changes to the water.

Step 2

Gently press the bag filled with air. Observe any changes to the air.

Step 3

Turn the block on its side. Squeeze it. Observe any changes to the block. **Compare** the changes to the water, the air, and the block.

Inquiry Skill

Comparing things helps you see how they are alike and how they are different.

Reading in Science

VOCABULARY

matter
property
mass

 READING FOCUS SKILL

COMPARE AND CONTRAST Look for ways different forms of matter are alike and ways they are different.

Forms of Matter

All things are made of **matter**. The books you read, the air you breathe, and the water you drink are all made of matter. Even people are made of matter.

What things in this picture are made of matter?

Matter has three forms. It can be a solid, a liquid, or a gas. The balloons, cars, hills, trees, and grass are solids. The water in the lake is a liquid. The air in the sky and inside the balloons is a gas.

 **COMPARE AND CONTRAST** How are the objects in this picture alike? How are they different?

Properties of Matter

Matter has properties. A **property** is one part of what something is like. It describes the matter that the thing is made of.

All matter has two main properties—it takes up space, and it has mass. **Mass** is the amount of matter in an object.

Matter has other properties. Color, size, and shape are properties of matter. The way something feels is also a property.

Find an object that is hard and bumpy and is shaped like a star. Now find an object that is shiny and smooth and is red, blue, and yellow. Properties can help you tell objects apart.

 COMPARE AND CONTRAST
What two properties do all kinds of matter have?

Matter and Space
Choose three classroom objects. Arrange them in order from the one that takes up the least space to the one that takes up the most space. Tell a classmate why you ordered the objects the way you did.

Measuring Mass

You can use a balance to find the mass of a solid. Put a solid object on one side of the balance. Add masses to the other side until both sides are even. Each mass has a number on it. Add the numbers to find the mass of the object you chose.

COMPARE AND CONTRAST Does a person have more or less mass than this shell?

Focus Skill

1. COMPARE AND CONTRAST Copy and complete this chart. Tell how forms of matter are alike and how they are different.

Matter

alike

All matter takes up **Ⓐ** _____.

All matter has **Ⓑ** _____.

different

Matter can be a solid, a **Ⓒ** _____, or a **Ⓓ** _____.

2. SUMMARIZE Use the chart to write a lesson summary.

3. VOCABULARY Describe the block by naming some of its **properties**.

Test Prep

4. How can you measure the mass of a solid?

Links

Writing

List of Clues

Draw a picture of a classroom object. On the other side of the paper, write a list of its properties as clues. Ask a classmate to read your clues and guess the object.

1. It is not a liquid.
2. It is not a gas.
3. It does not take up much space.
4.

For more links and activities, go to **www.hspscience.com**

What Are Solids?

Fast Fact

Sculptures are made from solid matter, such as wood, clay, metal, or stone. Measuring solid objects can help you find out their size and mass.

Measure a Solid

You need

- 4 objects

- balance

Step 1

Use the balance to **measure** the mass of each object.

Step 2

Put the objects in order from the least mass to the most mass.

Step 3

Make a chart to show the order of the objects from least mass to most mass.

Inquiry Skill

You can use a balance to **measure** the mass of a solid.

READING FOCUS SKILL

COMPARE AND CONTRAST Look for ways solids are alike and ways they are different.

Properties of Solids

A solid is a form of matter. All matter has mass and takes up space. A **solid** is the only form of matter that has its own **shape**. The shape of a solid will not change unless you cut it, bend it, break it, or change it in another way.

You can see and feel a solid. Some solids are hard, and some are soft. Solids can have different colors, sizes, and shapes. They can have different textures, too. **Texture** is the way something feels when you touch it.

⭐ *(Focus Skill)* **COMPARE AND CONTRAST**
How are solids alike? How are they different?

Insta-Lab

Sort Classroom Objects

With a partner, gather some classroom objects. Take turns describing their properties. Then sort the objects in different ways, such as by color, by shape, by size, and by texture.

Measuring Solids

Solids do not all have the same mass. You can use a balance to measure the mass of a solid. This boy is measuring the mass of a clay cat.

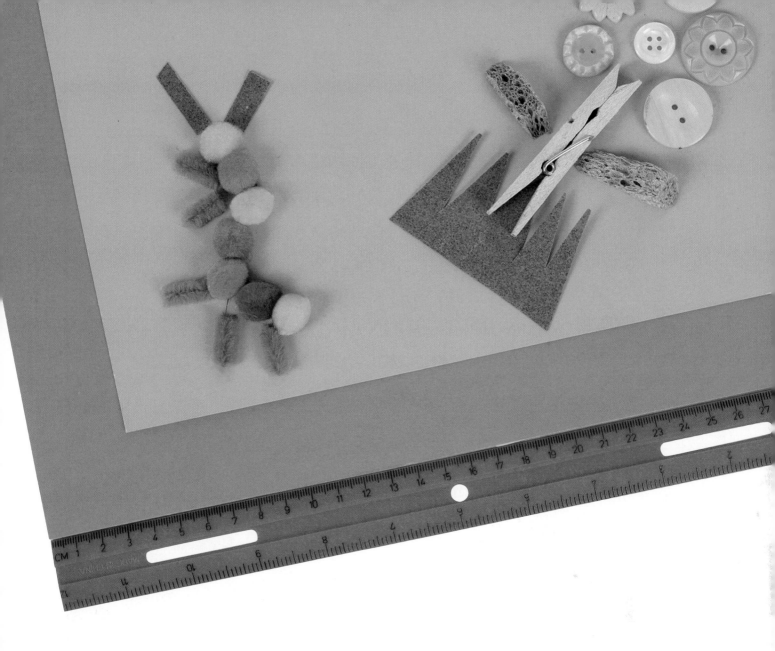

You can measure how long, high, or wide a solid is. You can use a ruler, a meterstick, or a yardstick to measure.

A **centimeter** is a unit used to measure length. An inch is a unit of length, too. This ruler measures both centimeters and inches.

COMPARE AND CONTRAST How are a balance and a ruler alike? How are they different?

Different Textures

Some rocks feel smooth. Other rocks feel rough. You can compare the textures of rocks by looking at them and feeling them. A hand lens lets you see more details. How are the textures of these rocks different? How can you tell?

◀ rough rock

▲ smooth rock

For more links and activities, go to
www.hspscience.com

1. COMPARE AND CONTRAST Copy and complete this chart.

Solids

alike

All solids have **A** _____.

All solids take up **B** _____.

All solids have their own **C** _____.

different

Solids can be different colors, sizes, and **D** _____.

Some solids are hard, and some are **E** _____.

2. DRAW CONCLUSIONS How are a rock, a block, and a ball alike?

3. VOCABULARY Use the term **centimeter** to tell about this picture.

Test Prep

4. What property does a solid have that other forms of matter do **NOT** have?

A. It has mass.

B. It takes up space.

C. It has its own shape.

D. It can be measured.

Links

Math

Measure How Big Around
Wrap a string around the outside of an object. Measure the length of the string with a ruler to find out how big around the object is. Then draw a picture of the object and record how big around it is.

The ball is 26 centimeters around.

For more links and activities, go to www.hspscience.com

What Are Liquids?

Fast Fact

Iguazú Falls in South America is one of the largest waterfalls in the world. The shape of the falling water is always changing. Making inferences helps you figure out why matter changes.

Measure a Liquid

You need

- colored water
- measuring cup
- 3 different clear containers
- black marker

Step 1

Measure $\frac{1}{2}$ cup water. Pour the water into a container. Mark the level on the outside of the container.

Step 2

Repeat Step 1 for the other two containers.

Step 3

Is the water level the same in all three containers? Why or why not? What can you infer?

Inquiry Skill

When you infer, you use what you have observed to figure out what happened.

READING FOCUS SKILL

MAIN IDEA AND DETAILS Look for details about the properties of liquids.

Properties of Liquids

Liquids are a form of matter. Like all matter, a **liquid** has mass and takes up space. A liquid does not have its own shape. It takes the shape of its container.

A liquid in a bottle has the same shape as the bottle. If you tilt the bottle, the liquid changes shape. If you pour the liquid into a glass, it takes the shape of the glass.

You can see and feel a liquid. If you pour liquid from one container into another, its shape changes. The amount of liquid stays the same. The amount does not change unless you add more liquid or take some away.

 MAIN IDEA AND DETAILS What shape does a liquid always take?

Measuring Liquids

You can measure the volume of a liquid. **Volume** is the amount of space a liquid takes up. A **milliliter** is a unit used to measure the volume of a liquid. An ounce is a unit of volume, too.

A measuring cup may show milliliters on one side and ounces on the other side.

 MAIN IDEA AND DETAILS What can you use to measure the volume of a liquid?

Measure Two Ways

Use a measuring cup to find out about how many milliliters equal 5 ounces. Tell a classmate how you found the amount.

1. MAIN IDEA AND DETAILS Copy and complete this chart. Tell details about the main idea.

Main Idea and Details

Liquids are a form of matter.

| A liquid has **A** _____. | It takes up **B** _____. | It does not have its own **C** _____. | You can measure it to find its **D** _____. |

2. SUMMARIZE Write two sentences that tell what this lesson is about.

3. VOCABULARY Use the terms **volume**, **liquid**, and **milliliter** to tell about this picture.

Test Prep

4. How can you tell that a liquid does not have its own shape?

Links

Health

Measure Your Liquids

Liquids help your body stay healthy. You should drink six to eight cups of water or other liquids each day. Keep a chart for a few days. Record each time you drink a liquid and about how much you drink.

7:00	1 cup
12:00	2 cups
3:00	1 cup
6:30	2 cups
8:00	1 cup

For more links and activities, go to **www.hspscience.com**

What Are Gases?

Fast Fact

You can twist balloons into different shapes because the air inside does not have its own shape. Making inferences can help you learn about air.

Measure a Gas

You need

- **balance**   • **balloon filled with air**   • **balloon without air**

Step 1

Place the balloon filled with air on one side of the balance. Place the balloon without air on the other side.

Step 2

Observe both balloons. What can you **infer** about why their masses are different? Record what you **infer**.

Step 3

Communicate to a classmate what you **infer**.

Inquiry Skill

When you **infer**, you use what you observed to figure out why something happened.

311

VOCABULARY
gas

 READING FOCUS SKILL

MAIN IDEA AND DETAILS Look for details about the properties of gases.

Gases and Air

Gases are a form of matter. Like all matter, a **gas** takes up space and has mass. It is the only kind of matter that always fills all the space of its container. When you blow up a balloon, the gas spreads out inside. It takes the shape of the balloon. A gas does not have its own shape.

▼ Gases are in this drink. Can you find them?

Air is made up of gases. It is all around you. Often you can not see, smell, or feel the air around you. But you can see and feel what it does. Moving air lifts the girl's hair. Moving air also makes a pinwheel spin.

 MAIN IDEA AND DETAILS
Focus Skill **What happens when air is put into a balloon?**

Observe Air

Tightly pack a paper towel into the bottom of a cup. Turn the cup upside down. Push it straight down into a bowl of water. Then pull it straight out. What happens to the paper towel? Why?

Comparing Forms of Matter

This chart tells about the three forms of matter. How are they alike? How are they different?

⭐ **Focus Skill** **MAIN IDEA AND DETAILS** What are two details about each type of matter?

Forms of Matter

	solid	liquid	gas
mass	has mass	has mass	has mass
space	takes up space	takes up space	takes up space
shape	has its own shape	takes the shape of its container	spreads out to fill its container
ways it can be measured	mass—balance size—ruler	mass—balance volume— measuring cup	mass—balance

1. MAIN IDEA AND DETAILS Copy and complete this chart. Tell details about the main idea.

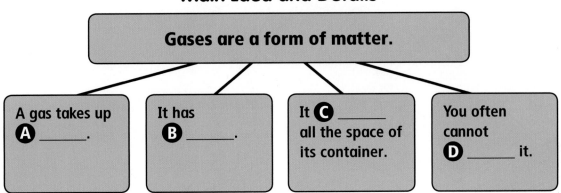

Main Idea and Details

Gases are a form of matter.

| A gas takes up **A** _____. | It has **B** _____. | It **C** _____ all the space of its container. | You often cannot **D** _____ it. |

2. DRAW CONCLUSIONS What shape is the air inside a bubble?

3. VOCABULARY Use the term **gas** to tell about a balloon.

Test Prep

4. How is a gas like all matter?
   A. It takes up space.
   B. It has its own shape.
   C. You can always see it.
   D. You can always feel it.

Links

Art

Make a Windsock

Decorate a sheet of paper. Tape it together to make a tube. Tape paper strips to one end. Make three holes in the other end. Tie string in the holes. Then tie the windsock to a stick. Show how wind makes the windsock move.

 For more links and activities, go to www.hspscience.com

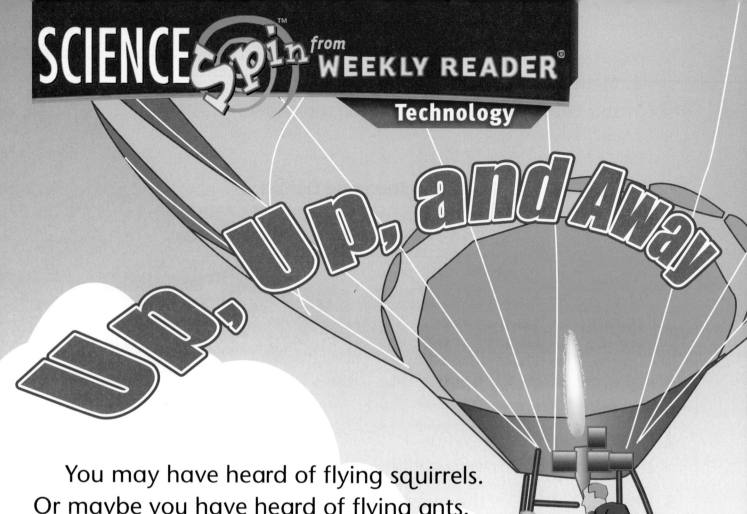

Up, Up, and Away

You may have heard of flying squirrels. Or maybe you have heard of flying ants. But have you ever heard of a flying dog?

Meet Buster the terrier. Buster has visited about 30 states, mostly from hundreds of feet above the ground in a hot-air balloon.

Not Afraid of Heights

Buster regularly takes to the air in his owner's hot-air balloon. His owner, Don Edwards, owns a hot-air balloon business in Florida. Buster is a great flier, says his owner. Even the loud noise of the balloon's burner does not bother the dog.

Buster, who always wears a leash when in the balloon's gondola, or basket, can't wait to fly. His owner says, "When Buster flies, he is like a little kid."

How It Works

The burner is used to heat up the air inside the balloon's giant, colorful envelope. Hot air is lighter than cold air and makes the balloon rise. To keep the balloon rising, the air inside the balloon must be reheated from time to time. As the air in the balloon cools, the pilot can reheat it by firing the burner.

Think About It

What makes a hot-air balloon float upward into the sky?

Find out more! Log on to **www.hspscience.com**

What's in a Bubble?

What's in a bubble? Nothing, right? Not really, as Catherine Ho found out recently at a visit to a science museum.

Catherine saw an exhibit that makes bubbles if you press a button. She learned that bubbles are like balloons. They are filled with gas and they take up space. But not all bubbles are alike.

Bubbles can be made into many shapes and sizes. Catherine saw that some bubbles are rounded. Bubbles can also be made into square shapes with different bubble wands.

You Can Do It!

Hot Air and Cold Air

What to Do

1. Stretch a balloon over the top of an empty bottle.

2. Place the bottle in a bowl. Watch an adult pour hot water into the bowl. **CAUTION:** Be careful near the hot water! Wait a few minutes. What happens?

3. Wait for the adult to empty the hot water. Then fill the bowl with ice. What happens?

Materials

- plastic bottle
- balloon
- bowl
- hot water
- ice cubes

Draw Conclusions

What can you infer about the way temperature changes air?

Classifying Matter

Make a chart like this one. Look through old magazines and newspapers to find pictures that show each kind of matter. Cut out the pictures, and glue them in the correct places on the chart. Label each picture.

Kinds of Matter		
solids	liquids	gases

Review and Test Preparation

Vocabulary Review

Use the terms below to complete the sentences. The page numbers tell you where to look if you need help.

matter p. 290   **texture** p. 299

mass p. 292   **liquid** p. 306

solid p. 298   **gas** p. 312

1. Matter that has its own shape is a _____.

2. The way something feels is its _____.

3. Everything in the world is made up of _____.

4. Matter that always fills all the space of its container is a _____.

5. A balance measures an object's _____.

6. Matter you can see that does not have its own shape is a _____.

Check Understanding

7. 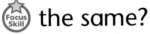 How are all the things in the picture the same?

    A. They are all liquids.

    B. They are all solids.

    C. They are all gases.

    D. They are all made of matter.

8. 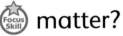 What are two properties of all matter?

    F. Matter has mass and color.

    G. Matter has color and its own shape.

    H. Matter has mass and takes up space.

    J. Matter has texture and no shape of its own.

Critical Thinking

9. Jon has a fish tank. Tell how it shows all three kinds of matter.

10. How can you use a ruler, a balance, and a measuring cup to learn about matter?

10 Changes in Matter

Lesson 1 How Can Matter Change?

Lesson 2 How Can Water Change?

Lesson 3 What Are Other Changes to Matter?

Vocabulary

mixture
evaporation
water vapor
condensation
burning

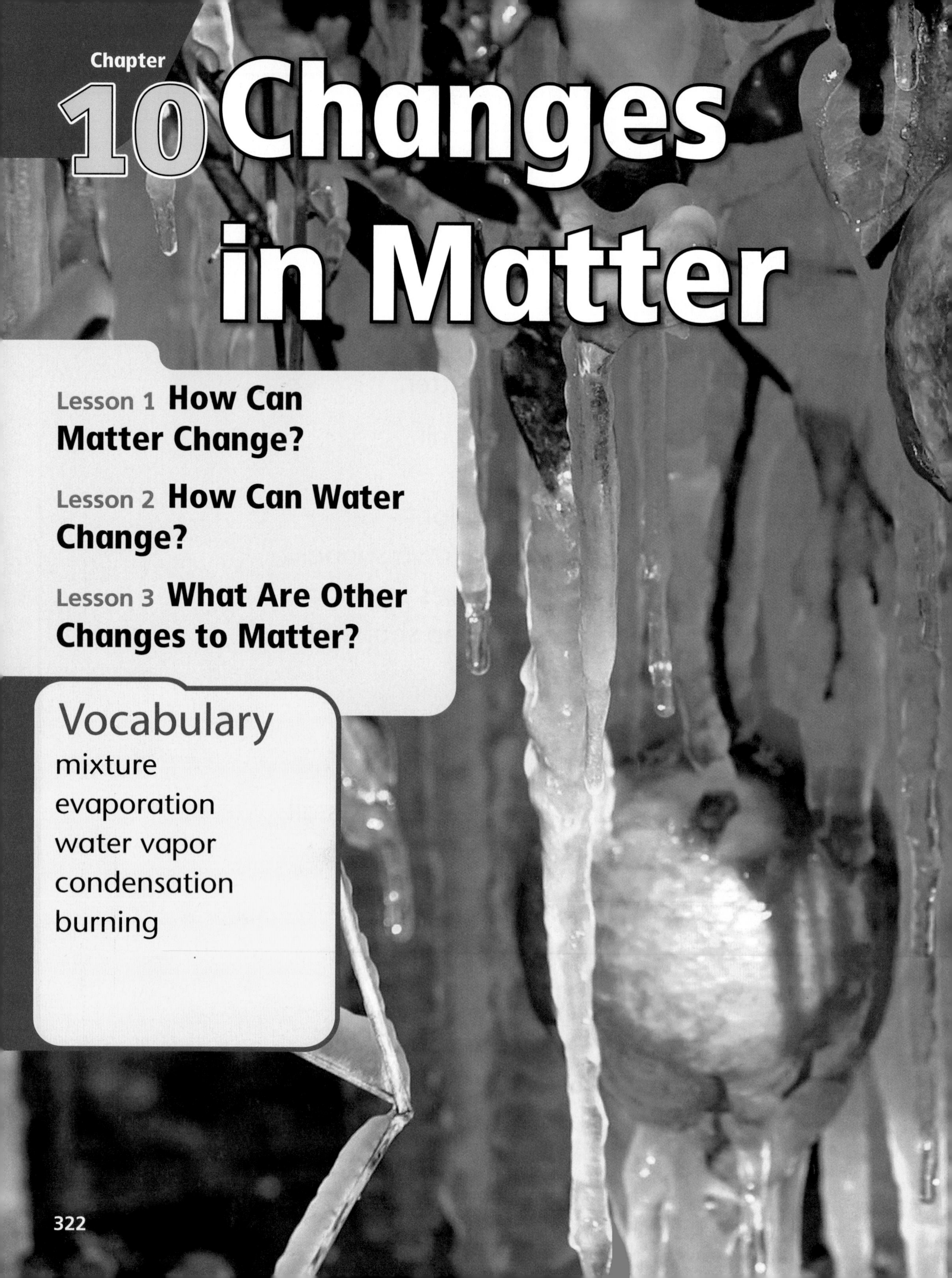

I wonder...

Why does water change to ice?

What do **you** wonder?

How Can Matter Change?

Fast Fact

The children's pasta with sauce and cheese is a mixture. The green salad is also a mixture. You can communicate about foods you like when you make tasty mixtures.

Make a Mixture

You need

- dried fruits and seeds
- measuring cup
- zip-top bag

Step 1

Use the measuring cup to measure the same amounts of dried fruits and seeds.

Step 2

Put the foods into the bag. Close the bag tightly, and shake it.

Step 3

Observe. What has changed? What has stayed the same? **Communicate** to your classmates what you see.

Inquiry Skill

When you **communicate** your observations, you share with others what you have learned.

VOCABULARY
mixture

 READING FOCUS SKILL

CAUSE AND EFFECT Look for ways matter can change. Find the cause of each change.

Mixing Matter

When you mix two or more kinds of matter, you make a **mixture**. Solids, liquids, and gases can all be parts of mixtures. Fruit salad is a mixture of solids. You make it by mixing pieces of fruit. You can separate fruit salad into pieces. Each piece is the same size and shape as it was in the mixture. Substances you put in a mixture do not become new substances.

Lemonade is a mixture. You make it with water, lemon juice, and sugar. The sugar is a solid. You mix it with the two liquids. You no longer see the sugar, but it is there. If you take a sip, you will taste the sugar.

 CAUSE AND EFFECT What happens to fruit pieces when you mix them together?

Mix It Up

Mix four spoonfuls of cornstarch with two spoonfuls of water. Roll the mixture in your hands. Pour it from hand to hand. What happens? Describe the cornstarch and water before and after you mixed them.

Kinds of Changes

You change matter when you cut it. Cutting a watermelon changes its size and shape. Look at these other ways to change matter.

 CAUSE AND EFFECT How does matter change when you cut it or break it?

Break it.

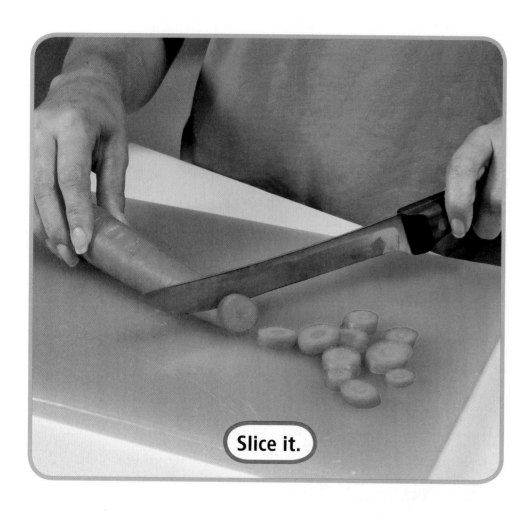

Slice it.

Shape it.

Tear it.

Cut it.

Measuring Matter

When you change only the shape of matter, its mass stays the same. The pieces of cheese on both sides of this balance were once alike. They were blocks that had the same shape and mass. Then one block of cheese was changed. It was cut into cubes. Its shape changed. But the balance shows that its mass did not change.

CAUSE AND EFFECT What stayed the same when the cheese was cut into cubes? How do you know it stayed the same?

1. CAUSE AND EFFECT Copy and complete this chart. Tell the effect of each cause.

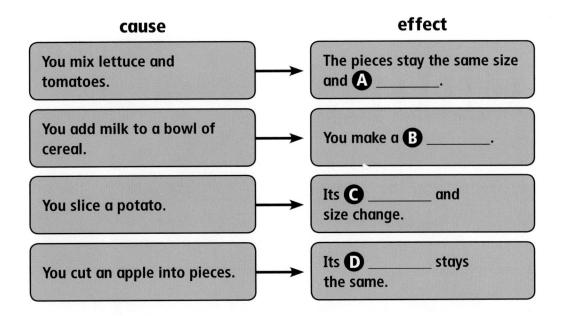

cause	effect
You mix lettuce and tomatoes.	The pieces stay the same size and **A** _____.
You add milk to a bowl of cereal.	You make a **B** _____.
You slice a potato.	Its **C** _____ and size change.
You cut an apple into pieces.	Its **D** _____ stays the same.

2. SUMMARIZE Write two sentences that tell what this lesson is about.

3. VOCABULARY Use the term **mixture** to tell about the picture.

Test Prep

4. When the shape of matter is changed, what stays the same?

Links

Writing

Snack Recipe

Make up a healthful snack that is a mixture of different foods. Write your recipe. List what you need. Write steps to tell how to make it. Share your recipe with your classmates.

Margie's Munchy Mix

What you need

1 cup pumpkin seeds
1 cup raisins
cereal

 For more links and activities, go to www.hspscience.com

How Can Water Change?

Fast Fact

Water is the only matter that is naturally found in three forms on Earth. The forms are solid, liquid, and gas. You can predict which form the ice in this pond will become when it gets warmer.

What Freezing Does

You need

- **plastic tub with lid**

- **water**

- **marker**

Step 1

Fill a plastic tub halfway with water. Mark the water level on the side of the tub.

Step 2

Put a lid on the tub. Place the tub in the freezer. **Predict** what will happen to the water.

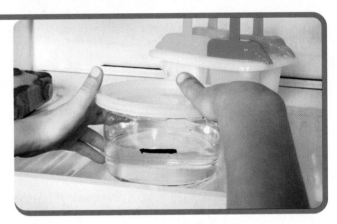

Step 3

Wait one day. Remove the tub from the freezer. Did the water change? Did the tub change? How did they change?

Inquiry Skill

When you **predict**, you tell what you think will happen.

Reading in Science

VOCABULARY

evaporation
water vapor
condensation

 READING FOCUS SKILL

CAUSE AND EFFECT Look for the causes that change water into a solid, a liquid, and a gas.

Freezing

Water has three forms. It can be a solid, a liquid, or a gas.

Water changes from a liquid to a solid when enough heat is taken away from it. The water freezes and becomes ice. Ice is water in its solid form.

The tray is filled with juice. Juice is mostly water. How will it change when it freezes?

The juice is no longer a liquid. It has changed to a solid. It is now an ice pop. When matter is a solid, it has its own shape.

 CAUSE AND EFFECT What caused the juice to change from a liquid to a solid?

Melting

The ice pop is now melting. Warm air is adding heat to the ice. Ice melts when its temperature is high enough.

The juice changes from a solid to a liquid. It no longer has a shape.

CAUSE AND EFFECT Why is the ice pop melting?

Which Melts Faster?

Set out two plates. Put one ice cube on each plate. Place a lamp over one of the plates. Wait five minutes. Which ice cube melted more? Why?

Evaporation and Boiling

Water changes from a liquid to a gas when enough heat is added to it. This change is called **evaporation**. When water is a gas, it is called **water vapor**. You can not see water vapor. It is in the air.

Water boils when its temperature gets high enough. The boiling water in this pot is evaporating. As long as the water keeps boiling, it will continue to evaporate.

Focus Skill **CAUSE AND EFFECT** What causes water to change to a gas?

Condensation

Water vapor changes from a gas to a liquid when heat is taken away from it. This change is called **condensation**.

This glass is filled with a cold drink. It takes heat away from the air around it. This changes the water vapor in the air into a liquid. The tiny drops of water on the outside of the glass show that water has condensed from water vapor.

CAUSE AND EFFECT What caused water drops to form on the outside of the glass?

338

1. CAUSE AND EFFECT Copy and complete this chart. Tell how water changes.

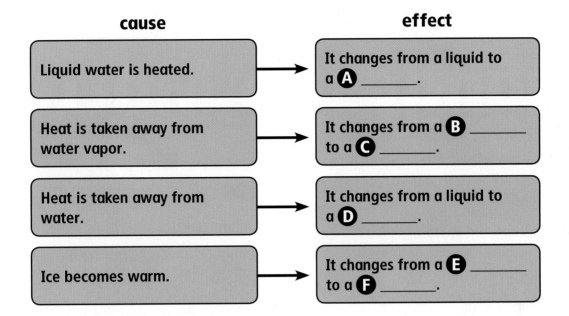

cause

effect

| Liquid water is heated. | → | It changes from a liquid to a **A** _____. |

| Heat is taken away from water vapor. | → | It changes from a **B** _____ to a **C** _____. |

| Heat is taken away from water. | → | It changes from a liquid to a **D** _____. |

| Ice becomes warm. | → | It changes from a **E** _____ to a **F** _____. |

2. DRAW CONCLUSIONS Can ice that becomes a liquid change back to a solid? Explain.

3. VOCABULARY Use the terms **water vapor** and **condensation** to tell about this picture.

Test Prep

4. How can you change water to a gas?

  A. Take heat away.
  B. Condense it.
  C. Add heat.
  D. Make ice.

Links

Math

Measure and Compare
Measure the temperature of a glass of water. Then measure the temperature of a bowl of ice. Compare. Does the water or the ice have the lower temperature?

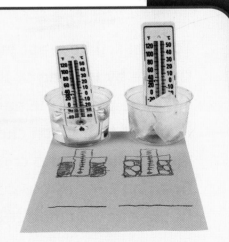

 For more links and activities, go to **www.hspscience.com**

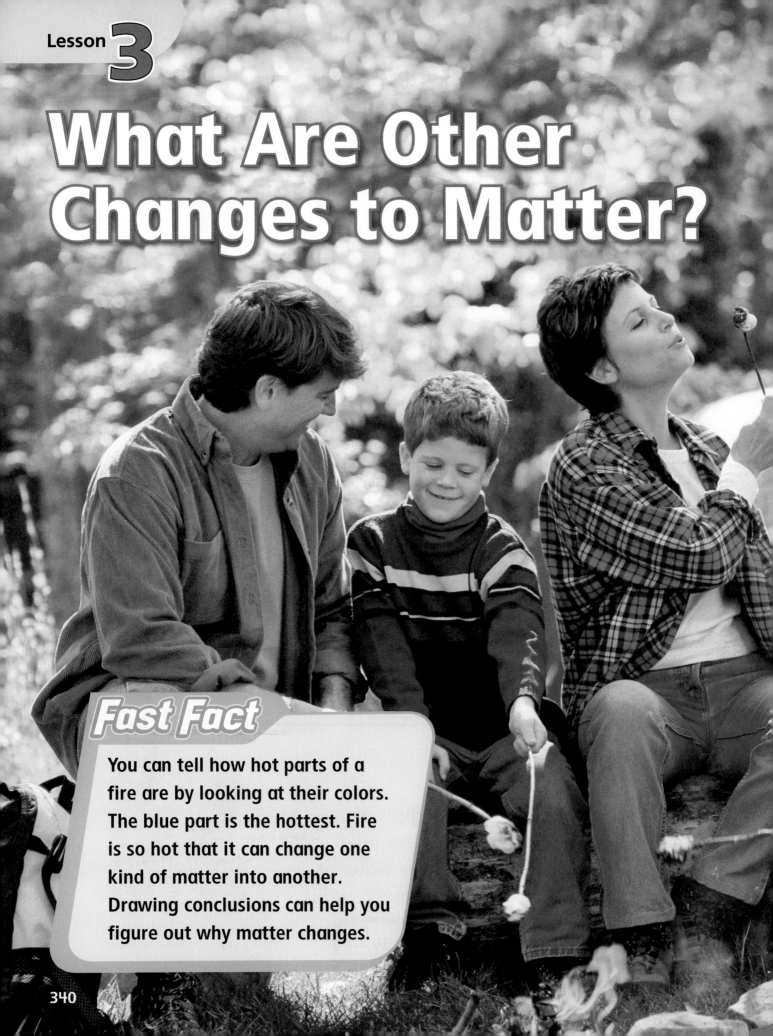

What Are Other Changes to Matter?

Fast Fact

You can tell how hot parts of a fire are by looking at their colors. The blue part is the hottest. Fire is so hot that it can change one kind of matter into another. Drawing conclusions can help you figure out why matter changes.

How Matter Can Change

You need

- black plastic bowl
- foil
- gelatin cube

Step 1

Place the foil, shiny side up, in the bowl.

Step 2

Place the gelatin cube on the foil in the bowl. Place the bowl outside in a sunny spot.

Step 3

Wait one hour. Observe the gelatin cube. Can you **draw conclusions** from what you observed? Explain.

Inquiry Skill

Use your observations and what you know to **draw conclusions**.

VOCABULARY

burning

 READING FOCUS SKILL

CAUSE AND EFFECT Look for the causes and effects of burning and cooking.

Burning and Cooking

Fire and cooking change matter into different matter. The new matter can not change back into what it was before.

The fire is burning this wood. **Burning** the wood changes it into ashes and smoke. The ashes and smoke can not change back into wood.

Cooking heats food. The heat changes the marshmallows. They change from white to brown. They can not change back to white.

The meat and vegetables were raw, or uncooked. Cooking changed them. Their color, shape, texture, size, and taste are different. They can never be raw again.

CAUSE AND EFFECT How and why does meat change when it is cooked?

Uncooked and Cooked

Draw pictures to show what spaghetti looks like before and after it is cooked. Tell a classmate how the spaghetti changes.

Making Muffins

1. **Mix the ingredients.**

2. **Pour the mixture into a pan.**

3. **Bake the mixture.**

What changes do you see? What caused these changes?

1

2

3

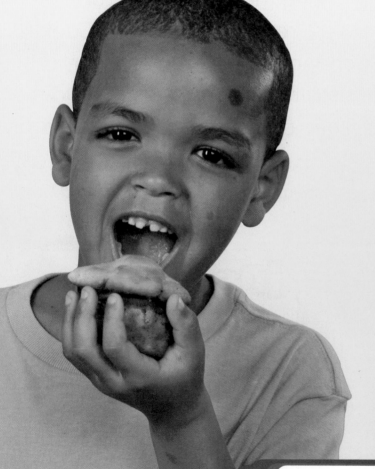

 For more links and activities, go to www.hspscience.com

Reading Review

1. CAUSE AND EFFECT Copy and complete this chart. Tell the effects of burning and cooking.

cause   **effect**

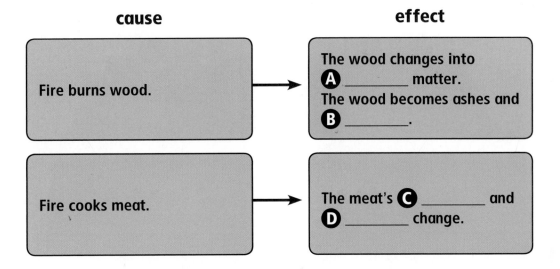

Fire burns wood.

The wood changes into
A _____ matter.
The wood becomes ashes and
B _____.

Fire cooks meat.

The meat's **C** _____ and
D _____ change.

2. SUMMARIZE Use the chart to write a summary of this lesson.

3. VOCABULARY Use the term **burning** to tell about this picture.

Test Prep

4. What happens when paper burns?

   A. Its shape stays the same.
   B. Its size stays the same.
   C. Its matter changes.
   D. Its color stays the same.

Links

Art

Before and After
Draw pictures of a food before and after it is cooked. Tell about the food's texture, size, color, shape, and taste. Share your work with a classmate.

Dough

Bread

For more links and activities, go to
www.hspscience.com

The Future of Bandages

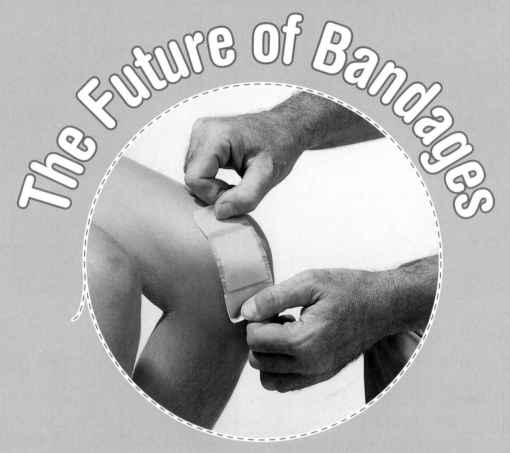

All kids get scrapes and cuts, especially when they're playing outside. When you get a scrape or a cut, you usually put a plastic bandage on. What happens when it is time to change that bandage? Ouch! Pulling off a plastic bandage can hurt.

Scientists have recently invented a new fabric bandage. This bandage is better than a plastic bandage. It never has to be taken off!

Tiny Strands

The new bandage is made up of thousands of tiny hair-like strands. The strands are 1,000 times thinner than a human hair. The strands are also found in a person's blood. The strands found in a person's blood act like a net across a cut to stop bleeding.

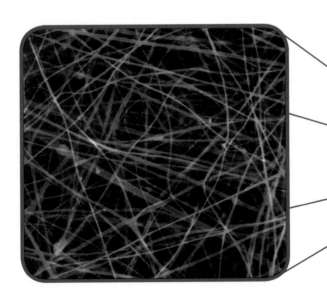

Think About It

How does the new bandage change as a cut heals?

The New Bandage in Town

The new bandage works like the body's own bandage—a scab. After a cut covered with the new bandage has healed, the body absorbs the fibers. The bandage simply disappears.

Find out more! Log on to **www.hspscience.com**

A Famous Scientist

Albert Einstein is one of the most famous scientists in history. It might surprise you to learn that Einstein didn't do well in some subjects in school. He loved math and science, though.

As he grew up, Einstein read a lot because he wanted to learn more about the things around him. He thought about things he could see. He thought about things that were much too small to see. He used his imagination to look at things in new ways. He thought about matter in ways that no one ever had before.

Mixing Matter

What to Do

1. Put a spoonful of salt into the warm water. Stir well.

2. Pour the mixture of salt and water into the pan.

3. Put the pan in a warm spot. Predict what will happen.

4. Wait two days. Then observe. Was your prediction correct?

You need
- $\frac{1}{2}$ cup warm water
- spoon
- salt
- pie pan

Draw Conclusions

What happened to the water? What was left in the pan?

Heat Changes Food

Place a cracker, an ice cube, some chocolate chips, and some butter on separate pieces of foil. Put them under a hot light. Check every five minutes. What changes do you see?

Review and Test Preparation

Vocabulary Review

Use the terms to complete the sentences. The page numbers tell you where to look if you need help.

mixture p. 326   **water vapor** p. 337

evaporation p. 337   **condensation** p. 338

1. When water changes from a liquid to a gas, the change is called _____.

2. Water in its gas form is called _____.

3. A mix of two or more things is a _____.

4. When water changes from a gas to a liquid, the change is called _____.

Check Understanding

5. How does water change when it (Focus Skill) is heated?

　　A. It changes from a liquid to a solid.

　　B. It changes from a gas to a solid.

　　C. It changes from a liquid to a gas.

　　D. It changes from a gas to a liquid.

6. What caused the bread to change?

   F. burning
   G. cutting
   H. freezing
   J. mixing

Critical Thinking

7. What changes would these icicles go through to become water vapor?

8. How does an egg change when it is cooked?

PHYSICAL SCIENCE

Energy in Motion

Chapter 11 Light and Heat

Chapter 12 Sound

Chapter 13 Motion

Holgate Toy Company

TO: dwayne@hspscience.com

FROM: ryan@hspscience.com

RE: Kane, Pennsylvania

Dear Dwayne,

My class went to a place where they make toys. We walked through the museum and saw very old toys. I got a square yo-yo to take home with me.

Your pen pal,

Ryan

NEIGHBORHOOD TROLLEY

National Baseball Hall of Fame

TO: charlie@hspscience.com

FROM: elise@hspscience.com

RE: Cooperstown, New York

Dear Charlie,

Congratulations on your home run in last week's game. Next time you visit, we'll take you to the Baseball Hall of Fame. You can see a bat Babe Ruth used to hit a homer.

Batter up!

Elise

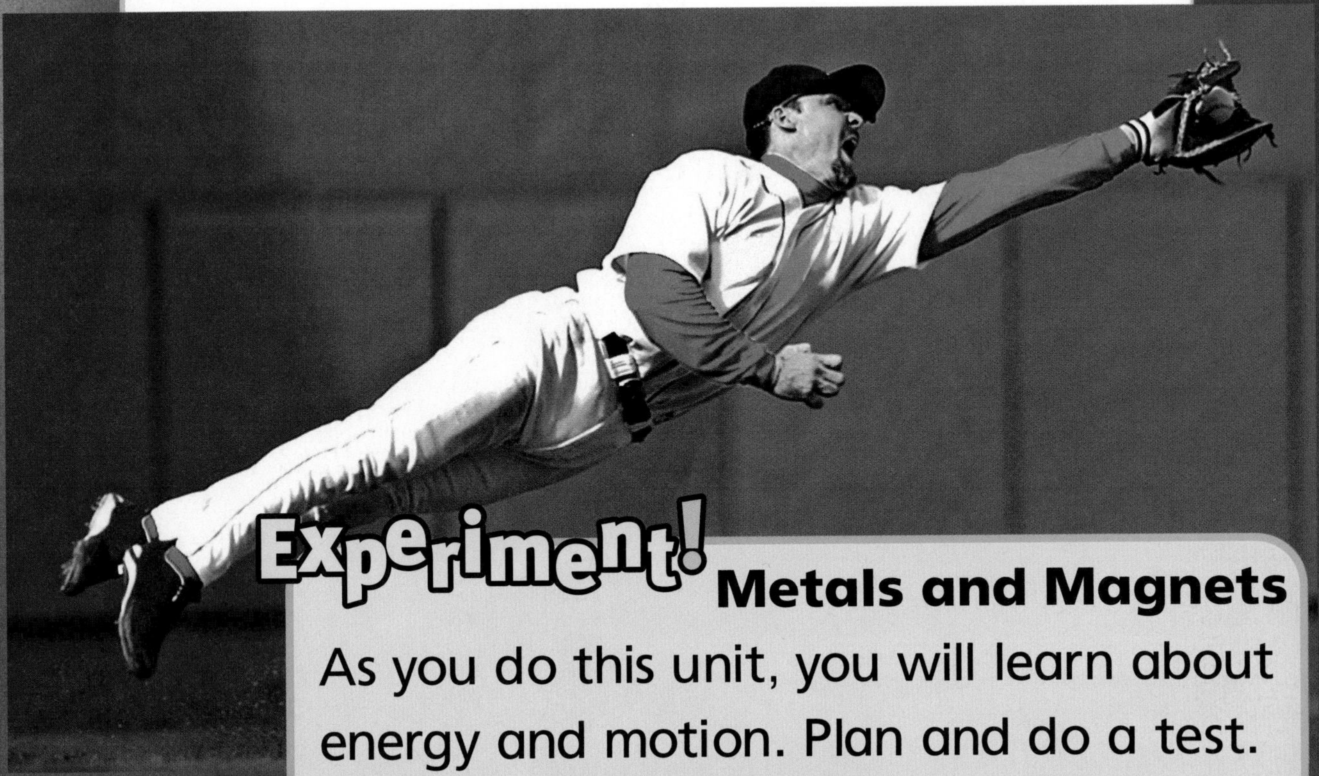

Experiment! Metals and Magnets

As you do this unit, you will learn about energy and motion. Plan and do a test. Find out how magnets make things move.

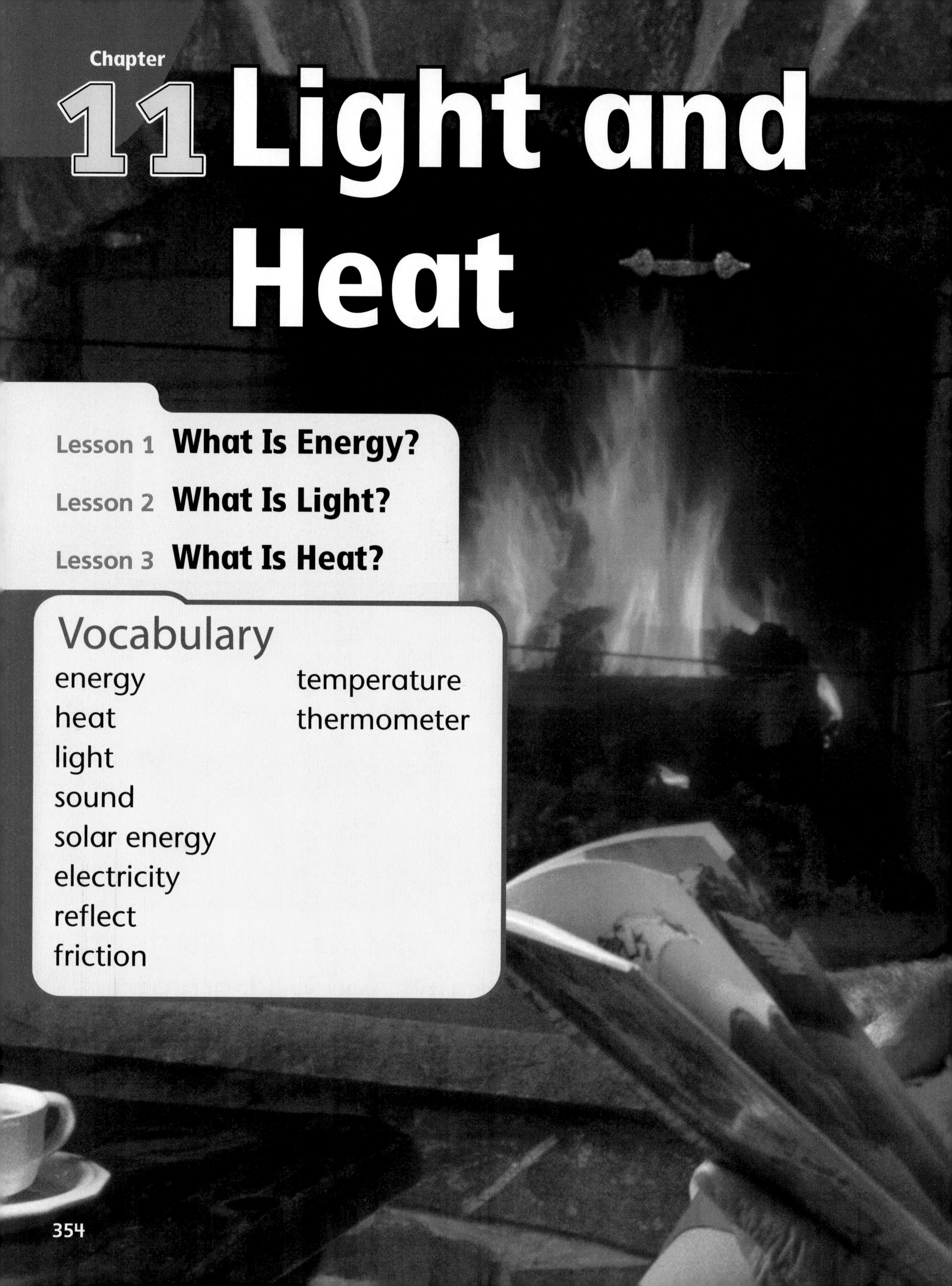

Chapter 11

Light and Heat

Lesson 1 **What Is Energy?**

Lesson 2 **What Is Light?**

Lesson 3 **What Is Heat?**

Vocabulary

energy
heat
light
sound
solar energy
electricity
reflect
friction
temperature
thermometer

I wonder...

Why do people make fires in fireplaces?

What do YOU wonder?

355

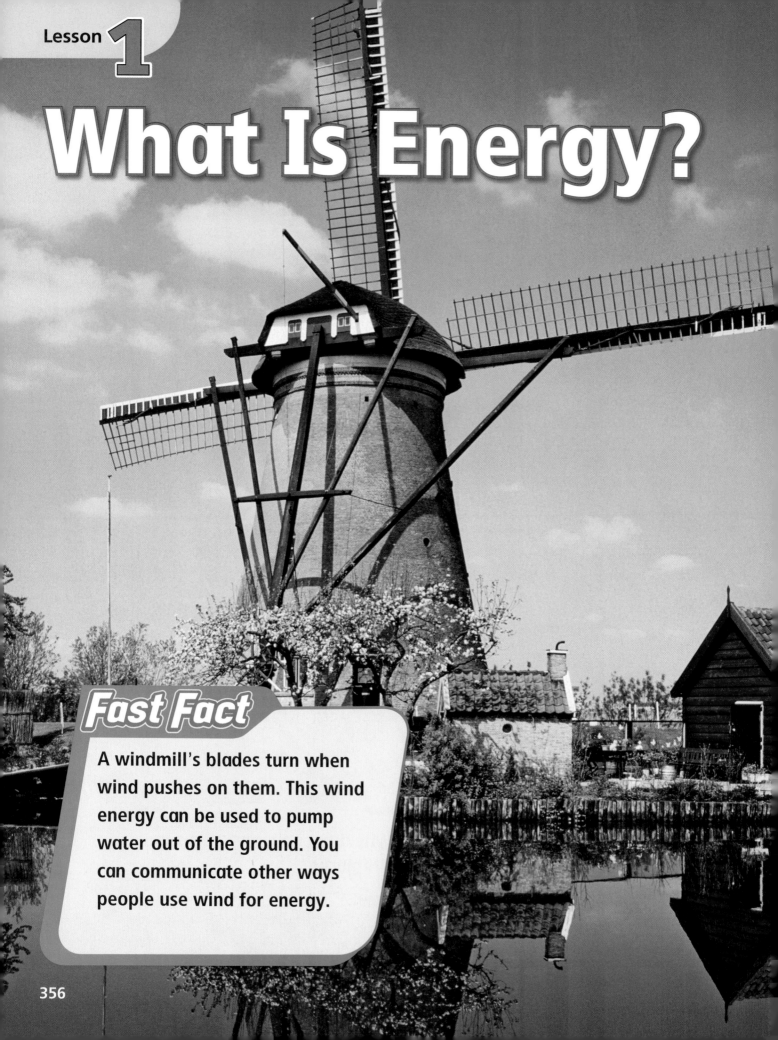

What Is Energy?

Fast Fact

A windmill's blades turn when wind pushes on them. This wind energy can be used to pump water out of the ground. You can communicate other ways people use wind for energy.

Energy from Wind

You need

• **toy car**

• **clay**

• **toothpicks**

• **paper**

Step 1

Plan an investigation.
Think of a way to use the clay, toothpicks, and paper to make a sail for the toy car.

Step 2

Carry out the plan you made in Step 1.

Step 3

Blow on the sail. Observe what happens. Then communicate what made the car move.

Inquiry Skill

You decide how to experiment when you plan an investigation.

357

Reading in Science

VOCABULARY

energy
heat
light
sound
solar energy
electricity

READING FOCUS SKILL

MAIN IDEA AND DETAILS Look for details about the forms of energy and about where energy comes from.

Energy

Energy is something that can cause matter to move or change. Energy has different forms. Heat, light, and sound are some forms of energy.

Heat is energy that makes things warmer. People use heat to warm their homes and cook their food. Heat can boil water and melt things, such as wax and ice. Heat can also burn things.

Heat makes water boil. ▶

Pittsburgh, Pennsylvania ▲

Light is energy that lets you see. The sun gives off light. Fires and electric lights give off light, too.

Sound is energy that you can hear. You hear sound when it travels to your ears. What kind of energy is the lion producing?

★ **MAIN IDEA AND DETAILS** What are some forms of energy?

Where Energy Comes From

Almost all energy on Earth comes from the sun. Energy from the sun is called **solar energy**. Most living things need solar energy to live. They need the sun's heat to stay warm. Plants use the sun's light to make their food. People and animals eat the plants to get energy.

Energy also comes from wind and moving water. They can make things move by pushing on them. How do wind and water move the kiteboard?

▲ gasoline pump

▲ sun

◀ kiteboarding

360

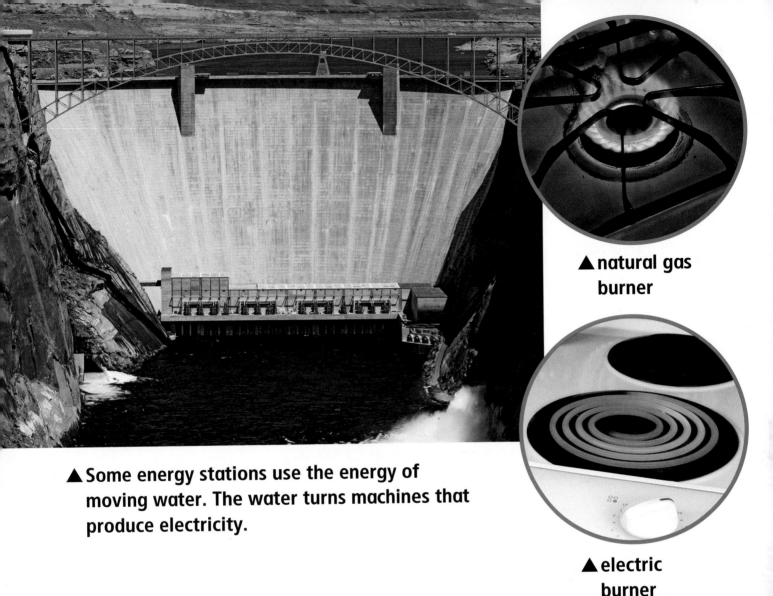

▲ natural gas burner

▲ electric burner

▲ Some energy stations use the energy of moving water. The water turns machines that produce electricity.

Energy also comes from fuels, such as coal and oil. Gasoline is a fuel made from oil. Most cars use energy from gasoline to move. Some people use natural gas fuel to heat their homes and cook their food.

 MAIN IDEA AND DETAILS
Where does energy come from?

Insta-Lab

Water Power

Place three small objects in the middle of a pan. Pour some water into the pan at one end. Observe what happens to the objects.

Electricity

Electricity is a form of energy. People produce electricity by using energy from other sources, such as wind or coal. Electricity provides power for many of the things you use each day. These things change electricity into heat, light, sound, and other forms of energy. Electricity moves from outlets, through plugs and wires, into these things.

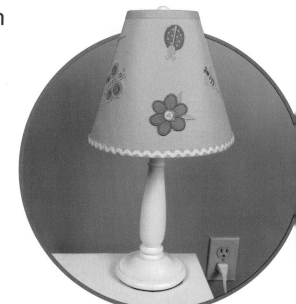

▲ lamp

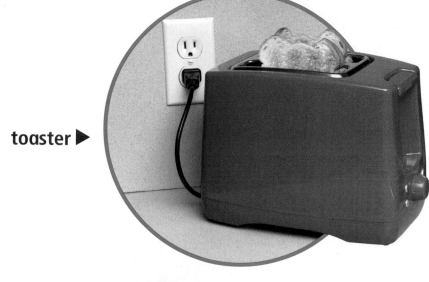

toaster ▶

▲ outlet

◀ radio

The flashlight and other things below need electricity to work. But you do not plug them into outlets. Instead, you put batteries inside them.

Batteries store energy and change it to electricity. Batteries come in different shapes and sizes. Some have more energy than others.

Car Battery

 MAIN IDEA AND DETAILS What kinds of energy can electricity be changed into?

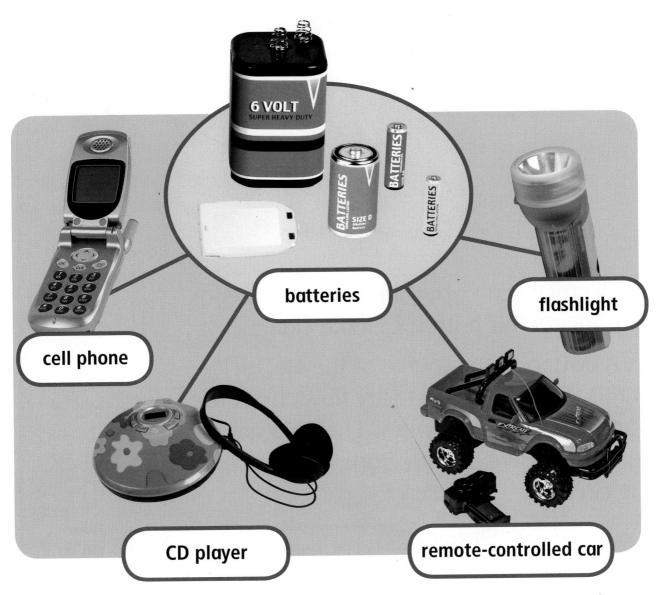

cell phone

batteries

flashlight

CD player

remote-controlled car

Electric Circuit

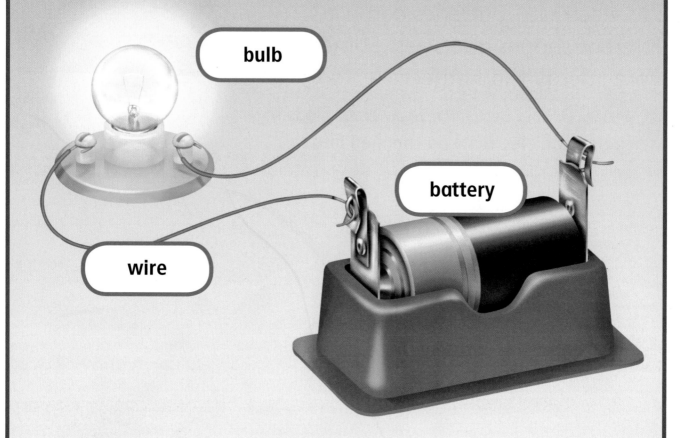

bulb

battery

wire

Electricity can travel in a path with ends that meet. This path is called a circuit.

A battery is the source of the electricity in this circuit. The electricity flows from the battery through the wires. The bulb will not light up if there are any gaps, or breaks, in the circuit.

 For more links and activities, go to www.hspscience.com

1. MAIN IDEA AND DETAILS Copy and complete this chart. Tell details about energy.

Main Idea and Details

Energy is something that can cause matter to move or change.

Three forms of energy are heat, **A** _____, and **B** _____.

Energy can come from the sun, wind, and moving **C** _____.

Energy can also come from gasoline and other **D** _____.

2. SUMMARIZE Write a summary of this lesson. Begin with the sentence **Energy has many forms**.

3. VOCABULARY Use the term **electricity** to tell about this picture.

Test Prep

4. How does heat change things?

  A. It makes them colder.

  B. It makes them warmer.

  C. It makes them slower.

  D. It makes them smaller.

Links

Writing

Electricity Chart

Look around the classroom. Which things get electricity from batteries? Which things get electricity from an outlet? Make a chart to show your observations. Compare your chart with your classmates' charts.

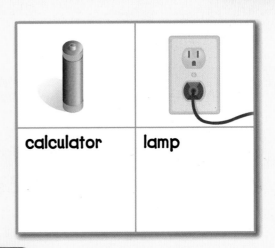

| calculator | lamp |

 For more links and activities, go to www.hspscience.com

What Is Light?

Fast Fact

Light moves in straight lines. When something stops light from moving forward, it makes a shadow. You can draw conclusions about the way light moves.

How Light Moves

You need

• small mirror

• flashlight

Step 1

Choose a spot on the wall on which you want light to shine. Then hold up the mirror.

Step 2

Have a partner shine the flashlight onto the mirror. Move the mirror so that light shines onto the spot you chose.

Step 3

Draw conclusions about the way light moves.

Inquiry Skill

Use your observations and what you know to draw conclusions.

Reading in Science

 READING FOCUS SKILL

MAIN IDEA AND DETAILS Look for details about how light moves.

Light

Light is a form of energy that lets you see. Most light seems to have no color, but it can actually be made up of many colors.

You can see the colors in light when you look at a rainbow. A rainbow forms when sunlight passes through drops of water in the air. The water splits the light into all of its colors. What colors do you see in the rainbow?

A glass prism acts like drops of water in the air. It splits the light into all of its colors. ▼

rainbow

Light travels in straight lines. A flashlight shines light toward the spot at which you point it.

When light hits most objects, the objects **reflect**, or bounce, light. You can see objects because they reflect light. Different objects reflect different amounts of light. A white, smooth surface reflects more light than a dark, rough one. Most mirrors are smooth and flat. They reflect most of the light that hits them.

 MAIN IDEA AND DETAILS How does light move?

Shadows

Light can pass through some objects but not others. An object that blocks light makes a shadow. When trees block sunlight, they make shadows on the ground.

Look at the picture of the people in the room. Light can pass through the glass windows. What is blocking the light? How can you tell?

 MAIN IDEA AND DETAILS
What makes a shadow?

Insta-Lab

What Does Light Shine Through?

Shine a flashlight onto different materials. You might try wax paper, plastic wrap, newspaper, and construction paper. Which ones does light pass through? Communicate your results.

1. MAIN IDEA AND DETAILS Copy and complete this chart. Tell details about light.

Main Idea and Details

Light is a form of energy.

| Light lets people **A** _____. | Sunlight is made up of many **B** _____. | Light travels in **C** _____ lines. | Most objects **D** _____ light. | When an object blocks light, it makes a **E** _____. |

2. DRAW CONCLUSIONS How can you tell if light cannot pass through an object?

3. VOCABULARY Use the term **reflect** to tell about light.

Test Prep

4. Why do only some objects make shadows?

Links

Math

Measure Shadows

Stand a pencil in a piece of clay. Put it in a sunny place. Measure its shadow. Record in a chart the time and the shadow's length. Wait one hour. Measure the shadow again, and record its length. Repeat one hour later.

A Pencil's Shadow

time	length of shadow
9:00	5 inches
10:00	4 inches
11:00	3 inches

 For more links and activities, go to www.hspscience.com

What Is Heat?

Fast Fact

Some colors absorb, or take in, more heat than others. This makes objects of some colors get warmer than objects of other colors. You can measure to find out which of two colors makes objects get warmer.

Color and Heat

You need

- 2 cups, water
- 2 thermometers
- black and white paper
- tape

Step 1

Fill each cup halfway with water. Place a thermometer in each cup.

Step 2

Tape black paper on the outside of one cup. Tape white paper on the other cup. Put both cups in a sunny place.

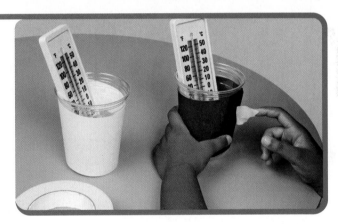

Step 3

After 30 minutes, measure the temperature of the water in each cup. Which temperature is higher?

Inquiry Skill

You can use a thermometer to measure temperature.

VOCABULARY
friction
temperature
thermometer

 READING FOCUS SKILL

MAIN IDEA AND DETAILS Look for details about how heat moves and how it is measured.

Heat and Burning

Heat makes things warmer. In the daytime, you can feel heat that comes from the sun. The sun's heat warms land, water, air, and living things.

Objects can produce heat when they rub against each other. This heat comes from friction. **Friction** is a force that slows down objects that rub against each other. It also causes them to get warmer.

People also produce heat when they burn fuel. Oil, natural gas, and wood are some fuels. They give off heat as they burn.

▼ Rubbing your hands together warms them.

gas grill

▲ oil lantern

▲ forest fire

Many people burn oil or natural gas to warm homes, schools, and other buildings. Natural gas is also used to cook food. As the gas burns, it gives off heat that cooks the food.

Wood comes from trees. It burns very easily. Trees in a forest can catch fire if people are not careful. People burn wood in fireplaces to warm their homes.

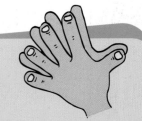

Insta-Lab

Making Heat

How do your hands feel? Are they warm or cool? Rub them together for 20 seconds. Then tell how they feel and how they changed.

MAIN IDEA AND DETAILS
Focus Skill

How can people produce heat?

Heat and Electricity

Many energy stations use heat to produce electricity. Heat changes water into steam, which turns machines that produce electricity. During this process, some heat is lost. It goes into the air or water.

Electricity moves from the energy station through power lines, or thick wires. The power lines carry electricity to homes, schools, and other buildings.

▼ nuclear energy station

▼ power lines

Electricity flows through wires in walls, floors, and ceilings. Many wires go to outlets.

Electricity flows to lamps and other objects when they are plugged into outlets. These objects change the electricity to heat, light, or sound. An electric stove changes electricity to heat. Then the heat cooks the food.

⭐ **Focus Skill** **MAIN IDEA AND DETAILS** How do energy stations produce electricity?

How Heat Moves

Heat moves from warmer objects to cooler ones. When someone warms up cold stew, heat moves from the stove's burner to the pot. Then it moves from the pot to the cold stew. As the heat moves, the stew becomes warm.

Heat moves more easily and quickly through some things than others. Heat moves easily through metal. The metal spoon in the stew will get hot right away. Heat does not move as easily through plastic or wood.

◄ wooden spoon

metal spoon ▶

◄ plastic spoon

Heat from an oven can make metal pots, pans, and trays very hot. People can burn their hands if they touch the metal. To protect their hands, people wear oven mitts.

Oven mitts are made from a thick material. Heat cannot move easily through it. A person who is wearing the mitts can move a hot tray and not get burned. Most of the heat from the tray cannot get to the person's hands.

 **MAIN IDEA AND DETAILS** How does heat move?

Temperature

Temperature is a measure of how hot or cold something is. A **thermometer** is a tool that measures an object's temperature. You can measure the temperature of air, food, and even your body. Temperature can be measured in degrees Fahrenheit and degrees Celsius.

Things that are hot have high temperatures. Things that are cold have low temperatures. Fire has a high temperature. Ice has a low temperature.

MAIN IDEA AND DETAILS Why do people use thermometers?

▲ This thermometer shows temperature in degrees Fahrenheit and degrees Celsius.

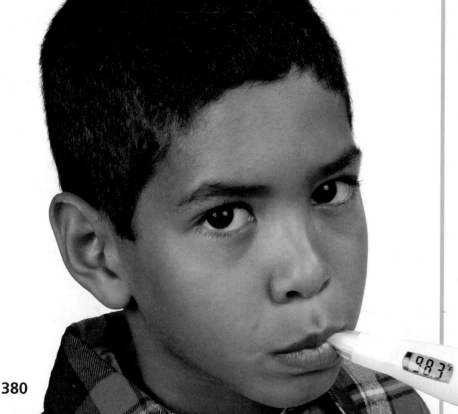

▼ digital thermometer

1. MAIN IDEA AND DETAILS Copy and complete this chart. Tell details about heat.

Main Idea and Details

Heat is a form of energy that makes things warmer.

| Objects produce heat when they **A** _____ against each other. | People produce heat when they **B** _____ fuel. | Energy stations use heat to produce **C** _____. | Heat moves from warmer objects to **D** _____ ones. |

2. SUMMARIZE Use the chart to write a lesson summary.

3. VOCABULARY Use the terms **friction** and **heat** to tell about this picture.

Test Prep

4. What can you use to measure heat?
  A. friction
  B. temperature
  C. thermometer
  D. wires

Links

Math

Measure Temperatures
Fill a cup with cold water. Use a thermometer to measure the temperature of the water. Set the cup in a pan of warm water. After five minutes, measure the temperature again. How did it change? Why? Share your results.

For more links and activities, go to www.hspscience.com

Liar, Liar, Face on Fire!

When kids catch another kid lying, they sometimes chant, "Liar, liar, pants on fire." That childhood saying, however, might soon change to "Liar, liar, face on fire."

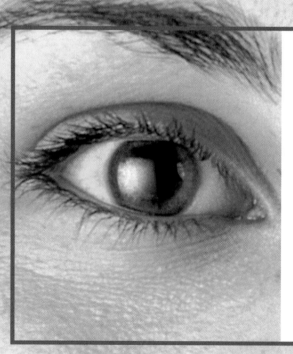

Eye Am a Camera

Scientists have learned that when people lie, blood rushes to the area around their eyes. As the warm blood flows to that area, that part of the face heats up.

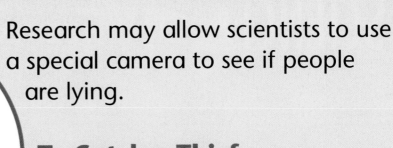

Research may allow scientists to use a special camera to see if people are lying.

To Catch a Thief

Scientists used a special camera that can detect heat. The heat-sensing camera was tested on 20 people. During the test, scientists asked eight of the people to take something in the laboratory without asking. The people were then told to lie about what they had taken.

All 20 people were then asked if they had taken something. While the people were asked questions, the special heat-sensing camera filmed their faces. The camera filmed a rise in temperature around the eyes of six of the eight liars. The camera did not find an increase in temperature in the people who told the truth.

Think About It

How else might a heat-sensing camera be used?

Find out more! Log on to
www.hspscience.com

A Hot Idea

James Joule was a scientist who lived more than 180 years ago. He studied many things, but he was especially interested in electricity. He found that electricity produces heat.

In his research, Joule came up with an idea about heat and electricity that is called Joule's law. It helps people figure out how much heat will be produced when electricity is used.

You Can Do It!

Heat on the Move

Materials
- bowl of hot water
- metal, plastic, and wooden spoons

What to Do

1. Wait while an adult fills a bowl with hot water. **CAUTION:** Be careful near hot water!

2. Place each kind of spoon in the hot water.

3. Wait two minutes. Then carefully feel and compare the handles of the spoons.

Draw Conclusions
What can you tell about how heat moves? How does heat move differently through different materials?

Shadows

Shine a flashlight on a wall, and tape a sheet of paper on that spot. Set an object between the wall and the light. Draw its shadow on the paper. Then move the object close to the light and far from the light. Draw and label its shadow each time. How does the shadow change? Why?

Review and Test Preparation

Vocabulary Review

Use the terms to complete the sentences. The page numbers tell you where to look if you need help.

energy p. 358   **friction** p. 374

solar energy p. 360   **thermometer** p. 380

1. Energy from the sun is _____.

2. A force that slows down objects that rub against each other is _____.

3. Something that can cause movement or change is _____.

4. A tool that measures temperature is a _____.

Check Understanding

5. What are two ways to produce heat?

6. Why do these pots and pans have plastic handles?

7. Which of these is a

 correct detail?

A. Friction is a form of energy.

B. Sound is a form of energy.

C. A shadow is a form of energy.

D. Color is a form of energy.

8. Why do trees make shadows?

F. Light is made up of many colors.

G. Light can not pass through trees.

H. Light can pass through trees.

J. Light comes from the sun.

Critical Thinking

9. Why do people sometimes use electricity from batteries instead of outlets?

10. What would happen to Earth if there were no sun?

Chapter
12 Sound

Lesson 1 What Causes Sound?

Lesson 2 How Does Sound Travel?

Lesson 3 How Do We Make Different Sounds?

Vocabulary
sound
vibrate
sound wave
loudness
pitch

I wonder...

Why can people who are far away from this train hear the sounds it makes?

What do YOU wonder?

What Causes Sound?

Fast Fact

You can hear sounds all around you. Sometimes you can feel sounds, too. You can communicate what you observe about sound.

How Sound Is Made

You need

- **wax paper**
- **tube with holes**
- **rubber band**

Step 1

Put wax paper over one end of a tube. Use a rubber band to hold the wax paper in place.

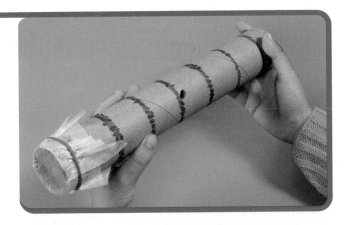

Step 2

Hum into the open end of the tube. What do you hear? Feel the wax paper. What do you feel? Stop humming. What changed?

Step 3

Communicate your observations to a classmate.

Inquiry Skill

When you **communicate**, you share your ideas through writing, drawing, or speaking.

391

READING FOCUS SKILL

CAUSE AND EFFECT Look for the causes of sounds.

Vibrations Make Sound

Sound is energy that you can hear. You may hear a dog barking or a bell ringing. You may hear music playing or people talking. The sounds are different, but they are made in the same way. All sound is made when something **vibrates**, or moves quickly back and forth.

What things in these pictures are making sounds?

What things in these pictures are making sounds?

Objects make sounds when they vibrate. The top of a drum vibrates when you hit it. A guitar string vibrates when you pluck it. The vibrations make sounds. When the vibrations stop, the sounds stop. Some things, such as a drum or thunder, make sounds so loud that you can feel them, too.

CAUSE AND EFFECT What causes sound?

Insta-Lab

Make Vibrations

Hold a ruler on a desk so that one end hangs over the edge. Push that end down, and then let it go. What do you see, hear, and feel?

393

The Ear

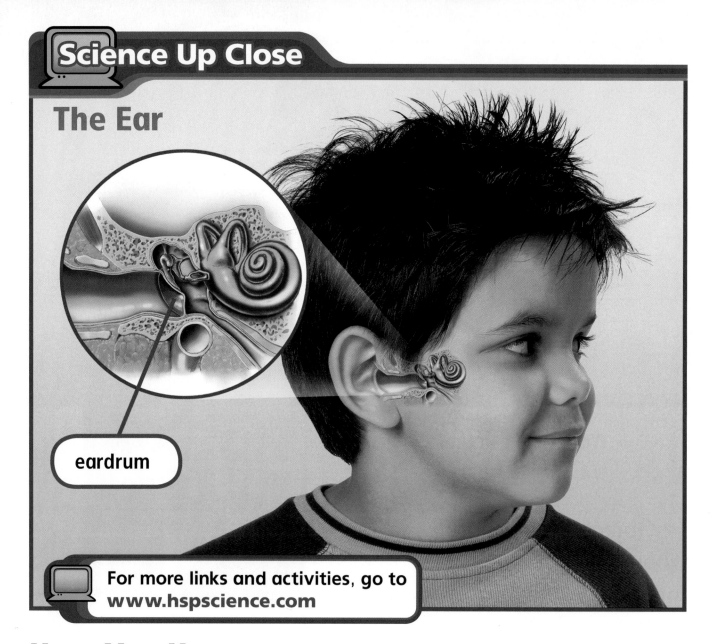

eardrum

For more links and activities, go to
www.hspscience.com

How You Hear

You hear sounds with your ears. Sound
vibrations move through the air into your
ear. They move from your outer ear to your
inner ear. The vibrations cause the eardrum
and the tiny bones in your ear to vibrate.
The inner ear sends signals to the brain.
You hear a sound.

 CAUSE AND EFFECT What causes you to hear
a sound?

1. CAUSE AND EFFECT Copy and complete this chart. Tell the effect of each cause.

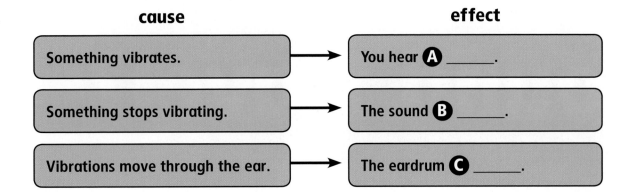

cause	effect
Something vibrates.	You hear **A** _____.
Something stops vibrating.	The sound **B** _____.
Vibrations move through the ear.	The eardrum **C** _____.

2. SUMMARIZE Write two sentences that tell what this lesson is about.

3. VOCABULARY Use the terms **vibrate** and **sound** to tell how sound is made.

Test Prep

4. What happens when a guitar string stops vibrating?
   A. The sound gets louder.
   B. The sound stops.
   C. The eardrum vibrates.
   D. The sound gets softer.

Links

Writing

Description of Sounds
Sit quietly, and listen to the sounds around you. Then write about the sounds you hear. Describe the way they sound.

I hear a door squeak.

A dog barks outside.

 For more links and activities, go to www.hspscience.com

How Does Sound Travel?

Fast Fact

Most sound you hear travels through the air to reach your ears. Sound can also travel through solids, such as wood, and through liquids, such as water. You can use what you know to predict how a sound will travel.

How Sound Travels

You need

- tape measure

- masking tape

Step 1

Use the tape measure to measure 50 centimeters on your desk. Mark each end with tape.

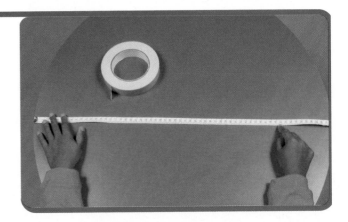

Step 2

Scratch at one tape mark and listen at the other. **Predict** whether you will hear the sound if you put your ear on the desk. Try it.

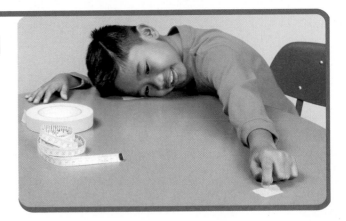

Step 3

What did you observe? Was your **prediction** correct?

Inquiry Skill

To **predict**, think about what you already know and then tell what you think will happen.

VOCABULARY
sound wave

 READING FOCUS SKILL

MAIN IDEA AND DETAILS Look for the different kinds of matter that sound can travel through.

Sound Travels Through Air

Sound can travel through different kinds of matter. Sound can travel through gases, such as air. When an object vibrates, it produces sound waves. **Sound waves** are vibrations that are moving through matter. The sound waves travel through the air to your ears, and you hear the sound.

Sound moves in all directions. When a rooster crows, people all around the rooster can hear it.

Sound waves can be blocked. Some people use ear coverings to protect their ears from loud sounds. This keeps some of the sound waves from reaching their eardrums.

 MAIN IDEA AND DETAILS How does sound move?

Sound Travels Through Water

Sound travels through liquids, such as water. Sound travels faster through water than through air.

Dolphins make sounds to find things underwater. The sounds travel through the water. When they hit objects, they bounce off. The bounced sounds are called echoes. The dolphins listen to the echoes to tell how far away things are.

▲ **Sound waves from the tuning fork move through the water. They make the water vibrate.**

▼ **dolphin**

▲ humpback whales

Humpback whales also make sounds underwater. Their sounds are like songs. The whales may sing for many hours at a time. Their songs can reach other whales that are far away.

⭐ **Focus Skill** **MAIN IDEA AND DETAILS** **What is one liquid that sound can travel through?**

Make Waves

Fill a cup with water. Gently touch the water with a pencil eraser. What do you see? Tell a classmate how the ripples are moving. How are these little waves like sound waves?

Sound Travels Through Solids

Sound travels through solids, such as wood and glass. Sound travels faster through most solids than through gases or liquids.

Have you ever talked on a string telephone? A string connects two cans. One person talks into a can. The sound waves make the air in the can vibrate. This makes the can vibrate, and then the can makes the string vibrate.

The sound waves travel through the string and make the other can and the air in it vibrate. The vibrations travel into that person's ear, and he or she hears the sound.

 MAIN IDEA AND DETAILS **In a string telephone, how does sound travel from one can to the other?**

1. MAIN IDEA AND DETAILS Copy and complete the chart. Tell about the kinds of matter that sound can travel through.

Main Idea and Details

Sound travels through different kinds of matter.

Sound can travel through air, which is a **A** _____.	Dolphins make sounds that travel through water, a **B** _____.	Sound travels through **C** _____, such as wood and glass.

2. DRAW CONCLUSIONS How can you tell that sound travels in all directions?

3. VOCABULARY Use the term **sound waves** to tell about the picture.

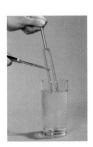

Test Prep

4. Which kind of matter does sound travel through the fastest?
- **A.** solids
- **B.** liquids
- **C.** gases
- **D.** liquids and gases

Links

Math

Order from Least to Most
Sound travels at different speeds through different kinds of matter. Use the chart to order the speeds from slowest to fastest.

Speed of Sound in Meters per Second

kind of matter	speed
water	1,433
glass	5,030
air	343
gold	3,240
rubber	1,600

For more links and activities, go to **www.hspscience.com**

How Do We Make Different Sounds?

Fast Fact

Guitar strings make different sounds because they are not all the same. Some are thick. Some are thin. Some are tighter than others. You can hypothesize why sounds are different.

Why Sounds Are Different

You need

- colored water
- 3 glasses
- wooden spoon

Step 1

Pour a different amount of water into each glass. **Hypothesize** whether all the glasses will sound the same when you tap them.

Step 2

Use the spoon to tap each glass on the side. Was your **hypothesis** correct?

Step 3

Find a way to make all the glasses sound the same.

Inquiry Skill

When you **hypothesize**, you make an explanation that you can test.

READING FOCUS SKILL

CAUSE AND EFFECT Look for what causes different sounds.

Loud or Soft

Sounds are different. They may be loud or soft. A shout is a loud sound. A whisper is a soft, or quiet, sound.

The **loudness** of a sound is how loud or soft it is. It takes more energy to make a loud sound than a soft sound.

The closer you are to what makes a sound, the louder the sound you hear. It's hard to hear people talk when you are far away from them. As you move closer, you can hear them more easily.

 CAUSE AND EFFECT What happens when a lot of energy is used to make a sound?

Loud and Soft

Clap as loudly as you can. Then clap as softly as you can. Does it take more energy to clap loudly or to clap softly?

High or Low

Sounds are also different in **pitch**, or how high or low they are. A whistle makes a sound with a high pitch. A big drum makes a sound with a low pitch.

The speed of an object's vibration makes its sound's pitch low or high. Thicker or longer strings vibrate more slowly. They make a sound with a low pitch. Thinner or shorter strings vibrate faster. They make a sound with a high pitch.

(Focus Skill) CAUSE AND EFFECT What makes a sound's pitch high or low?

A xylophone has long and short bars. The long bars make sounds with low pitches. The short bars make sounds with high pitches. ▼

408

1. CAUSE AND EFFECT Copy and complete this chart. Tell what sound is the effect of each cause.

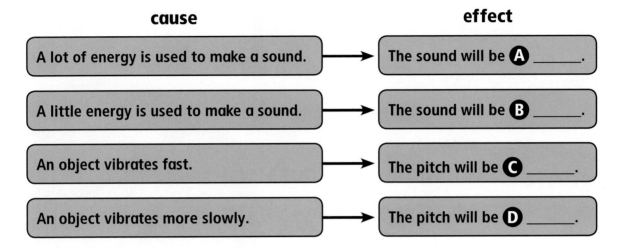

cause	effect
A lot of energy is used to make a sound.	→ The sound will be **Ⓐ** _____.
A little energy is used to make a sound.	→ The sound will be **Ⓑ** _____.
An object vibrates fast.	→ The pitch will be **Ⓒ** _____.
An object vibrates more slowly.	→ The pitch will be **Ⓓ** _____.

2. SUMMARIZE Write a summary of this lesson. Begin with the sentence **Sounds are different**.

3. VOCABULARY Explain the meanings of the terms **loudness** and **pitch**.

Test Prep

4. What happens when a string vibrates very quickly?

   A. It makes a high sound.

   B. It makes a low sound.

   C. It makes no sound.

   D. It makes a soft sound.

Links

Social Studies

Too Many Sounds

Too many sounds can cause noise pollution. Make a list of problems caused by too much sound. Then, for each sound problem, write a way people could solve it.

Noise Pollution	
problem	solution
The radio and television are both on.	Turn one off.

For more links and activities, go to www.hspscience.com

The Sounds Spring Brings

In spring, birds are very busy flying about and making nests. Scientists who study birds often try to record bird songs to study later. To capture those songs, scientists use equipment such as microphones, headphones, and recording machines.

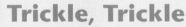

Trickle, Trickle

Spring brings warmer weather. Warm weather melts any snow and ice left from winter. The melted water trickles through streams and rivers and into lakes and oceans.

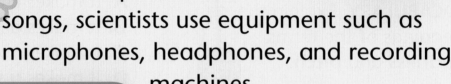

Whoosh, Whoosh

Spring brings whooshing winds. The wind blows clouds and kites in the sky. Wind also helps plants spread their seeds. When seeds land, they grow into new plants and flowers.

Buzz, Buzz

Spring brings new plants and flowers. Busy bees buzz from flower to flower collecting nectar. Nectar is a sweet liquid made by flowers. The buzzing bees collect nectar for food to eat.

Phonics Fun

Whoosh has the *sh* sound. What are five other words with the same sound?

Think About It

What are some sounds heard in other seasons?

Find out more! Log on to
www.hspscience.com

A Call to Invent

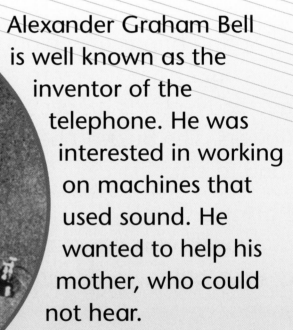

Alexander Graham Bell is well known as the inventor of the telephone. He was interested in working on machines that used sound. He wanted to help his mother, who could not hear.

About 130 years ago, Bell was trying to improve a machine called a telegraph. It was during this work that he made a discovery. Bell found out that he could send speech over a charged wire. This led to the invention of the telephone.

Moving Sound

What to Do

1. Stretch plastic wrap over the open end of the can. Use the rubber band to keep the plastic tight.

2. Put a spoonful of sugar on the plastic.

3. Hold the metal tray near the can, and bang on the tray with the spoon.

4. Observe what happens to the sugar.

Materials

- plastic wrap
- empty metal can
- rubber band
- sugar
- metal tray
- wooden spoon

Draw Conclusions

What happened? Why did this happen?

How Long Does Sound Last?

Hold a triangle by its string. Tap the triangle gently. Count and record the seconds the sound lasts. Tap a bit harder, and record the seconds. Hit the triangle very hard, and record the seconds. Which sound lasts longest? Why?

How Long Sounds Last

tap	seconds
gentle tap	2
medium tap	
hard tap	

Review and Test Preparation

Vocabulary Review

Use the terms below to complete the sentences. The page numbers tell you where to look if you need help.

sound p. 392   **sound waves** p. 398

vibrate p. 392   **pitch** p. 408

1. When guitar strings move back and forth, they _____.

2. Energy that you can hear is _____.

3. The highness or lowness of a sound is its _____.

4. Vibrations that move through matter are called _____.

Check Understanding

5. What causes the sound a drum makes?

    A. ears

    B. loudness

    C. pitch

    D. vibrations

6. What can sound move through?

    F. only air and water

    G. only air and solids

    H. only water and solids

    J. air, water, and solids

Critical Thinking

7. Does it take more energy to whisper or to shout? Explain.

8. Tell how ears can hear the sounds of a harp.

Lesson 1 What Are Ways Things Move?

Lesson 2 What Makes Things Move?

Lesson 3 How Do Magnets Move Things?

Vocabulary
motion
speed
force
gravity
friction
magnet
pole
attract
repel

I wonder...

What makes things move?

What do YOU wonder?

What Are Ways Things Move?

Fast Fact

A rolling ball will move in a straight line if it is not touched. You can plan an investigation to find different ways a ball can move.

How Things Can Move

You need

● golf ball

● classroom objects

Step 1

Roll the ball in a straight line.

Step 2

In how many different ways can you make the ball move? **Plan an investigation** to find out. Use classroom objects to help you.

Step 3

Follow your plan. Communicate your observations.

Inquiry Skill

When you **plan an investigation**, you think of a way to answer a question.

READING FOCUS SKILL

MAIN IDEA AND DETAILS Look for details about the ways things can move.

Kinds of Motion

When something moves, it is in **motion**. A ball is in motion when it is rolling.

Objects can move in many paths. A toy car can move in a straight line. A swing moves back and forth in a curved path. The hands of a clock move in a circle. A bike moves in a curved path when it turns a corner. A ball curves and may zigzag up and down as it bounces.

How are objects moving in this picture?

 MAIN IDEA AND DETAILS What are some different ways an object can move?

straight

YOU PUTT GOLF

circle

back and forth

curve

zigzag

421

Fast and Slow

Speed describes how fast something moves. Different things move at different speeds. A car can move faster than a bike. A skater can move faster than a person who is walking.

⭐ **Focus Skill** **MAIN IDEA AND DETAILS**

What do the words <u>fast</u> and <u>slow</u> describe?

Insta-Lab

Watch It Go!

Write a list of things that can go fast. Exchange lists with a partner. See how many things you and your partner wrote on your lists.

422

1. MAIN IDEA AND DETAILS Copy and complete this chart. Tell details about how things move.

Main Idea and Details

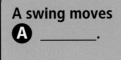

Objects can move in different paths and at different speeds.

| A toy car can move in a straight line. | A swing moves **A** _____. | The hands of a clock move in a **B** _____. | Objects can move quickly or **C** _____. |

2. SUMMARIZE Write two sentences that tell what this lesson is about.

3. VOCABULARY Explain the meanings of the terms **motion** and **speed**.

Test Prep

4. What are some different ways things can move?

Links

Writing

Description of Ways Things Move

Look at things outside that move. Write sentences that tell about the direction and speed of the moving objects.

I see a plane flying in a straight line. It is moving very fast.

 For more links and activities, go to www.hspscience.com

What Makes Things Move?

Fast Fact

A person moves a kayak by pulling one end of the paddle and then the other. You can classify the way you move an object as a push or a pull.

How You Move Objects

You need

- **paper and pencil**

Make a chart like this one.

What I Moved	Push or Pull?

Move some objects in the classroom. For each object, did you use a push or a pull? Use the chart to **classify** each movement.

Which did you use more often to move objects—pushes or pulls? Compare your results with a classmate's results.

Inquiry Skill

When you **classify** movements, you can see how they are alike.

425

VOCABULARY
force
gravity
friction

 READING FOCUS SKILL

CAUSE AND EFFECT Look for the causes of motion.

Forces and Motion

A **force** is a push or pull. You can use pushes and pulls to change where an object is. If you push a swing, it moves away from you. If you pull a swing, it moves toward you.

You can use force to change the direction of a moving object. When you kick a ball, you push it. A push on the right side of the ball will make it go to the left. A push on the left side will make it go to the right.

pull

push

426

The more force you use, the farther and faster an object will move. A strong kick will push a ball farther and faster than a gentle kick. You need a small force to move a light ball quickly. You need more force to move a heavy ball just as quickly.

Focus Skill **CAUSE AND EFFECT** What causes objects to move?

Insta-Lab

More or Less?

Push a book gently across a table. Then push a pile of two or three books across the table. Did you use more or less force to move the pile than you used to move the single book?

Gravity

Gravity is a force that pulls things toward the center of Earth. It makes things fall unless something holds them up. When you let go of something, gravity causes it to fall to the ground. Gravity causes a ball to roll downhill. It pulls your body down a slide. Gravity keeps people on the ground, too.

 CAUSE AND EFFECT How does gravity cause objects to move?

Friction

Friction is a force that slows down or stops things that are moving. This happens when two things rub against each other. A bike chain rubs against the gears. A rusty chain makes a bike harder to pedal.

Smooth surfaces cause less friction than rough ones. Smooth surfaces do not slow down moving things as much. It is easier to ride a bike with a smooth clean chain than a rusty one.

CAUSE AND EFFECT **What effect does friction have on moving objects?**

Bike Brakes

Bike brakes use friction to stop a bike. When you ride a bike, the brakes do not touch the wheels. There is no friction between them.

To stop the bike, you press the brakes against the wheels. The brakes rub against the wheels and cause friction. The wheels turn more and more slowly until they stop moving.

brakes off

brakes on

For more links and activities, go to
www.hspscience.com

1. CAUSE AND EFFECT Copy and complete this chart. Tell what causes each effect.

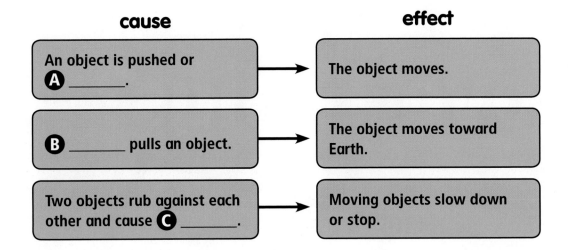

cause

An object is pushed or **A** _____.

→ The object moves.

B _____ pulls an object.

→ The object moves toward Earth.

Two objects rub against each other and cause **C** _____.

→ Moving objects slow down or stop.

effect

2. DRAW CONCLUSIONS Why can a skater on a smooth surface go faster than one on a rough surface?

3. VOCABULARY How is **force** being used in the picture?

Test Prep

4. What causes a book to fall to the ground when you drop it?
   A. friction
   B. gravity
   C. pushing
   D. speed

Links

Math

Measure Motion

Roll a toy car down a ramp. Use a meterstick to measure how far the car moved after it reached the bottom. Record the distance in a chart. Place a towel over the ramp and repeat. Why is the second distance different from the first? What is the difference between the distances?

How Far a Car Moves

without a towel	2 meters
with a towel	

 For more links and activities, go to **www.hspscience.com**

431

How Do Magnets Move Things?

Magnets can move some objects without touching them. You can hypothesize how magnets will move other magnets.

How Magnets Work

You need

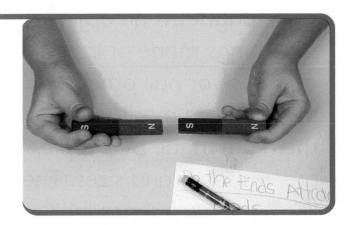

● **2 bar magnets**

Step 1

Hypothesize what will happen when you bring together the ends of two magnets.

Step 2

Make a chart like this one.

Do the Ends Attract or Repel?	
Ends	**Attract or Repel**
N end and S end	
N end and N end	
S end and S end	

Step 3

Bring the N end of one magnet toward the S end of the other one. Record what you observe. Repeat, using the two N ends and then the two S ends. Was your **hypothesis** correct?

Inquiry Skill

When you **hypothesize**, you make a statement you can test.

VOCABULARY

magnet
pole
attract
repel

 READING FOCUS SKILL

MAIN IDEA AND DETAILS Look for details about magnets.

Magnets

A **magnet** is an object that can pull things made of iron or steel. It can also push or pull other magnets. Many magnets are made of metal. Most of them are made by people. They come in many shapes and sizes. They may look like bars, horseshoes, balls, or rings.

Lodestone is a kind of rock that is a magnet. Lodestone is found in nature.▼

All magnets have two **poles**, or ends. One end is the north-seeking pole, or N pole. The other end is the south-seeking pole, or S pole.

Opposite poles **attract**, or pull, each other. The N pole of one magnet and the S pole of another magnet attract each other. The two N poles or the two S poles on different magnets **repel** each other, or push each other away.

 MAIN IDEA AND DETAILS What are magnets?

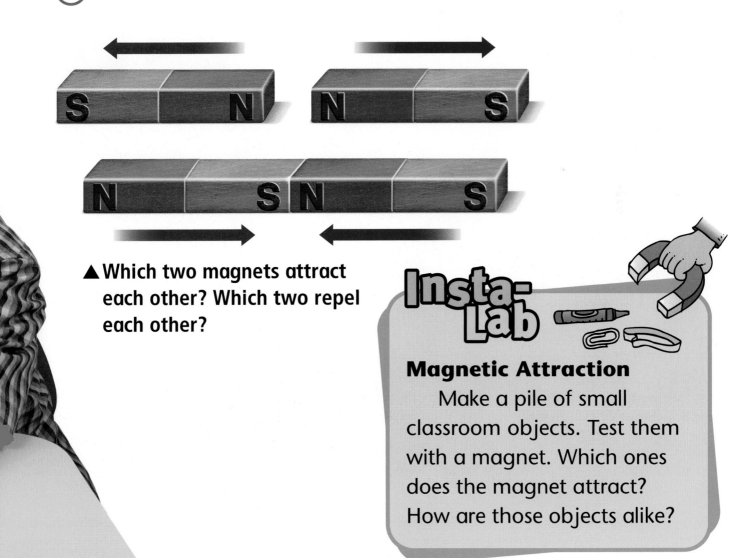

▲ Which two magnets attract each other? Which two repel each other?

Insta-Lab

Magnetic Attraction

Make a pile of small classroom objects. Test them with a magnet. Which ones does the magnet attract? How are those objects alike?

What Magnets Do

Magnets can pull iron and steel objects without touching them. They can also push and pull other magnets without touching them. Magnets can do this because their force can pass through air, water, and some solids.

The magnet below can pull the toy truck because the truck has iron in it. The magnet's force passes through the air, so the magnet pulls the truck without touching it.

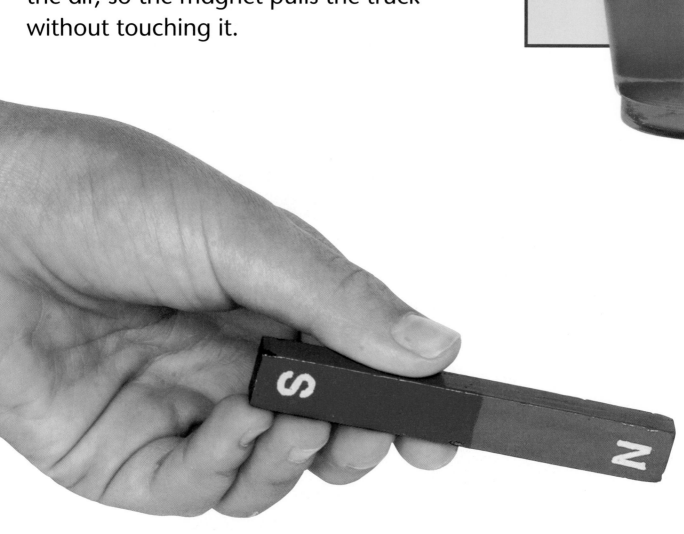

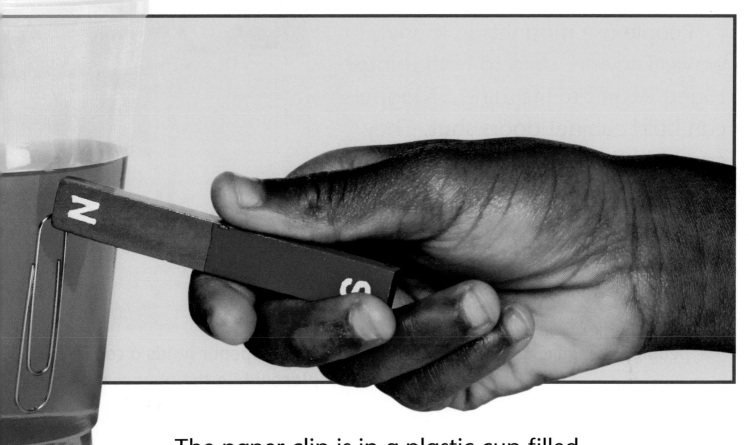

The paper clip is in a plastic cup filled with water. The magnet moved the paper clip from the bottom of the cup to the side of the cup without touching the paper clip. The pull of the magnet can pass through plastic and water.

MAIN IDEA AND DETAILS What can the force of a magnet pass through?

How People Use Magnets

People use magnets in many ways. They are used to hold things together and to lift things. Magnets can hold cabinet doors shut. They can hold things to surfaces made of iron or steel. Large magnets can help lift and move heavy metal objects, such as cars. Magnets are used in some doorbells and telephones.

⭐ **Focus Skill** **MAIN IDEA AND DETAILS** How do people use magnets?

A can opener holds a can in place while the opener cuts off its lid. Then a magnet holds the lid while someone pulls the can away.

A compass magnet is shaped like a needle. It always points north. ▼

A refrigerator magnet can hold up pieces of paper. ▼

1. **MAIN IDEA AND DETAILS** Copy and complete this chart. Tell details about magnets.

Main Idea and Details

Magnets can pull iron or steel. Magnets can push and pull other magnets.

| A magnet has an N pole and an **A** _____ pole. | Opposite poles **B** _____ each other. | The same poles on different magnets **C** _____ each other. | A magnet's force can move through air, water, and some **D** _____ . |

2. **SUMMARIZE** Use the chart to write a lesson summary.

3. **VOCABULARY** Use the terms **magnet**, **poles**, **attract**, and **repel** to tell about the picture.

Test Prep

4. How can magnets move objects?

Links

Art

Magnet Inventions

Invent a toy or a tool that uses a magnet. Draw a picture of it. Write a description of what it does and how to make it. Share your invention with the class.

Paper Clip Grabber
I made a tool that picks up paper clips that fall on the floor.
I taped a magnet to the end of a ruler.

For more links and activities, go to
www.hspscience.com

Swimmers Glide Like Sharks

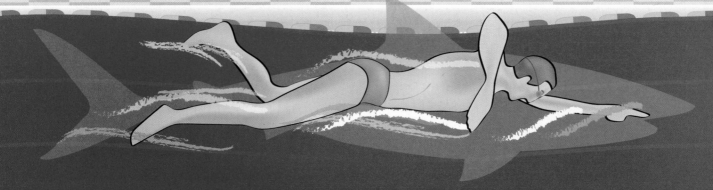

Scientists have invented a new swimsuit that helps Olympic athletes glide through the water. To make the suit, scientists turned to one of the best swimmers in nature, the shark. The new swimsuit, called Fastskin, looks and feels like a shark's skin.

SHARK'S SKIN SUIT

Sharks have tiny V-shaped ridges on their skin. The ridges turn water away from the shark so that the water does not slow down the fish.

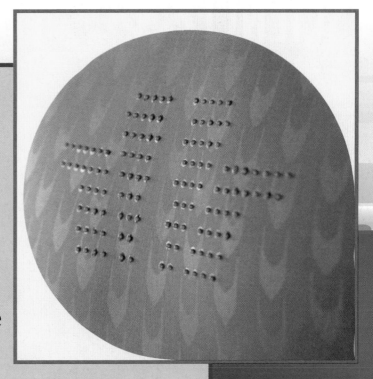

Studying Sharks

To make Fastskin, scientists first studied a real shark's skin under a big magnifier. Then they copied the pattern of the skin on the new swimsuit. The Fastskin has the same kind of ridges that a real shark's skin has.

Fastskin helps swimmers move through the water by cutting down on turbulence. One kind of turbulence is stirred-up water, which can slow down swimmers. Fastskin is made of synthetic, or human-made, fabrics. Fastskin is very tight and can take up to 15 minutes to squeeze into.

Think About It

How does less turbulence in the water help an Olympic swimmer?

Find out more! Log on to
www.hspscience.com

Playing with MAGNETS

Magnets have many uses, such as for keeping a door closed. But magnets can also be used for fun.

Amy Lopez likes to investigate magnets. She also likes puzzles. Some of the coolest puzzles she has seen have magnets in them.

One of Amy's favorite toys is a magnet kit. It has shiny metal balls and colored links. She connects hundreds of the links to each other. She can spell out her name or make a face with the magnets. "Making stuff with magnets is fun!" Amy says.

You Can Do It!

Materials

- straightened paper clip
- magnet
- small piece of plastic foam
- bowl of water

Make Your Own Compass

What to Do

1. Rub a magnet along a straightened paper clip. Rub 50 times in the same direction.

2. Put the plastic foam in water. Lay the paper clip on the foam.

3. Observe the direction to which the paper clip points. Turn the bowl. What happens?

Draw Conclusions

Why do you think the paper clip pointed the way it did?

Ramps and Rolling

Make a ramp with books. Roll a toy car down the ramp. Measure and record how far it rolls after it reaches the bottom. Make the ramp higher. Roll and measure again. Make the ramp even higher. Roll and measure a third time. Why does the car roll a different distance each time?

Distance Car Rolled

ramp with 2 books	3 feet
ramp with 3 books	
ramp with 4 books	

Review and Test Preparation

Vocabulary Review

Use the terms below to complete the sentences. The page numbers tell you where to look if you need help.

motion p. 420   **gravity** p. 428

speed p. 422   **magnet** p. 434

force p. 426   **pole** p. 435

1. A force that pulls things toward the center of Earth is _____.

2. The end of a magnet is a _____.

3. How fast something moves is its _____.

4. When something moves, it is in _____.

5. A push or pull is a _____.

6. An object that can push or pull things made of iron or steel is a _____.

Check Understanding

7. Which spoon may a magnet be able to pull?

8. Mae hits a baseball lightly. Then she
(Focus Skill) uses more force to hit the baseball.
What effect does this have on the
baseball?

A. The baseball moves more quickly.

B. The baseball moves more slowly.

C. The baseball does not move as far.

D. The baseball stops moving.

Critical Thinking

9. Why do you need gravity to swing?

10. Why do people need to drive their cars
slowly on icy or wet roads?

References

Contents

Health Handbook

Your Senses.. R1

Your Skeletal System R4

Your Muscular System...................... R5

Your Nervous System R6

Your Digestive System R7

Your Respiratory System R8

Your Circulatory System.................. R9

Staying Healthy R10

Keeping Clean R11

Caring for Your Teeth..................... R12

Reading in Science Handbook

Identify the Main Idea and Details...R14

Compare and Contrast.................. R15

Cause and Effect............................ R16

Sequence...................................... R17

Draw Conclusions.......................... R18

Summarize..................................... R19

Math in Science Handbook   R20

Safety in Science......................... R26

Glossary.. R27

Index R46

Your Senses

You have five senses that tell you about the world. Your five senses are sight, hearing, smell, taste, and touch.

Your Eyes

If you look at your eyes in a mirror, you will see an outer white part, a colored part called the iris, and a dark hole in the middle. This hole is called the pupil.

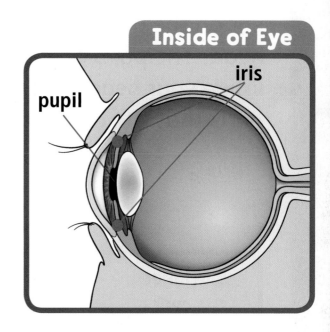

Inside of Eye

Caring for Your Eyes

• Have a doctor check your eyes to find out if they are healthy.

• Never look directly at the sun or at very bright lights.

• Wear sunglasses outdoors in bright sunlight and on snow and water.

• Don't touch or rub your eyes.

• Protect your eyes when you play sports.

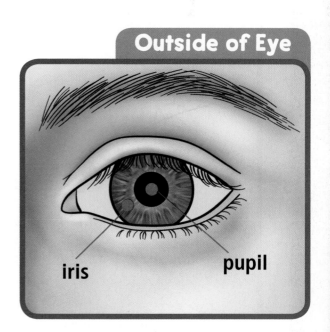

Outside of Eye

Your Senses

Your Ears

Your ears let you hear the things around you. You can see only a small part of the ear on the outside of your head. The parts of your ear inside your head are the parts that let you hear.

Caring for Your Ears

• Have a doctor check your ears.

• Avoid very loud noises.

• Never put anything in your ears.

• Protect your ears when you play sports.

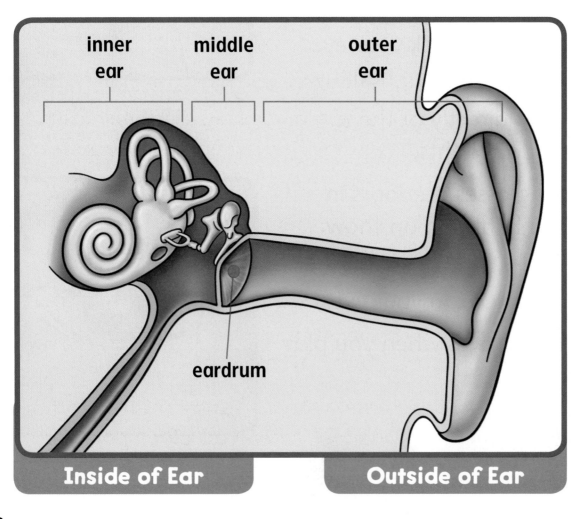

inner ear	middle ear	outer ear

eardrum

Inside of Ear   **Outside of Ear**

Your Senses of Smell and Taste

Your nose cleans the air you breathe and lets you smell things. Your nose and tongue help you taste things you eat and drink.

Your Skin

Your skin protects your body from germs. Your skin also gives you your sense of touch.

Caring for Your Skin

- Always wash your hands after coughing or blowing your nose, touching an animal, playing outside, or using the restroom.

- Protect your skin from sunburn. Wear a hat and clothes to cover your skin outdoors.

- Use sunscreen to protect your skin from the sun.

- Wear proper safety pads and a helmet when you play sports, ride a bike, or skate.

Your Skeletal System

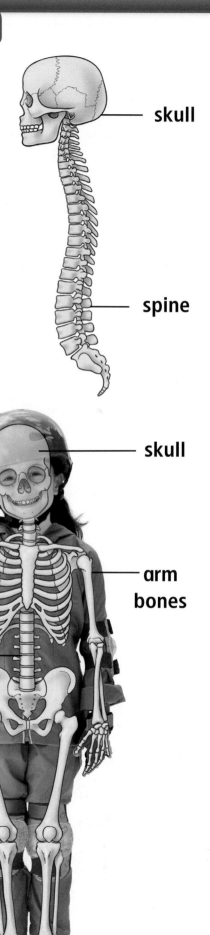

Inside your body are many hard, strong bones. They form your skeletal system. The bones in your body protect parts inside your body.

Your skeletal system works with your muscular system to hold your body up and to give it shape.

Caring for Your Skeletal System

- Always wear a helmet and other safety gear when you skate, ride a bike or a scooter, or play sports.

- Eat foods that help keep your bones strong and hard.

- Exercise to help your bones stay strong and healthy.

- Get plenty of rest to help your bones grow.

skull

spine

skull

arm bones

spine (backbone)

hip bones

leg bones

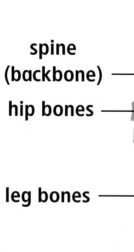

Your Muscular System

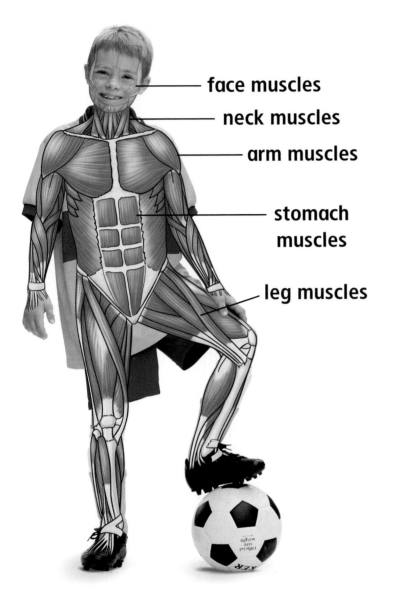

- face muscles
- neck muscles
- arm muscles
- stomach muscles
- leg muscles

Your muscular system is made up of the muscles in your body. Muscles are body parts that help you move.

Caring for Your Muscular System

- Exercise to keep your muscles strong.

- Eat foods that will help your muscles grow.

- Drink plenty of water when you play sports or exercise.

- Rest your muscles after you exercise or play sports.

Your Nervous System

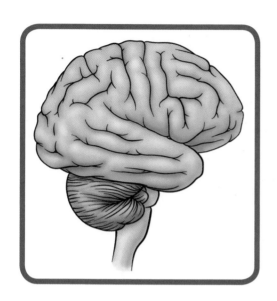

Your brain and your nerves are parts of your nervous system. Your brain keeps your body working. It tells you about the world around you. Your brain also lets you think, remember, and have feelings.

Caring for Your Nervous System

- Get plenty of sleep. Sleeping lets your brain rest.

- Always wear a helmet to protect your head and your brain when you ride a bike or play sports.

Your Digestive System

Your digestive system helps your body get energy from the foods you eat. Your body needs energy to do things.

When your body digests food, it breaks the food down. Your digestive system keeps the things your body needs. It also gets rid of the things your body does not need to keep.

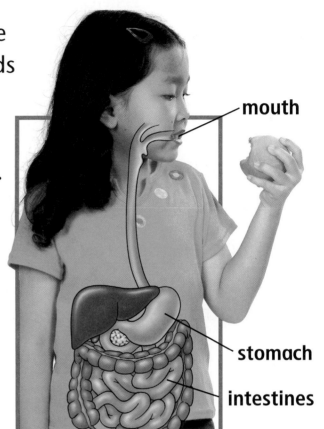

mouth

stomach

intestines

Caring for Your Digestive System

• Brush and floss your teeth every day.

• Wash your hands before you eat.

• Eat slowly and chew your food well before you swallow.

• Eat vegetables and fruits. They help move foods through your digestive system.

Your Respiratory System

You breathe using your respiratory system. Your mouth, nose, and lungs are all parts of your respiratory system.

Caring for Your Respiratory System

- Never put anything in your nose.

- Never smoke.

- Exercise enough to make you breathe harder. Breathing harder makes your lungs stronger.

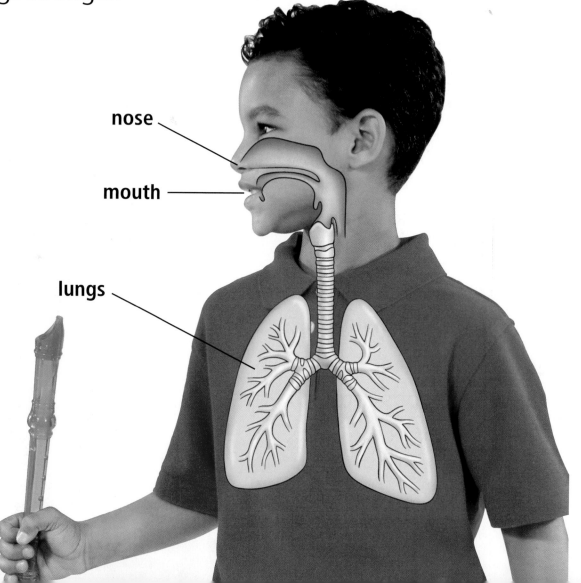

nose

mouth

lungs

Your Circulatory System

Your circulatory system is made up of your heart and your blood vessels. Your blood carries food energy and oxygen to help your body work. Blood vessels are small tubes. They carry blood from your heart to every part of your body.

Your heart is a muscle. It is beating all the time. As your heart beats, it pumps blood through your blood vessels.

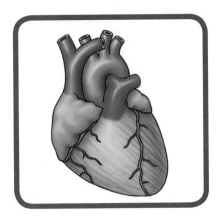

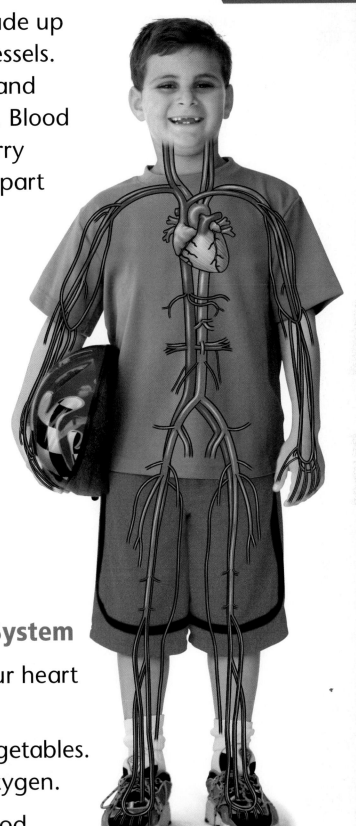

Caring for Your Circulatory System

• Exercise every day to keep your heart strong.

• Eat meats and green leafy vegetables. They help your blood carry oxygen.

• Never touch anyone else's blood.

Staying Healthy

You can do many things to help yourself stay fit and healthy.

You can also avoid doing things that can harm you.

If you know ways to stay safe and healthy and you do these things, you can help yourself have good health.

Getting enough rest

Staying away from alcohol, tobacco, and other drugs

Staying active

Keeping clean

Eating right

Keeping Clean

Keeping clean helps you stay healthy. You can pick up germs from the things you touch. Washing with soap and water helps remove germs from your skin.

Wash your hands for as long as it takes to say your ABCs. Always wash your hands at these times.

- Before and after you eat

- After coughing or blowing your nose

- After using the restroom

- After touching an animal

- After playing outside

Caring for Your Teeth

Brushing your teeth and gums keeps them clean and healthy. You should brush your teeth at least twice a day. Brush in the morning. Brush before you go to bed at night. It is also good to brush your teeth after you eat if you can.

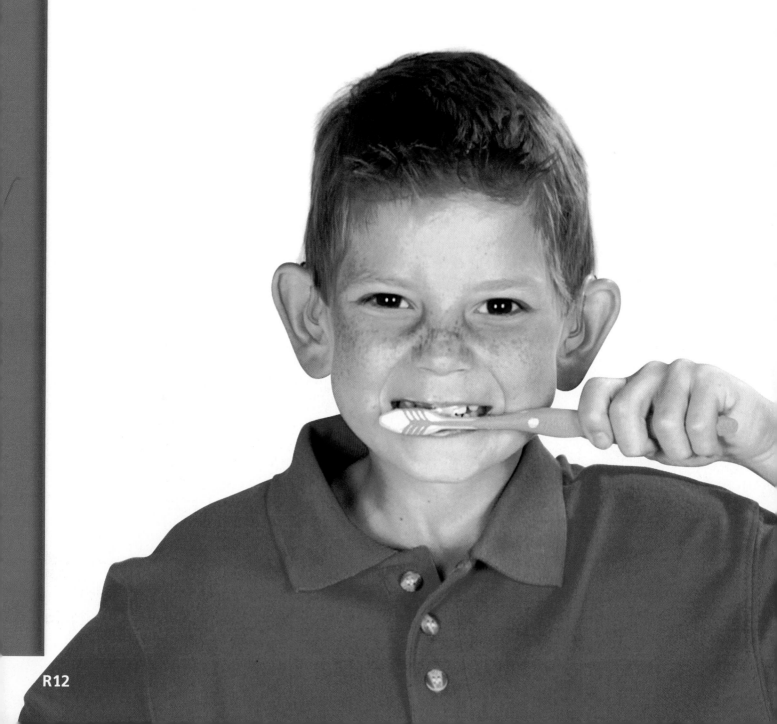

Brushing Your Teeth

Use a soft toothbrush that is the right size for you. Always use your own toothbrush. Use only a small amount of toothpaste. It should be about the size of a pea. Be sure to rinse your mouth with water after you brush your teeth.

❶ Brush the outsides of all of your teeth.

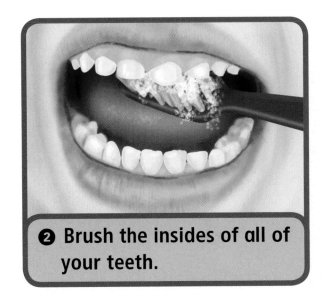

❷ Brush the insides of all of your teeth.

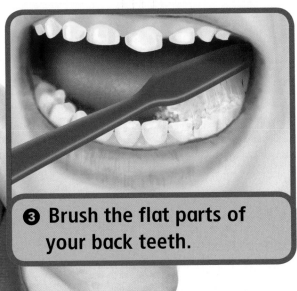

❸ Brush the flat parts of your back teeth.

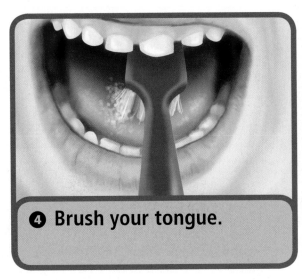

❹ Brush your tongue.

Identify the Main Idea and Details

Learning how to find the main idea can help you understand what you read. The main idea of a paragraph is what it is mostly about. The details tell you more about it. Read this paragraph.

> Snakes swallow their food whole. They cannot chew their food. Snakes' mouths are flexible. They can open their mouths very wide. They can move their jaws from side to side. Their skin can stretch to help open their mouths wide. Because it can open its mouth wide, a snake can swallow a larger animal.

This chart shows the main idea and details.

Detail Snakes cannot chew.	**Detail** Snakes' mouths are flexible.

Main Idea Snakes must swallow their food whole.

Detail Snakes' skin can stretch to help open their mouths wide.	**Detail** Snakes can open their mouths very wide.

Compare and Contrast

Learning how to compare and contrast can help you understand what you read. Comparing is finding what is alike. Contrasting is finding what is different. Read this paragraph.

The desert and the forest are both environments for living things. Many kinds of plants and animals live there. The desert is dry for most of the year. The forest has more rain. Plants such as cactuses live in the desert. Oak and maple trees live in the forest.

This chart shows comparing and contrasting.

Compare

alike
Both are environments.
Many kinds of plants and animals live in each environment.

Contrast

different
Deserts are dry.
Forests have more rain.
Plants such as cactuses live in the desert.
Oak and maple trees live in the forest.

Cause and Effect

Learning how to find cause and effect can help you understand what you read. A cause is why something happens. An effect is what happens. Some paragraphs have more than one cause or effect. Read this paragraph.

> People once used a poison called DDT to get rid of pests. Small birds eat bugs. Some large birds eat small birds. When small birds ate bugs sprayed with DDT, the DDT got into their bodies. When large birds ate small birds, the DDT got into their bodies, too. DDT caused birds to lay eggs that broke easily.

This chart shows cause and effect.

Cause

Small birds ate bugs sprayed with DDT.

Effects

Large birds that ate small birds got DDT into their bodies. The DDT made the birds lay eggs that broke easily.

Sequence

Learning how to find sequence can help you understand what you read. Sequence is the order in which something happens. Some paragraphs use words that help you understand order. Read this paragraph. Look at the underlined words.

> Ricky and his grandpa made a special dessert. <u>First</u>, Grandpa peeled apples and cut them into small chunks. <u>Next</u>, Ricky put the apple chunks and some raisins in a bowl. <u>Then</u>, Grandpa put the bowl into a microwave oven for about ten minutes. <u>Last</u>, when the bowl was cool enough to touch, Ricky and Grandpa ate their dessert.

This chart shows sequence.

1. <u>First</u>, Grandpa peeled apples and cut them into chunks.

2. <u>Next</u>, Ricky put apple chunks and raisins in a bowl.

3. <u>Then</u>, Grandpa put the bowl in a microwave oven for ten minutes.

4. <u>Last</u>, Ricky and Grandpa ate their dessert.

Draw Conclusions

When you draw conclusions, you tell what you have learned. What you learned also includes your own ideas. Read this paragraph.

> The body coverings of many animals can help them hide. One kind of moth has wings with a pattern that looks like tree bark. The moth is hard to see when it is resting on a tree. A polar bear's white coat can make it hard to see in the snow. Being hard to see can help protect an animal or help it hunt other animals.

This chart shows how to draw conclusions.

What I Read
The body coverings of a moth and a polar bear can help them hide.

What I Know
I have seen an insect that looks like a leaf. The insect was very hard to see when it was on a tree branch.

Conclusion
Some animals that live near my own home have body coverings that help them hide.

 Summarize

When you summarize, you tell the main idea and details you remember from what you read. Read this paragraph.

> The leaves of a tree grow in the summer. They provide food for the growing tree. Leaves trap energy from the sun. They get water from the ground. They take in gases from the air. Leaves use these things to make food for the tree.

This chart shows how to summarize.

Recall Detail	Recall Detail	Recall Detail
Leaves grow in the summer.	Leaves trap sunlight.	Leaves collect water from the ground and gases from the air.

Summary Leaves use sunlight, water, and gases to make food for the tree.

Using Tables, Charts, and Graphs

Gathering Data

When you investigate in science, you need to collect data.

Suppose you want to find out what kinds of things are in soil. You can sort the things you find into groups.

Things I Found in One Cup of Soil

Parts of Plants

Small Rocks

Parts of Animals

By studying the circles, you can see the different items found in soil. However, you might display the data in a different way. For example, you could use a tally table.

Reading a Tally Table

You can show your data in a tally table.

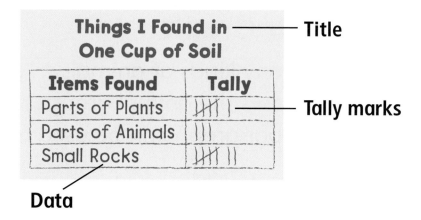

Things I Found in — Title
One Cup of Soil

Items Found	Tally
Parts of Plants	|||||	— Tally marks
Parts of Animals	|||
Small Rocks	||||| ||

Data

How to Read a Tally Table

1. **Read** the tally table. Use the labels.

2. **Study** the data.

3. **Count** the tally marks.

4. **Draw conclusions**. Ask yourself questions like the ones on this page.

Skills Practice

1. How many parts of plants were found in the soil?

2. How many more small rocks were found in the soil than parts of animals?

3. How many parts of plants and parts of animals were found?

Using Tables, Charts, and Graphs

Reading a Bar Graph

People keep many kinds of animals as pets. This bar graph shows the animal groups most pets belong to. A bar graph can be used to compare data.

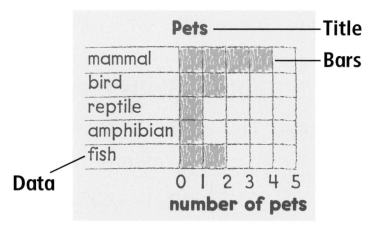

How to Read a Bar Graph

1. **Look** at the title to learn what kind of information is shown.

2. **Read** the graph. Use the labels.

3. **Study** the data. Compare the bars.

4. **Draw conclusions**. Ask yourself questions like the ones on this page.

Skills Practice

1. How many pets are mammals?

2. How many pets are birds?

3. How many more pets are mammals than fish?

Reading a Picture Graph

Some second-grade students were asked to choose their favorite season. They made a picture graph to show the results. A picture graph uses pictures to show information.

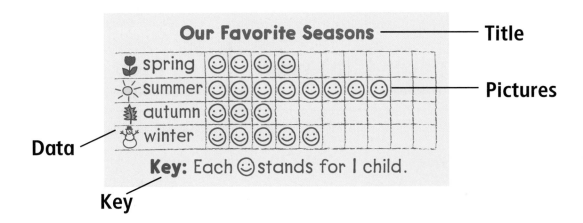

How to Read a Picture Graph

1. **Look** at the title to learn what kind of information is shown.

2. **Read** the graph. Use the labels.

3. **Study** the data. Compare the number of pictures in each row.

4. **Draw conclusions**. Ask yourself questions like the ones on this page.

Skills Practice

1. Which season did the most students choose?

2. Which season did the fewest students choose?

3. How many students in all chose summer or winter?

Measurements

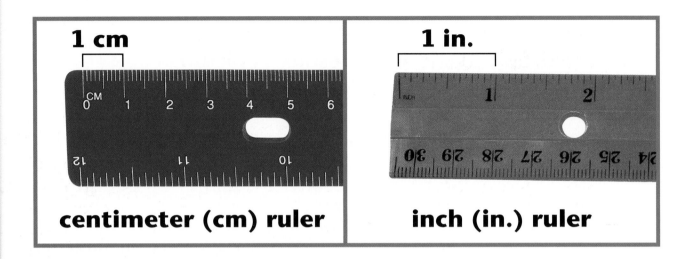

centimeter (cm) ruler

inch (in.) ruler

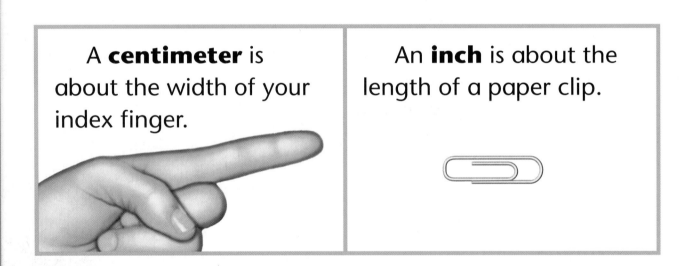

A **centimeter** is about the width of your index finger.

An **inch** is about the length of a paper clip.

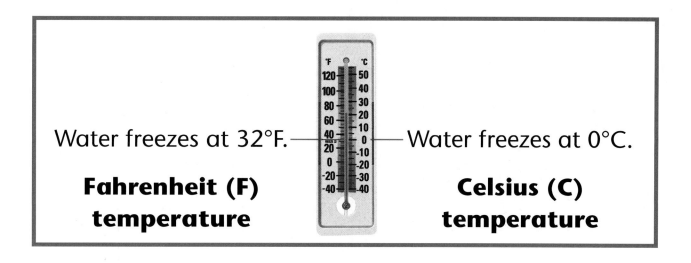

Water freezes at 32°F. —— Water freezes at 0°C.

**Fahrenheit (F)
temperature**

**Celsius (C)
temperature**

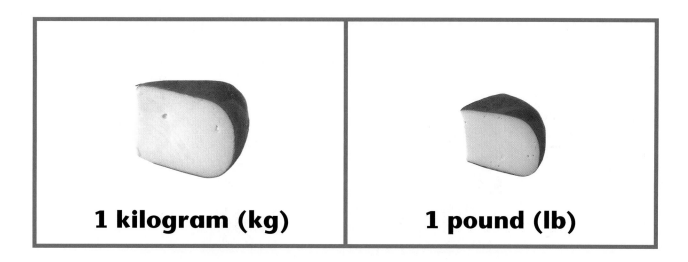

1 kilogram (kg)

1 pound (lb)

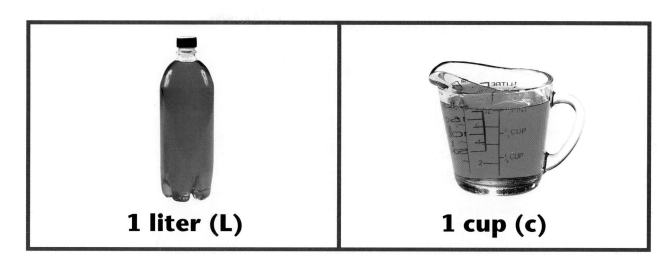

1 liter (L)

1 cup (c)

Safety in Science

Here are some safety rules to follow when you do activities.

1. **Think ahead.** Study the steps and follow them.

2. **Be neat and clean.** Wipe up spills right away.

3. **Watch your eyes.** Wear safety goggles when told to do so.

4. **Be careful with sharp things.**

5. **Do not eat or drink things.**

Visit the Multimedia Science Glossary to see illustrations of these words and to hear them pronounced.
www.hspscience.com

Glossary

A

adapt (uh•DAPT)

To change. Animals and plants adapt over time to live in their environments. (123)

aquarium (uh•KWAIR•ee•uhm)

A tank filled with water in which plants and animals live.

amphibian (am•FIB•ee•uhn)

The group of animals with smooth, wet skin. Young amphibians live in the water, and most adults live on land. (68)

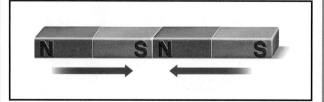

attract (uh•TRAKT)

To pull something. Opposite poles of two magnets attract each other. (435)

B

bird (BERD)

The group of animals with feathers on their bodies and wings. Most birds can fly. (60)

boulder (BOHL•der)

A very large rock. (162)

burning (BER•ning)

The change of a substance into ashes and smoke. (342)

C

centimeter (SEN•tuh•mee•ter)

A unit used to measure how long a solid is. Centimeters are marked on many rulers. (301)

condensation (kahn•duhn•SAY•shuhn)

The change of water from a gas to a liquid. Condensation happens when heat is taken away from water vapor. (338)

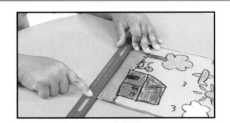

condense (kuhn•DENS)

To change from water vapor gas into liquid water. Water vapor condenses when heat is taken away. (238)

C

constellation
(kahn•stuh•LAY•shuhn)

A group of stars that form a pattern. (256)

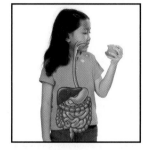

digest (dy•JEST)

To break down food to get energy and nutrients from it. (R7)

drought (DROWT)

A long time when it does not rain. During a drought the land may become dry, and plants may die. (240)

D

desert (DEZ•ert)

An environment that is very dry because it gets little rain. (128)

dinosaur (DY•nuh•sawr)

An animal that lived on Earth millions of years ago. Dinosaurs have become extinct. (170)

E

earthquake (ERTH•kwayk)

A shaking of Earth's surface that can cause land to rise and fall. (156)

E

electricity
(uh•lek•TRIH•sih•tee)

A form of energy. People produce electricity by using energy from other sources. (362)

endangered (en•DAYN•jerd)

In danger of not being alive anymore. People can help endangered animals by protecting the places they live. (207)

energy (EN•er•jee)

Something that can cause matter to move or change. Heat, light, and sound are forms of energy. (358)

environment
(en•VY•ruhn•muhnt)

All the living and nonliving things in a place. (120)

erosion (uh•ROH•zhuhn)

A kind of change that happens when wind and water move sand and small rocks to a new place. (155)

evaporate (ee•VAP•uh•rayt)

To change from liquid water into a gas. Water evaporates when heat is added. (238)

E

evaporation
(ee•vap•uh•RAY•shuhn)

The change of water from a liquid to a gas. Evaporation happens when heat is added to liquid water. (337)

extinct (ek•STINGT)

No longer living. Dinosaurs are extinct because none of them lives anymore. (170)

F

fish (FISH)

The group of animals that live in water and get oxygen through gills. Fish have scales and use fins to swim. (69)

flowers (FLOW•erz)

The plant parts that help a plant make new plants. Part of the flower makes seeds that grow into new plants. (91)

food chain (FOOD CHAYN)

A diagram that shows the order in which animals eat other living things. (138)

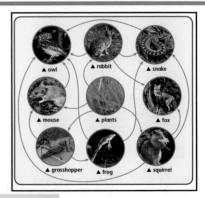

food web (FOOD WEB)

A diagram that shows how food chains are connected. (140)

F

force (FAWRS)

A push or pull that makes something move. Magnetism is one kind of force. (426)

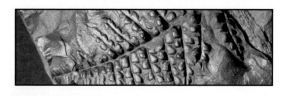

fossil (FAHS•uhl)

What is left of an animal or plant that lived long ago. A fossil can be a print in a rock or bones that have turned to rock. (170)

friction (FRIK•shuhn)

A force that slows down objects when they rub against each other. Friction also causes the objects to get warmer. (374, 429)

G

gas (GAS)

The only form of matter that always fills all the space of its container. (312)

germinate (JER•muh•nayt)

To start to grow. A seed may germinate when it gets water, warmth, and oxygen. (102)

grassland (GRAS•land)

An open environment covered with grass. (130)

G

gravity (GRAV•ih•tee)

A force that pulls things toward the center of Earth. (428)

H

habitat (HAB•ih•tat)

A place where a living thing has the food, water, and shelter it needs to live. (121)

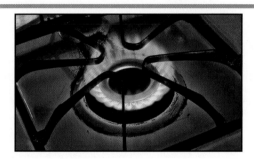

heat (HEET)

Energy that makes things warmer. Heat can be used to cook food or melt things. (358)

I

inquiry skills
(IN•kwer•ee SKILZ)

A set of skills people use to find out information. (4)

investigate (in•VES•tuh•gayt)

To plan and do a test. Scientists investigate to answer a question. (20)

L

leaves (LEEVZ)

The parts of a plant that make food for the plant. Leaves use light, oxygen, and water to make food. (91)

L

life cycle (LYF SY•kuhl)

All the stages of a plant's or an animal's life. (74, 102)

light (LYT)

A form of energy that lets you see. The sun and fires give off light energy. (359)

liquid (LIK•wid)

A form of matter that takes the shape of its container. (306)

living (LIV•ing)

Alive. Plants and animals are living things because they need food, water, and oxygen. (32)

loudness (LOWD•nuhs)

How loud or soft a sound is. (406)

M

magnet (MAG•nit)

An object that can pull things made of iron and steel. (434)

M

mammal (MAM•uhl)

The group of animals with hair or fur on their bodies. (58)

mass (MAS)

The amount of matter in an object. Mass can be measured using a tool called a balance. (292)

matter (MAT•er)

The material all things are made of. Matter can be a solid, a liquid, or a gas. (290)

milliliter (MIL•ih•leet•er)

A unit used to measure the volume of a liquid. Milliliters are marked on many measuring cups. (308)

mineral (MIN•er•uhl)

Solid matter found in nature that was never living. Rocks are usually made of many different minerals. (163)

mixture (MIKS•cher)

A mix of different kinds of matter. Substances in a mixture do not become other substances. (326)

M

moon (MOON)

A huge ball of rock that orbits Earth. The moon takes almost one month to go all the way around Earth. (266)

motion (MOH•shuhn)

Movement. When something moves, it is in motion. (420)

N

natural resource
(NACH•er•uhl REE•sawrs)

Anything in nature people can use to meet their needs. (186)

nonliving (nahn•LIV•ing)

Not alive. Air, water, and rocks are nonliving. (34)

nutrients (NOO•tree•uhnts)

Substances that plants and animals need to survive. Animals get nutrients from food. Plants get nutrients from the soil. (44)

O

ocean (OH•shuhn)

A large body of salt water. Fish and other animals live in oceans. (132)

orbit (AWR•bit)

The path a planet takes as it moves around the sun. Earth's orbit around the sun takes one year. (255)

oxygen (AHK•suh•juhn)

A gas in the air and water. Most living things need oxygen. (32)

pitch (PICH)

How high or low a sound is. (408)

planet (PLAN•it)

A large ball of rock or gas that moves around the sun. Earth is our planet. (254)

pole (POHL)

An end of a magnet. All magnets have a north-seeking pole and a south-seeking pole. (435)

pollution (puh•LOO•shuhn)

Waste that harms the air, water, or land. (196)

P

pond (PAHND)

A small, freshwater environment. Beavers and water lilies may live in a pond. (134)

precipitation
(prih•sip•uh•TAY•shuhn)

Water that falls from the sky. Rain, snow, sleet, and hail are kinds of precipitation. (234)

property (PRAH•per•tee)

One part of what something is like. Color, size, and shape are each a property. (292)

R

rain forest
(RAYN FAWR•ist)

An environment, with many tall trees, that gets rain almost every day. (129)

recycle (ree•SY•kuhl)

To use the materials in old things to make new things. (205)

reduce (ree•DOOS)

To use less of a resource. (204)

R

reflect (rih•FLEKT)

To bounce off. Light reflects when it hits most objects. (369)

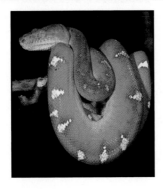

reptile (REP•tyl)

The group of animals with dry skin covered in scales. (66)

reuse (ree•YOOZ)

To use a resource again. (204)

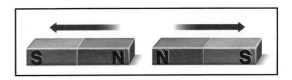

repel (rih•PEL)

To push away. Poles that are the same on two magnets repel each other. (435)

resource (REE•sawrs)

Anything people can use to meet their needs. (186)

roots (ROOTS)

The parts of a plant that take in water and nutrients. Most roots grow underground and help hold the plant in place. (90)

rotate (ROH•tayt)

To spin around like a top. Earth rotates one time every 24 hours. (260)

science tools (SY•uhns TOOLZ)

Tools people use to find information. (12)

season (SEE•zuhn)

A time of year that has a certain kind of weather. The four seasons are spring, summer, fall, and winter. (223, 275)

shelter (SHEL•ter)

A safe place to live. Birds may use a nest for shelter. (39)

shrub (SHRUHB)

A bush. Shrubs have many woody stems. (97)

soil (SOYL)

Bits of rocks mixed with matter that was once living. (164)

S

solar energy

(SOH•ler EN•er•jee)

Energy from the sun. (360)

solar system

(SOH•ler SIS•tuhm)

The sun, its planets, and other objects that move around the sun. (254)

solid (SAHL•id)

The only form of matter that has its own shape. (298)

sound (SOWND)

Energy you can hear. Sounds are made when an object vibrates. (359, 392)

sound wave

(SOWND WAYV)

Vibrations moving through matter. When sound waves reach your ears, you can hear sound. (398)

speed (SPEED)

How fast something moves. (422)

S

star (STAR)

A big ball of hot gases that give off light and heat energy. The sun is the closest star to Earth. (256)

stems (STEMZ)

The parts of a plant that carry water and nutrients from the roots to the leaves. (90)

survive (ser•VYV)

To stay alive. Animals need food and water to survive. (38)

T

tadpole (TAD•pohl)

A young frog. Tadpoles hatch from eggs and use gills to get oxygen from water. (76)

temperature (TEM•per•uh•cher)

A measure of how hot or cold something is. (231, 380)

terrarium (tuh•RAIR•ee•uhm)

A container in which plants and animals live on soil. (119)

T

texture (TEKS•cher)

The way something feels when you touch it. (299)

thermometer (ther•MAHM•uh•ter)

A tool that measures an object's temperature. (231, 380)

trunk (TRUHNK)

The one main stem of a tree. (97)

tundra (TUHN•druh)

An environment that is cold and snowy. Plants that live in a tundra are short. The animals have thick fur that helps them stay warm. (131)

V

vibrate (VY•brayt)

To move back and forth quickly. (392)

volcano (vahl•KAY•noh)

A place where hot melted rock called lava comes out of the ground onto Earth's surface. (157)

V

volume (VAHL•yoom)

The amount of space something takes up. (308)

water vapor
(WAWT•er VAY•per)

Water in the form of a gas. (337)

weather pattern
(WEH•ther PAT•ern)

A change in the weather that repeats. (222)

W

water cycle
(WAW•ter SY•kuhl)

The movement of water from Earth's surface into the air and back to Earth's surface. (238)

weather (WEH•ther)

What the air outside is like. The weather in summer is often sunny and hot. (222)

weathering (WEH•ther•ing)

A kind of change that happens when wind and water break down rock into smaller pieces. (154)

W

wind (WIND)

Air that is moving. (232)

Index

A

Adapt, 123
Air
 animals' need for, 32
 as gas, 312–313
 as natural resource, 186
 as nonliving things, 34
 plants' need for, 33
 pollution, 196
 sound traveling through, 398–399
 water in, 237
Amphibians, 68
 body covering, 68, 70
 compared to reptiles and fish, 70
 egg, 70
 frog, 68, 76–77
 green tree frog, 129
 oxygen, 68, 70
 salamander, 68
Anemometer, 233
Animals
 adapt to environment, 123–124
 classify, 65
 in desert, 128
 endangered, 207
 in food chain, 138–139
 food for, 32, 37, 38, 137–140
 in food web, 140
 fossils of, 171–173
 in grassland, 130
 growth of, 36–41
 learning about, from fossils, 174
 life cycle of some, 74–79
 as living things, 32
 as natural resource, 192
 in ocean, 132–133
 oxygen for, 32, 40
 in ponds, 134
 prairie dog, 39
 in rain forest, 129
 space and shelter for, 39
 surviving in different places, 126–135
 in tundra, 131
 water for, 32, 38
 where animals live, 119
 See also Amphibians; Birds; Fish; Insects; Mammals; Reptiles
Attract, 435
Awendaw, South Carolina, 115

B

Balance, 16
Batteries, 363
Bay, 158
Big Dipper, 256
Birds
 beaks, 124
 blue jay, 61
 characteristics of, 60–61
 compared to mammals, 62
 eggs, 60–61, 62
 feathers, 60, 62
 food for, 37
 heron, 60
 penguin, 61
Body coverings of animals
 amphibians, 68, 70
 birds, 60, 62
 fish, 70
 mammals, 58–59, 62
 reptiles, 66–67, 70
Body systems
 caring for your teeth, R12–R13
 circulatory system, R9
 digestive system, R7
 ears, R2
 eyes, R1
 hearing, 394, R2
 keeping clean, R11
 nervous system, R6
 respiratory system, R8
 sense of smell, R3
 sense of taste, R3
 skeletal and muscular systems, R4–R5
 staying healthy, R10
Boiling, 337
Boulder, 162
Breckenridge, Colorado, 216
Burning, 342–343
 heat and, 374–375
Butterfly
 how color helps, 127

C

Cape Romain National Wildlife Refuge, 115
Cause and effect, R16
Celsius, 380
Centimeter, 301
Chicago, Illinois, 27
Chicago Botanic Garden, 27
Circuit, 364
Circulatory system, R9
Classify, 4
 leaves, 95, 96
 roots, 98
 stems, 97
Clay, 164
 as natural resource, 189
Coal, 361
Color
 butterfly and, 127
 heat and, 373
 in light, 368
Compare, 4, R15
Conclusions, drawing, 6, R18
Condensation, 338
Contrast, R15

Cooking, 342–343
Cooperstown, New York, 353
Copper, 188

D

Day
  Earth's rotation, 260–261
Daylight. *See* **Sunlight**
Delta, 158
Desert, 128
Details, R14
Digestive system, R7
Dinosaurs, 170
Drought, 240

E

Eardrum, 394, R2
Ears, 394, R2
Earth, 254
  moon's orbit around, 266–268
  orbit around sun, 272–273
Earth's rotation
  changes in shadows, 262
  day and night, 260–261
Earth's surface
  changes to, 152–159
  earthquakes and volcanoes, 156–157
  how land shapes change, 153
  rocks and soil, 160–167
  types of landforms, 158
  weathering and erosion, 154–155
Earth's tilt, 271, 273
  seasons change and, 274–276
Earthquakes, 156
Echoes, 400
Eggs
  amphibians, 70
  birds, 60–61, 62
  fish, 69, 70
  frog, 76
  reptiles, 66–67, 70, 78

Electricity, 362–363
  circuit, 364
  heat and, 376–377
Endangered animals, 207
Energy
  batteries, 363
  characteristics of, 358
  circuit, 364
  conserving, 206–207
  electricity, 362–363
  gas, natural gas, coal, 361
  heat, 358, 372–381
  light as, 359, 366–371
  solar, 360
  sound as, 359
  from sun, 360
  from water, 360
  where energy comes from, 360–361
  from wind, 357, 360
Environments, 120–125
  characteristics of, 120
  desert, 128
  grassland, 130
  habitats in, 121
  living things surviving in different places, 126–135
  oceans, 132–133
  people and, 122
  ponds, 134
  rain forest, 129
  tundra, 131
  water hyacinths, 122
Erosion, 154–155
Evaporation, 337
  Unit Experiment, 217
Eyes, R1

F

Fahrenheit, 380
Fall, 225, 275
  weather in, 225
Feathers
  birds, 60, 62

  compared to hair, 57
Fish
  angelfish, 69
  body covering, 70
  characteristics of, 69
  compared to amphibians and reptiles, 70
  eggs, 69, 70
  jellyfish, 132
  octopus, 132
  oxygen for, 40, 69, 70
  red pigfish, 123
  shark, 69, 133
Flood, 241
Flowers, 91
  parts of, 92
  tulip, 97
Food
  for animals, 32, 38, 137–140
  for birds, 37
  for plants, 33
Food chain, 138–139
Food web, 140
Force
  characteristics of, 426–427
  friction, 429
  gravity, 428
Fossils, 168–175
  how fossils form, 172–173
  uncovering, 169
  what we find out from, 170–171, 174
Freezing, 333–335
Friction, 429
  bike brakes, 430
  heat, 374
Fuel, 361

G

Gases, 291, 310–315
  air as, 312–313
  measure, 311
  properties of, 312
Gasoline, 375

Gateway Arch, 284
Germinate, 102
Granite, 163
Grassland, 130
Gravity, 428
Greenbrier, Arkansas, 26
Growth
 of animals, 36–41
 of cat, 74–75
 of frog, 76–77
 of plants, 42–47
 of sea turtle, 78

Habitats, 121
Hair
 compared to feathers, 57
Hardness
 of rocks, 161
Hearing, 394, R2
Heat, 372–381
 burning and, 374–375
 characteristics of, 358
 color and, 373
 condensation, 338
 electricity and, 376–377
 as energy, 358
 evaporation, 337
 freezing, 334
 friction, 374
 how heat moves, 378–379
 melting, 336
 temperature and, 380
Holgate Toy Company, 352
Humus, 165
Hypothesis, 6, 20

Inches, 301
Inquiry Skill, 4–8, 37, 43
 classify, 4, 31, 65, 95, 425
 communicate, 8, 101, 137,
  169, 271, 325, 391

compare, 4, 19, 57, 229, 289
draw conclusions, 6, 161, 185,
 341, 367
hypothesize, 6, 405, 433
infer, 6, 127, 237, 253, 305, 311
make a model, 5, 265
measure, 5, 297, 373
observe, 3, 4, 89, 153, 195, 221,
 259
plan an investigation, 8, 203,
 357, 419
predict, 7, 11, 333, 397
sequence, 5, 73
Insects
 water striders, 134
Insta-Lab, 7, 13, 21, 33, 39, 45,
 60, 67, 77, 97, 105, 123, 130,
 139, 157, 165, 173, 191, 197,
 205, 223, 232, 241, 255, 261,
 267, 276, 293, 299, 308, 313,
 327, 336, 343, 361, 370, 375,
 393, 401, 407, 422, 427, 435
**International Snow Sculpture
 Championships,** 216
Intestines, R7
Investigate, 20–22
Island, 158

**Jasmine Moran Children's
 Museum,** 285
Jupiter, 254

Kane, Pennsylvania, 352

Landforms
 changes to, 153
 kinds of, 158
Lava, 157
Leaves, 91

classify, 95
 kinds of, 96
 in life cycle, 103
Lexington, Kentucky, 148
Lexington Children's Museum,
 148
Life cycles
 of bean plant, 101–103
 of cat, 74–75
 of dragonfly, 77
 of frog, 76–77
 of pine tree, 104–105
 of sea turtle, 78
 sequencing, 73
Light, 366–371
 characteristics of, 359, 368
 colors in, 368
 as energy, 359
 how light moves, 366–367
 for plants, 45
 reflect, 369
 shadows, 370
 stars and, 253
 See also Sunlight
Limestone, 163
Liquids, 291, 304–309, 314
 measure, 305, 308
 properties of, 306–307
 See also Water
Little Dipper, 256
Living things, 30–35
 animals as, 32
 in environment, 120
 food chain, 138–139
 needs of, 32
 plants as, 33
 surviving in different places,
  126–135
 See also Animals; Plants
Lodestone, 434
Loudness, 406–407

Magnets
attract and repel, 435
characteristics of, 434–435
how magnets work, 433–435
how people use magnets, 438
poles of, 435
what magnets do, 436–437
Main idea, R14
Mammals
bats, 129
bear, 124
beaver, 134
body coverings, 58–59, 62
caribou, 131
characteristics of, 58–59
cheetahs, 130
chipmunk, 58
compared to birds, 62
dolphin, 59, 400
elephants, 130
horse, 124
humpback whales, 401
life cycle of cat, 74–75
lion, 58
manatee, 59
monkeys, 129
polar bears, 131
sea otter, 123
teeth, 124
tiger, 124
Marble, 163
Mars, 254
Mass, 292
measure, 294, 300
Math in Science Handbook,
R20–R25
Matter, 288–294
burning and cooking,
342–343
changes to, 324–331, 340–345
changes to water, 332–339
comparing forms of, 314
forms of, 290–291

kinds of, 289–290
make a mixture, 325–327
measure, 330
properties of, 292–293
Measure, 5
gases, 311
liquids, 305, 308
mass, 294, 300
matter, 330
precipitation, 234
rain, 234
solids, 297, 300–301
temperature, 229, 231
weather, 228–235
wind, 232–233
Melting, 336
Mercury, 254
Milliliter, 308
Minerals, 163
kinds of, 163
for plants, 44
Mixture
making, 325–327
Moon
characteristics of, 266–267
orbit around Earth, 266–268
phases of, 266–268
why moon seems to shine,
265, 266
Motion, 418–423
bike brakes, 430
forces, 426–427
friction, 429
gravity, 428
how magnets move things,
432–439
how things can move, 419
how you move objects, 425
kinds of, 420–421
speed of, 422
what makes things move,
424–431
Mountains, 158
Muscular system, R4–R5

National Baseball Hall of Fame,
353
Natural gas, 361, 375
Natural resources, 186
air and water as, 186–187
animals as, 192
building and, 199
conserving, 206–207
how people harm natural
resources, 194–201
how people use, 184–193
people protecting, 202–209
plants as, 190–191
pollution, 195–197
reducing pollution, 208
reuse, reduce and recycle,
203–205
rocks and soil, 188–189
wasting, 198–200
ways we use water, 185
Neptune, 254
Nervous system, R6
**New Martinsville, West
Virginia,** 114
Night
Earth's rotation, 260–261
Nonliving things, 31, 34
in environment, 120
Nutrients, 44

Obsidian, 163
Oceans, 132–133
Orbit, 254
Earth around sun, 272–273
moon around Earth, 266–268
Ores, 188
Orion, 256, 257
Oxygen
for amphibians, 68, 70
for animals, 32, 40
for fish, 40, 69, 70

for plants, 33
for reptiles, 70

P

People
  environments and, 122
  harming natural resources,
    194–201
  protecting natural resources,
    202–209
  use magnets, 438
  using natural resources, 184–193
  See also Body systems
People in Science, 50, 82, 110,
  144, 178, 212, 280, 348, 384,
  412, 442
Pine cones
  in life cycle, 104–105
Pitch, 408
Planets, 254
  orbit, 254
  in solar system, 254–255
Plants
  adapt to environment, 123
  bean plant, 101–103
  cactus, 97, 128
  carrot, 98
  classify leaves, 95, 96
  classify roots, 98
  classify stems, 97
  corn, 98
  in desert, 128
  flowers, 91–92
  in food chain, 138–139
  food for, 33
  as food for animals,
    137–140
  in food web, 140
  fossils of, 170
  in grassland, 130
  how plants differ, 94–99
  leaves, 91
  life cycle of bean plant,
    101–103

life cycle of pine tree, 104–105
light for, 45
as living things, 33
as natural resource, 190–191
nutrients for, 44, 90, 91
oak tree, 106
in ocean, 132–133
oxygen for, 33
parts of, 88–93
plants look like parents, 106
in ponds, 134
in rain forest, 129
room to grow, 46
roots, 90
rose plant, 90
shrub, 97
soil for growing in, 166
stems, 91
surviving in different places,
  126–135
tulip, 97
in tundra, 131
water for, 33, 44, 90, 91
water hyacinths, 122
water lilies, 134
what plants need to grow,
  42–47
Pluto, 254
Poles, 435
Pollution, 195–197
  air, 196
  reducing, 208
  trash, 197
  Unit Experiment, 115
  water, 196
  what happens to, 195
Ponds, 134
Precipitation
  measuring, 234
Properties
  of gases, 312
  of liquids, 306–307
  of matter, 292–293
  of solids, 298–299

R

Rain
  measuring, 234
Rain forest, 129
Rain gauge, 234
Reading in Science Handbook
  cause and effect, R16
  compare and contrast, R15
  draw conclusions, R18
  main idea and details, R14
  sequence, R17
  summarize, R19
Recycle, 204–205
Reduce, 204–205
Reflect, 369
Repel, 435
Reptiles
  body covering, 66–67, 70
  characteristics of, 66–67
  compared to amphibians and
    fish, 70
  corn snake, 66
  eggs, 66–67, 70, 78
  life cycle of sea turtle, 78
  lizards, 128
  oxygen, 70
  sea turtle, 78
  snakes, 66–67
  turtle, 67
  veiled chameleon, 128
Resource, 186
Respiratory system, R8
Reuse, 204
  how to, 203
**Riddle's Elephant and Wildlife
  Sanctuary,** 26
Rocks
  hardness of, 161
  minerals, 163
  as natural resource, 188–189
  as nonliving things, 34
  size of, 162
  soil, 164–166
  weathering and erosion,

154–155
Roots, 90, 166
  kinds of, 98
Rotation of Earth, 260–261

S

Safety
  Safety in Science, R26
St. Louis, Missouri, 284
Sand, 162
  as part of soil, 165
Sandstone, 163
Santa Fe, New Mexico, 149
Saturn, 254
Science and Technology, 48–49,
  80–81, 108–109, 142–143,
  176–177, 210–211, 244–245,
  278–279, 316–317, 346–347,
  382–383, 410–411, 440–441
Science Projects for Home or
  School, 51, 83, 111, 145, 179,
  213, 247, 281, 319, 349, 385,
  413, 443
Science safety, R26
Science tools, 12–16
  balance, 16
  dropper, 15
  forceps, 13
  hand lens, 12
  magnifying box, 13
  measuring cup, 15
  ruler, 14
  tape measure, 14
  thermometer, 16
Science Up Close
  bike brakes, 430
  circuit, 364
  different textures, 302
  hearing, 394
  how fossils form, 172–173
  life cycle of frog, 76–77
  making muffins, 344
  parts of a flower, 92
  phases of moon, 268

wasting resources, 200
what happens during water
  cycle, 239
Seasons, 223, 275
  Earth's tilt and change of,
    274–276
  fall, 225
  spring, 223
  summer, 224
  weather and, 223
  winter, 226
Seeds
  germinate, 102
  in life cycle, 102
Seminole, Oklahoma, 285
Senses
  hearing, R2
  sight, R1
  smell, R3
  taste, R3
Sequence, 5, R17
Shadows, 370
  changes in, 259, 262
  Earth's rotation, 262
Shelter
  for animals, 39
Shrub, 97
Silt, 164
Skeletal system, R4
Slate, 163
Smell, R3
Snow
  measuring, 234
Soda Dam, 149
Soil, 164–166
  for growing things, 166
  kinds of, 164–165
  as natural resource, 188–189
Solar energy, 360
Solar system
  changes in moon, 264–269
  changes in shadows, 259, 262
  Earth's rotation, 260–261
  planets in, 254–255
  stars, 256
  what causes day and night,

258–263
what causes seasons, 270–277
Solids, 291, 296–303, 314
  measuring, 297, 300–301
  properties, 298–299
  sound travels through, 402
Sound
  causes of, 390–395
  as energy, 359
  hearing, 394
  high or low, 408
  how sound is made, 391–393
  how sound travels, 396–403
  loud or soft, 406–407
  pitch, 408
  travels through air, 398–399
  travels through solids, 402
  travels through water, 400–401
  vibrations make, 392–393
  why sounds are different, 405
Sound waves, 398
Space
  for animals, 39
  for plants, 46
Speed
  force and, 427
  of motion, 422
Spring, 223, 274
  weather in, 223
Stars
  characteristics of, 256
  constellations, 256
  light and, 253
Stems, 91
  kinds of, 97
  in life cycle, 103
Storms, 242
Summarize, R19
Summer, 224, 274, 276
  daylight in, 276
  weather in, 224
Sun, 254
  Earth's orbit around, 272–273
  energy from, 360
  heat from, 374
  solar energy, 360

as star, 256
Sunlight
  Earth's rotation, 260–261
  in summer, 276
  in winter, 276

Tadpole, 76
Taste, R3
Teeth, 124
  caring for, R12–R13
Temperature, 231, 380
  measuring, 229, 231
Texture, 299, 302
Thermometer, 231, 380
Thistle Dew Farm, 114
Trees
  life cycle of pine tree, 104–105
  as natural resource, 190–191
  oak tree, 106
  wasting resource of, 198–199
Trunk, 97
Tundra, 131

Unit Experiment
  evaporation, 217
  magnets, 353
  plants and erosion, 149
  plants and light, 27
  solids in water, 285
  water pollution, 115
Uranus, 254

Venus, 254
Vibrations
  pitch, 408
  sounds made by, 392–393
  sound travels through solids,
    402
  sound waves, 398

Volcanoes, 157
Volume
  liquids, 308

Water
  in air, 237
  for animals, 38
  animals need for, 32
  boiling, 337
  changes to, 332–339
  condensation, 338
  energy from, 360
  evaporation, 337
  freezing, 333–335
  melting, 336
  as natural resource, 187
  as nonliving things, 34
  for plants, 33, 44, 90, 91
  pollution, 196
  sound travels through, 400–401
  Unit Experiment, 115
  wasting, 200
  ways we use, 185
  See also Water cycle
Water cycle, 236–243
  characteristics of, 238–239
  drought, 240
  flood, 241
  storms, 242
  water in air, 237
Water vapor, 337
Weather, 222
  changes in, 221
  drought, 240
  fall, 225
  flood, 241
  how does weather change,
    220–227
  measuring precipitation, 234
  measuring temperature, 229,
    231
  measuring wind, 232–233
  seasons, 223

spring, 223
  storms, 242
  summer, 224
  water cycle, 236–243
  why we measure, 228–235
  winter, 226
Weathering, 154–155
Weather pattern, 222, 230
Weather vane, 232
Wind, 186, 232
  energy from, 206, 357, 360
  measuring, 232–233
Winter, 226, 275, 276
  daylight in, 276
  weather in, 226
Wood, 375

FAMILY Meerkats are very social animals.

DESCRIPTION Meerkats are about 12 inches tall when they are standing.

Meerkats have sharp, curved claws.

HABITAT Meerkats build burrows, where they stay at night.